Creative Beading, Vol. 3

The best projects from a year of *Bead&Button* magazine

© 2008 Kalmbach Publishing Co.
All rights reserved. This book may
not be reproduced in part or in whole
without written permission of the
publisher, except in the case of brief
quotations used in reviews. Published
by Kalmbach Publishing Co., 21027
Crossroads Circle, Waukesha, WI
53186. These books are distributed to
the book trade by Watson-Guptill.

12 11 10 09 08   1 2 3 4 5

Publisher's Cataloging-In-Publication Data

Creative beading. Vol. 3 : the best
projects from a year of Bead&Button
magazine.

    p. : col. ill. ; cm.

    "The material in this book has
previously appeared in Bead&Button
magazine."
    Includes index.
    ISBN: 978-0-87116-262-5

1. Beadwork--Handbooks, manuals,
etc. 2. Beads--Handbooks, manuals,
etc. 3. Jewelry making--Handbooks,
manuals, etc. I. Title: Bead&Button
magazine.

TT860 .C7438 2008
745.594/2

Printed in China.

Cont

ents

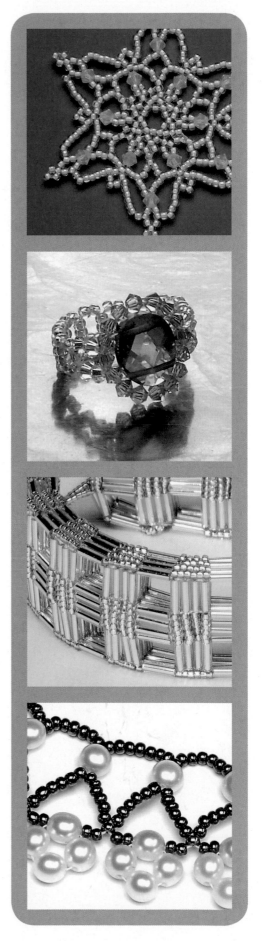

Introduction

Bead&Button readers tell us that they are most interested in learning and refining jewelry-making techniques. We have taken our readers' interests to heart to compile *Creative Beading, Vol. 3*, a lasting collection of *Bead&Button* projects.

While stitching is among beaders' greatest passions, wirework, stringing, and loomweaving are ever popular as well. Of course, the variety of ways to use bead-stitching techniques is practically endless. Just add creativity and voilà — another new design is conceived. We present all of this, and more, in this third collection of projects from our magazine.

Creative Beading, Vol. 3, is rich in both style and substance. Like volumes 1 and 2, we have organized this book by technique. It seems natural to categorize the projects this way, and it serves a dual purpose. Many beaders learn one technique at a time, completing several different projects in the same stitch, in order to master that stitch. By arranging our designs by technique, we help you establish your own learning curve.

We've included 50 stitching projects in 10 individual stitches, plus combined stitching techniques. It's possible to learn all of the contemporary stitches — crossweave, chevron chain, netting, ladder stitch, square stitch, right-angle weave, daisy chain, peyote stitch, herringbone stitch, and spiral rope stitch — just by making some of the projects in this book. Nineteen additional projects also enable you to make chic wirework and strung styles. In addition, you can learn bead crochet, kumihimo, macramé, and bead embroidery with detailed instructions for even more options.

The projects are from the pages of *Bead&Button*, which ensures that great care has been taken to test every design from the first bead picked up to the last one added. You receive complete and accurate materials lists, instructions, photographs, and illustrations to help you complete each project accurately.

In the end, what really matters is the sense of accomplishment and the skills you acquire in creating your new pieces of jewelry. Once you have learned how to make our designers' beautiful works, you can start to design your own!

Ann Dee Allen
Editor
Bead&Button magazine

Tools and materials

Excellent tools and materials for making jewelry are available in bead and craft stores, through catalogs, and on the Internet. Here are the essential supplies you'll need for the projects in this book.

TOOLS

Chainnose pliers have smooth, flat inner jaws, and the tips taper to a point. Use them for gripping and for opening and closing loops and jump rings.

Roundnose pliers have smooth, tapered, conical jaws used to make loops. The closer to the tip you work, the smaller the loop will be.

On **diagonal wire cutters,** use the front of the blades to make a pointed cut and the back of the blades to make a flat cut. Do not use your jewelry-grade wire cutters on memory wire, which is extremely hard; use heavy-duty wire cutters or bend the memory wire back and forth until it breaks.

Crimping pliers have two grooves in their jaws that are used to fold or roll a crimp into a compact shape.

Use **split-ring pliers** to simplify opening split rings by inserting a curved jaw between the wires.

Beading needles are coded by size. The higher the number, the finer the beading needle. Unlike sewing needles, the eye of a beading needle is almost as narrow as its shaft. In addition to the size of the bead, the number of times you will pass through the bead also affects the needle size that you will use – if you pass through a bead multiple times, you need to use a smaller needle.

FINDINGS

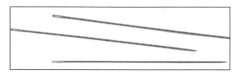

A **head pin** looks like a long, blunt, thick sewing pin. It has a flat or decorative head on one end to keep beads on. Head pins come in different diameters, or gauges, and lengths.

Eye pins are just like head pins except they have a round loop on one end instead of a head. You can make your own eye pins from wire.

A **jump ring** is used to connect two loops. It is a small wire circle or oval that is either soldered or comes with a split so you can twist the jump ring open and closed.

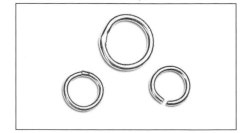

Split rings are used like jump rings but are much more secure. They look like tiny key rings and are made of springy wire.

Crimp beads are small, large-holed, thin-walled metal beads designed to be flattened or crimped into a tight roll. Use them when stringing jewelry on flexible beading wire.

Clasps come in many sizes and shapes. Some of the most common are the toggle, consisting of a ring and a bar; the lobster claw, which opens when you pull on a tiny lever; the S-hook, which links two soldered jump rings or split rings; the box, with a tab and a slot; and the slide, consisting of one tube that slides inside another.

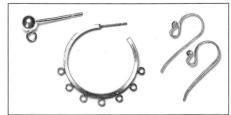

Earring findings come in a huge variety of metals and styles, including post, lever-back, French hook, and hoop. You will almost always want a loop (or loops) on earring findings so you can attach beads.

WIRE

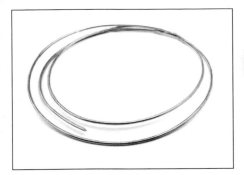

Wire is available in a number of materials and finishes, including brass, gold, gold-filled, gold-plated, fine silver, sterling silver, anodized niobium (chemically colored wire), and copper. Brass, copper, and craft wire are packaged in 10–40-yd. (9.1–37m) spools, while gold, silver, and niobium are sold by the foot or ounce. Wire thickness is measured by gauge – the higher the gauge number, the thinner the wire – and is available in varying hardnesses (dead-soft, half-hard, and hard) and shapes (round, half-round, and square).

STRINGING MATERIALS

Selecting beading thread and cord is one of the most important decisions you'll make when planning a project. Review the descriptions below to evaluate which material is best for your design.

Threads come in many sizes and strengths. Size (diameter or thickness) is designated by a letter or number. OO and A/O are the thinnest; B, D, E, F, and FF are subsequently thicker. **Cord** is measured on a number scale; 0 corresponds in thickness to D-size thread, 1 equals E, 2 equals F, and 3 equals FF.

Parallel filament nylon, such as Nymo or C-Lon, is made from many thin nylon fibers that are extruded and heat set to form a single-ply thread. Parallel filament nylon is durable and easy to thread, but it can be prone to fraying and stretching. It is best used in bead weaving and bead embroidery.

Plied nylon thread, such as Silamide, is made from two or more nylon threads that are extruded, twisted together, and coated or bonded for further security. It is strong and durable and some brands have had the stretch removed. It is more resistant to fraying than parallel filament nylon. It's a good material for twisted fringe, bead crochet, and beadwork that needs a lot of body.

Plied gel-spun polyethylene (GSP), such as Power Pro or DandyLine, is made from polyethylene fibers that have been spun into two or more threads that are braided together. It is almost unbreakable, it doesn't stretch, and it resists fraying. The thickness can make it difficult to make multiple passes through a bead. It is ideal for stitching with larger beads, such as pressed glass and crystals.

Parallel filament GSP, such as Fireline, is a single-ply thread made from spun and bonded polyethylene fibers. It's extremely strong, it doesn't stretch, and it resists fraying. However, crystals will cut through parallel filament GSP, and it can leave a black residue on your hands and your beads. It's most appropriate for bead stitching.

Polyester thread, such as Gutterman, is made from polyester fibers that are spun into single yarns and then twisted into plied thread. It doesn't stretch and comes in many colors, but it can become linty with use. It is best for bead crochet or bead embroidery when the thread must match the fabric.

Flexible beading wire is composed of wires twisted together and covered with nylon. This wire is stronger than thread and does not stretch; the higher the number of inner strands (between 7 and 49), the more flexible and kink-resistant the wire. It is available in a variety of sizes. Use .014 and .015 for most gemstones, crystals, and glass beads. Use thicker varieties, .018, .019, and .024, for heavy beads or nuggets. Use thinner wire, .010 and .012, for lightweight pieces and beads with very small holes, such as pearls.

Basics

WIREWORK

Crimping

Position the crimp bead in the hole of the crimping pliers that is closest to the handle. Holding the wires apart, squeeze the tool to compress the crimp bead, making sure one wire is on each side of the dent.

Place the crimp bead in the front hole of the tool, and position it so the dent is facing outward. Squeeze the tool to fold the crimp in half.

Tug on the wires to ensure that the crimp is secure.

Plain loops and jump rings: opening and closing

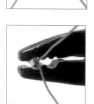

Hold a loop or jump ring with two pairs of chainnose pliers or with chainnose and bentnose pliers.

To open the loop or jump ring, bring the tips of one pair of pliers toward you and push the tips of the other pair away.

Reverse the steps to close the loop or jump ring.

Loops, plain

Using chainnose pliers, make a right-angle bend approximately ¼ in. (6mm) from the end of the wire.

Grip the tip of the wire in roundnose pliers. Press downward slightly, and rotate the wire into a loop.

Let go, then grip the loop at the same place on the pliers, and keep turning to close the loop.

The closer to the tip of the roundnose pliers that you work, the smaller the loop will be.

Loops, wrapped

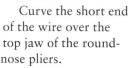

Using chainnose pliers, make a right-angle bend approximately 1¼ in. (3.2cm) from the end of the wire.

Position the jaws of your roundnose pliers in the bend.

Curve the short end of the wire over the top jaw of the round-nose pliers.

Reposition the pliers so the lower jaw fits snugly in the loop. Curve the wire downward around the bottom jaw of the pliers. This is the first half of a wrapped loop.

To complete the wraps, grasp the top of the loop with chain-nose pliers.

Wrap the wire around the stem two or three times. Trim the excess wire, and gently press the cut end close to the wraps with chainnose pliers.

Loops, wrapped above a top-drilled bead

Center a top-drilled bead on a 3-in. (7.6cm) piece of wire. Bend each wire end upward, crossing them into an X above the bead.

Using chainnose pliers, make a small bend in each wire end so they form a right angle.

Wrap the horizontal wire around the vertical wire as in a wrapped loop. Trim the excess wrapping wire.

Make a wrapped loop with the vertical wire, directly above these wraps.

STITCHES AND THREAD

Conditioning thread

Use either beeswax (not candle wax or paraffin) or Thread Heaven to condition nylon thread (Nymo). Beeswax smooths the nylon fibers and adds tackiness that will stiffen your beadwork slightly. Thread Heaven adds a static charge that causes the thread to repel itself, so don't use it with doubled thread. Stretch the thread, then pull it through the conditioner, starting with the end that comes off the spool first.

Ending/adding thread

To end a thread, weave back into the beadwork, following the existing thread path and tying two or three half-hitch knots around the thread between beads as you go. Change directions as you weave so the thread crosses itself. Sew through a few beads after the last knot before cutting the thread.

To add a thread, start several rows prior to the point where the last bead was added. Weave through the beadwork, tying half-hitch knots as you go, and exit where you left off.

Stop bead

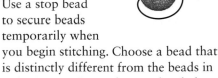

Use a stop bead to secure beads temporarily when you begin stitching. Choose a bead that is distinctly different from the beads in your project. String the stop bead about 6 in. (15cm) from the end of your thread, and go back through it in the same direction. If desired, go through it one more time for added security.

Brick stitch

Work off a stitched ladder (see Ladder stitch). Pick up two beads. Sew under the thread bridge between the second and third beads on the ladder from back to front. Sew up the second bead added and then down the first. Come back up the second bead.

For the row's remaining stitches, pick up one bead. Sew under the next thread bridge on the previous row from back to front. Sew back up the new bead.

Ladder stitch

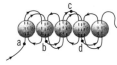

There are several ways to work a ladder. The common way is to pick up two beads, sew through the first bead again, and then sew through the second bead (a–b). Add subsequent beads by picking up one bead, sewing through the previous bead, and then sewing through the new bead (b–c). Continue for the desired length.

While this is the most common technique, it produces uneven tension along the ladder of beads because of the alternating pattern of a single thread bridge on the edge between two beads and a double thread bridge on the opposite edge between the same two

beads. You can easily correct the uneven tension by zigzagging back through the beads in the opposite direction. Doing this creates a double thread path along both edges of the ladder. This aligns the beads right next to each other but fills the bead holes with extra thread, which can cause a problem if you are using beads with small holes.

When you're using ladder stitch to create a base for brick stitch, having the holes filled with thread doesn't matter because the rows of brick stitch are worked off the thread bridges, not by sewing through the beads. If you're using the ladder as a base for Ndebele herringbone stitch, extra thread is potentially problematic, because you'll be sewing through the ladder base more than once.

There are two alternate methods for working ladder stitch, each of which produces beadwork with even tension.

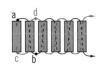

For the first, center a bead on a length of thread with a needle attached to each end. Pick up a bead with one needle, and cross the other needle through it (a–b and c–d). Add all subsequent beads in the same manner.

To begin the other alternative method, pick up all the beads you need to reach the length your pattern requires. Fold the last two beads so they are parallel, and sew through the second-to-last bead again in the same direction (a–b). Fold the next loose bead so it sits

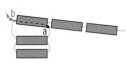

parallel to the previous bead in the ladder, and sew through the loose bead in the same direction (a–b). Continue sewing back through each bead until you exit the last bead of the ladder.

If you are working in tubular brick or Ndebele herringbone stitch, sew your ladder into a ring to provide a base for the new technique. With your thread exiting the last bead in your ladder, sew through the first bead and then back through the last bead, or cross the needles through the first bead if you are using the crossweave technique.

Ndebele herringbone: flat

Start with an even number of beads stitched into a ladder (see Ladder stitch). Turn the ladder, if necessary, so your thread exits the end bead pointing up.

Pick up two beads, and go down

through the next bead on the ladder (a–b). Come up through the third bead on the ladder, pick up two beads, and go down through the fourth bead (b–c). Repeat across the ladder.

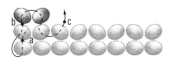

To make a turn, sew down through the end bead of the previous row and back through the last bead of the pair you just added (a–b). Pick up two beads, sew down through the next bead in the previous row, and sew up through the following bead (b–c). Continue adding pairs of beads across the row. You may choose to hide the edge thread by picking up an accent or smaller bead before you sew back through the last bead of the pair you just added.

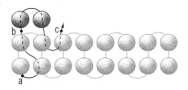

Basics

To make a turn without having thread show on the edge or adding an edge bead, sew down through the end bead in the previous row and up through the second-to-last bead in the previous row, and continue through the last bead added (**a–b**). Pick up two beads, sew down through the next bead in the previous row, and sew up through the following bead (**b–c**). Continue adding pairs of beads across the row. Using this turn will flatten the angle of the edge bead, making the edge stack look a little different than the others.

Ndebele herringbone: tubular

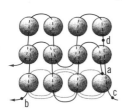

To work tubular Ndebele herringbone, you can start with either a ring or a ladder. To start with a ring, pick up the desired number of beads, and tie the tail and working thread together to form a circle.

To start with a ladder (see Ladder stitch), use an even number of beads, and stitch the first bead to the last bead to form a ring.

Pick up two beads, and go through the next bead on the previous row (the ladder). Come up through the next bead, and repeat. There will be two stitches when you've gone down through the fourth bead (**a–b**).

You need to work a step-up to be in position to start the next row. To do this, come up through the bead next to the one your needle is exiting and the first bead of the first stitch in the row above (**c–d**).

Continue adding two beads per stitch and stepping up at the end of each round.

Peyote: flat even-count

Pick up an even number of beads (**a–b**). These beads will shift to form the first two rows.

To begin row 3, pick up a bead, skip the last bead strung in the previous step, and sew through the next bead in the opposite direction (**b–c**). For each stitch, pick up a bead, skip a bead in the previous row, and sew through the next bead, exiting the first bead strung (**c–d**). The beads added in this row are higher than the previous rows and are referred to as "up-beads."

For each stitch in subsequent rows, pick up a bead, and sew through the next up-bead in the previous row (**d–e**). To count peyote stitch rows, count the total number of beads along both straight edges.

Peyote: flat odd-count

Odd-count peyote is the same as even-count peyote, except for the turn on odd-numbered rows, where the last bead of the row can't be attached in the standard way because there is no up-bead to sew into. The odd-row turn can be convoluted, so we've simplified it here. Please note that the start of this simplified approach is a little different in that the first beads you pick up are the beads in rows 2 and 3. In the next step, you work row 1 and do a simplified turn. After the turn, you'll work the rest of the piece, beginning with row 4.

Pick up an odd number of beads (**a–b**). These beads will shift to form rows 2 and 3 in the next step. If you're working a pattern with more than one bead color, make sure you pick up the beads for the correct rows.

To begin the next row (row 1), pick up a bead, skip the last bead strung in the previous step, and sew through the next bead in the opposite direction (**b–c**). Continue in this manner, exiting

the second-to-last bead strung in the previous row (**c–d**). For the final stitch in the row, pick up a bead, and sew through the first bead strung again (**d–e**). The beads added in this row are higher than previous rows and are referred to as "up-beads."

To work row 4 and all subsequent even-numbered rows, pick up one bead per stitch, exiting the end up-bead in the previous row (**a–b**).

To work row 5 and all subsequent odd-numbered rows, pick up one bead per stitch, exiting the end up-bead in the previous row (**b–c**). Pick up a bead, and sew under the thread bridge between the edge beads below (**c–d**). Sew back through the last bead added to begin the next row (**d–e**).

Peyote: tubular even-count

Pick up an even number of beads to equal the desired circumference. Knot the thread to form a ring, leaving some slack.

Put the ring over a form if desired. Go through the first bead to the left of the knot. Pick up a bead, skip a bead on the previous round, and go through the next bead. Repeat until you're back at the start.

Since you started with an even number of beads, you need to work a step-up to be in position for the next round. Go through the

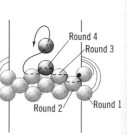

first beads on rounds 2 and 3. Pick up a bead, and go through the second bead on round 3. Repeat.

If you begin with an odd number of beads, you won't need to step up; the beads form a continuous spiral.

Peyote: two-drop

Work two-drop peyote stitch the same as basic peyote, but treat pairs of beads as if they were single beads.

Start with an even number of beads divisible by four.

Pick up two beads (stitch 1 of row 3), skip two beads, and go through the next two beads. Repeat across the row.

Peyote: rapid increase

At the point of increase, pick up two beads instead of one. Go through the next bead.

When you reach the two beads on the next row, go through the first bead, add a bead, and go through the second bead.

Peyote: rapid decrease

At the point of decrease, go through two beads on the previous row.

On the next row, when you reach the two-bead space, pick up one bead.

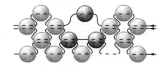

Peyote: flat odd-count, decrease at edge

Work across the row, stopping before you would add the last bead (a–b). Sew under the thread bridge directly below (b–c), and sew back through the bead you just exited and the last bead added (c–d).

Peyote: flat odd-count, increase at edge

To do an increase in flat, odd-count peyote, work three rows beyond the increase point, stopping before adding the last bead (a–b). Pick up three beads, sew under the thread bridge on the previous

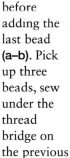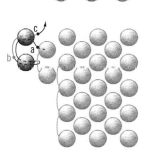

row, and sew back through the last bead added (b–c) and the second bead picked up (c–d). Sew back through the edge bead in the second-to-last row, and continue through the first and second bead picked up for this stitch (d–e).

Pick up two beads, sew under the thread bridge below, and sew back through the second bead picked up (a–b). Continue through the first bead picked up (b–c) to begin the next row.

Zipping up or joining flat peyote

To join two sections of a flat peyote piece invisibly, match up the two pieces so the edge beads fit together. "Zip up" the pieces by zigzagging through the up-beads on both edges.

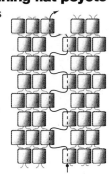

Right-angle weave

To start the first row, pick up four beads, and tie into a ring. Go through the first three beads again.

Pick up three beads. Go back through the last bead of the previous ring (a–b) and continue through the first two picked up for this stitch (b–c).

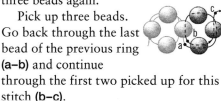

Continue adding three beads for each stitch until the first row is the desired length. You are sewing rings in a figure 8 pattern, alternating direction with each stitch.

To begin row 2, go through the last three beads of the last stitch on row 1, exiting the bead at the edge of one long side.

Pick up three beads, and go back through the bead you exited in the previous step (a–b). Continue through the first new bead (b–c).

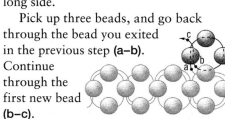

Pick up two beads, and go through the next top bead on the previous row and the bead you exited on the previous stitch (a–b). Continue through the two new beads and the next top bead of the previous row (b–c).

Basics

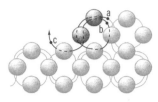

Pick up two beads, go through bead you exited on the previous stitch, the top bead on the previous row, and the first new bead. Keep the thread moving in a figure 8. Pick up two beads per stitch for the rest of the row. Don't sew straight lines between stitches.

Square stitch

String the required number of beads for the first row. Then pick up the first bead of the second row. Go through the last bead of the first row and the first bead

of the second row in the same direction as before. The new bead sits on top of the old bead, and the holes are parallel.

Pick up the second bead of row 2, and go through the next-to-last bead of row 1.

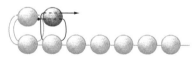

Continue through the new bead of row 2. Repeat this step for the entire row.

Beaded backstitch

To stitch a line of beads, come up through the fabric from the wrong side. Pick up three beads. Stretch the bead thread along the line where the beads will go, and go through the fabric right after the third bead. Come up through the fabric between the second and third beads, and go through the third bead again. String three more beads and repeat. For a tighter stitch, pick up only two beads at a time.

Whip stitch

Whip stitch is a method of hand sewing seams. Bring the needle through the material on the bottom side of the opening, and push it through the material on the upper side of the opening at an angle as shown. Repeat until the opening has been closed.

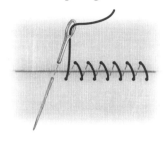

LOOMWORK

Set up the warp

Tie the end of the spool of thread to a screw or hook at one end of the loom.

Bring the thread over one spring and across to the spring at the other end of the loom. Wrap the thread around the back of the rod or screw at the other end of the loom. Go back over the spring in the other direction, and wrap the thread around the opposite screw or hook.

Continue wrapping the thread between springs, keeping the threads a bead's width apart until you have one more warp thread than the number of beads in the width of the pattern. Keep the tension even, but not too tight. Secure the last warp thread to a hook or screw on the loom, then cut the thread from the spool.

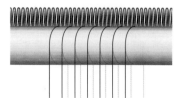

Weave the pattern

Tie the end of a 1-yd. (.9m) length of thread to the first warp thread just below the spring at the top of the loom. Bring the needle under the warp threads. String the first row of beads as

shown on the pattern and slide them to the knot.

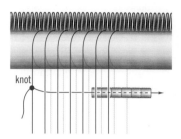

Push the beads up between the warp threads with your finger.

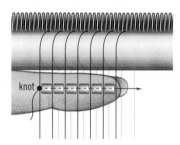

Sew back through the beads, keeping the needle above the warp threads. Repeat, following the pattern row by row.

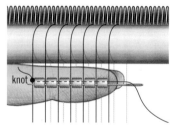

Once you complete the last row, secure the working thread by weaving it into the beadwork.

KNOTS

Half-hitch knot

Pass the needle under the thread between two beads. A loop will form as you pull the thread through. Cross over the thread between the beads, sew through the loop, and pull gently to draw the knot into the beadwork.

Lark's head knot

Fold a cord in half and lay it behind a ring, loop, bar, etc. with the fold pointing down. Bring the ends through the ring from back to front, then through the fold, and tighten.

Continuous lark's head knot

Loop the working cord around a bar, ring, or another cord from front to back, crossing it over itself at the base of the loop. Make another loop from back to front, and pull the working end through the loop just formed. Tighten.

Overhand knot

Make a loop at the end of the thread. Pull the short tail through the loop, and tighten.

Square knot

Cross the left-hand end of the thread over the right, and bring it around and back up.

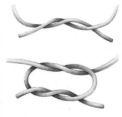

Cross the end that is now on the right over the left, go through the loop, and pull both ends to tighten.

Surgeon's knot

Cross the left-hand end of the thread over the right twice. Pull the ends to

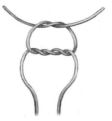

tighten. Cross the end that is now on the right over the left, go through the loop, and tighten.

BEAD CROCHET

Chain stitch

Make a loop in the thread, crossing the ball end over the tail. Put the hook through the loop, yarn over the hook, and draw through the first loop.

Yarn over the hook, and draw through the loop. Repeat for the desired number of chain stitches.

Bead chain stitch

Work as in regular chain stitch, but before doing the yarn over, slide a bead down to the hook. Yarn over the hook, and draw through the loop. Repeat for the desired number of chain stitches. The bead chain should curl into the shape of a backward comma.

Join into a ring

When your bead chain is the desired length, use a slip stitch to join it into a ring: Insert the hook to the left of the first bead. Flip the bead to the right. Slide a bead down to the hook. Yarn over, and bring the yarn through both

the stitch and the loop on the hook.

Slip stitch

Go into the next stitch. Yarn over, and draw the yarn through the stitch and the loop.

Bead slip stitch

Insert the hook to the left of the next bead, and flip that bead to the right. Slide a bead down to the hook, yarn over, and bring the yarn through both the stitch and the loop on the hook.

Bead single crochet

Insert the hook through the front and back loops of the next stitch. Slide a bead against the base of the loop on the hook.

Yarn over, and draw through the stitch. Yarn over, and draw through both remaining loops. The beads will be on the side facing away from you.

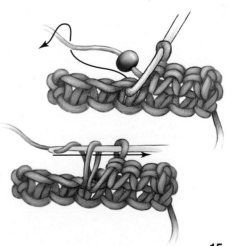

Lampwork and gemstones

Stone nuggets partner with lampworked beads in a classic necklace accented with a strand of silver tube beads.

designed by **Nancy Sells Puffer**

MATERIALS
necklace 19 in. (48cm)
- Hill Tribes silver pendant
- **4** 25 x 20mm (approx.) flat gemstone nuggets
- **6** 23 x 15mm (approx.) gemstone nuggets
- **9** 11 x 17mm lamp-worked beads
- **22** 5mm silver beads
- **2–3g** 3.8mm silver tube beads (Fire Mountain Gems, 800-355-2137, firemountaingems.com)
- **4–6** size 8º seed beads
- **18** 8mm flat silver spacers
- 13mm lobster claw clasp
- 1 in. (2.5cm) chain, 6mm links
- head pin
- 2 crimp beads
- flexible beading wire, .019
- alligator clip or tape
- chainnose pliers
- roundnose pliers
- crimping pliers (optional)
- wire cutters

step*by*step

[1] Determine the finished length of your necklace (mine is 19 in./48cm), add 4 in. (10cm), and cut a piece of beading wire to that length. Cut a second piece of beading wire 6 in. (15cm) longer than the first.

[2] Secure one end of the shorter wire with a clip or tape, and center the pendant on it. String one or more 8º seed beads to fill the pendant's bail so that the next beads strung will be positioned past the bail's edges **(photo a)**.

[3] String a 5mm silver bead, a 23 x 15mm gemstone nugget, a 5mm, an 8mm spacer, a lampworked bead, a spacer, a 5mm, a 25 x 20mm flat gemstone nugget, a 5mm, a spacer, a lampworked bead, and a spacer **(photo b)**. Repeat.

[4] String a 5mm and a 23 x 15mm nugget **(photo c)**. Secure the end of the wire with a clip or tape.

[5] Remove the clip or tape from the other end of the wire, and repeat steps 3 and 4.

[6] To attach the second wire, remove the clip or tape from one end of the beaded wire, and hold the ends of the two wires together. Over both ends, string two 5mms, a crimp bead, and the end link of 1 in. (2.5cm) of chain. Go back through the beads just strung **(photo d)**. Tighten the wires, and crimp the crimp bead (Basics, p. 10). Trim the excess wire.

[7] On the second wire, string approximately 3 in. (7.6cm) of silver tube beads. Skip the next few beads, and go through the second lamp-worked bead from the end and the spacers surrounding

it **(photo e)**. Make sure the strand of tube beads is long enough to arc gracefully over the larger beads. Repeat, going through the fourth lampworked bead and the spacers surrounding it.

[8] String approximately 1½ in. (3.8cm) of tube beads, and go through the pendant's loop. String the tube beads on the second half of the necklace to match the first.

[9] To attach the clasp, repeat step 6, substituting a lobster claw clasp for the chain.

[10] To add a dangle to the chain, string a spacer, a lamp-worked bead, and a spacer on the head pin. Make the first half of a wrapped loop (Basics), attach it to the end chain link, and finish the wraps. Trim the excess wire. ◍

a

b

c

d

e

Bejeweled
bangles

Strings of crystals float between picot-edged bangles.

designed by **Debbi Simon**

a

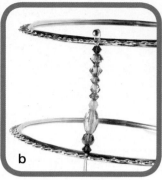

b

c

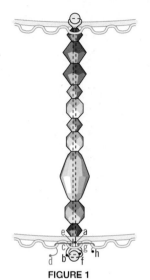

FIGURE 1

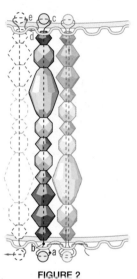

FIGURE 2

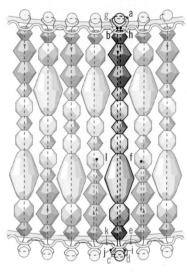

FIGURE 3

step*by*step

[1] Cut 10 ft. (3m) of beading wire, and center a 2mm silver bead on it. Fold the wire in half, aligning the ends. With both ends, go through one of the loops on a bangle (**photo a**).

[2] Over both ends, string a 3mm color D bicone crystal, two 4mm color C bicones, a 3mm color E bicone, a 3mm color G round crystal, an E, a 3mm color F round, a color A oval crystal, a 4mm color B round, and a D.

[3] Holding the wire ends together, go through a loop of the other bangle (**photo b**). Snug up the beads, and cross each end through a 2mm (**figure 1, a–b and e–f**).

[4] With each end, go back through the loop you just went through (**b–c and f–g**). Separate the ends. Then, going in opposite directions, take each end through the next loop from the inside to the outside (**c–d and g–h**).

[5] On one end, string a 2mm, and go back through the loop you just went through (**figure 2, a–b**). Snug up the 2mm.

[6] String a D, two Cs, an E, a G, an E, an F, an A, a B, and a D. Go through the corresponding loop on the other bangle (**b–c**).

[7] String a 2mm, and go back through the same loop (**c–d**). Snug up the beads. Use micro-tip tweezers to hold the wire taut (**photo c**),

keeping the beads snug while going through the next loop from the inside to the outside (**d–e**).

[8] Repeat steps 5–7 around the bangle until you have completed 28 rows.

[9] Using the other end of the wire, repeat steps 5–7, going in the opposite direction until there is one row remaining. Both ends should exit the same loop.

[10] Cross both ends through a 2mm, and go back through the loop (**figure 3, a–b and g–h**). With both ends together, pick up a D, two Cs, an E, a G, an E, an F, an A, a B, and a D, and go through the last corresponding loop on the bangle (**b–c and h–i**).

[11] Cross the ends through a 2mm (**c–d and i–j**), and go back through the loop (**d–e and j–k**). With each end, go through several beads in the adjacent row (**e–f and k–l**). Trim the excess wire. **○**

EDITOR'S NOTE:
Fashion a double-decker version of this cuff by inserting another bangle in the middle of the beading sequence. The center bangle will support a longer span of eye-catching crystals, allowing you to make the cuff wider.

Beachy bracelet

Shell buttons accent pearl or crystal dangles.

designed by **Julie Walker**

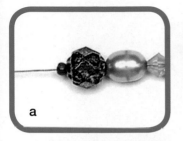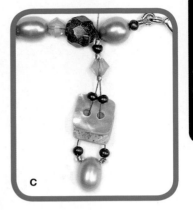

a

b

c

d

e

step*by*step

[1] On a comfortable length of Fireline, attach a stop bead (Basics, p. 10), and leave a 12-in. (30cm) tail.
[2] Pick up a color B cathedral-cut bead, a color A pearl or 6mm fire-polished bead, and a 4mm bicone crystal **(photo a)**. Repeat eight times.

[3] Pick up a B, an A, an 11º seed bead, a 15º seed bead, a small piece of French (bullion) wire, and the loop half of a toggle clasp. Sew back through the 15º, 11º, and A **(photo b)**, and pull tight to form a loop.
[4] Make a square dangle by picking up: a 15º, an 11º, a 15º, a crystal, a 15º, an 11º,

one hole each of two square buttons held back-to-back, an 11º, a 15º, a top-drilled pearl or briolette, a 15º, an 11º, the other hole of both buttons, and an 11º. Sew back through the 15º, crystal, 15º, 11º, and 15º **(photo c)**. Sew through the next B and crystal.
[5] Make a rectangular dangle by picking up a 15º, an 11º, one hole each of two back-to-back rectangular shell buttons, an 11º, a 15º, a crystal, a 15º, an 11º, the buttons' other holes, an 11º, and a 15º. Skip the next A and sew through the next B **(photo d)**.
[6] Make a square dangle, and sew through the next crystal and A.
[7] Make a rectangular dangle, skip the next B, and sew through the next crystal and A.

[8] Repeat steps 4–7, ending with step 4 until you reach the end of the bracelet. Remove the stop bead.
[9] Sew through the final B, and pick up an 11º and one to six 15ºs. (The extra 15ºs allow the bar half of the clasp to move freely, if needed.)
[10] Pick up a small piece of French (bullion) wire and the bar half of the clasp. Sew back through the 15ºs and 11º **(photo e)**, and pull tight.
[11] Making sure that there aren't any gaps between beads, and all of the drops hang correctly, tie a square knot (Basics) with the tails. Sew back through the bracelet with each tail, tie a few half-hitch knots (Basics), and trim. **o**

MATERIALS

bracelet 7 in. (18cm)
- **14** square and **12** rectangular Shellz two-hole buttons (blumenthallansing.com for store list)
- **7** 6mm top-drilled pearls or briolettes
- **10** 6mm pearls or round fire-polished beads, color A
- **10** 6mm cathedral-cut or round fire-polished beads, color B
- **22** 4mm bicone crystals
- **2g** size 11º seed beads
- **1g** size 15º seed beads
- toggle clasp
- French (bullion) wire (optional)
- Fireline 10 lb. test
- beading needles, #10 or #11

Art-glass focal bead

by **Julia Gerlach**

Display an art-glass bead on a multistrand necklace with fringe.

MATERIALS

necklace 20 in. (51cm)

- art-glass bead
- **2** large-hole 8mm silver beads
- assorted 3–8mm beads (in silver and colors to match the focal bead)
- **2** 4mm large-hole silver beads
- **14** 3mm silver beads
- 10g size 11º seed beads, aqua
- **2** hanks size 13º Charlottes, **1** each in dark aqua and turquoise
- clasp
- **2** cones with ⅜-in. (1cm) openings
- **6** in. (15cm) 20-gauge wire, half-hard
- **4** crimp beads
- **4** crimp covers (optional)
- Power Pro or DandyLine, .006
- **8** in. (20cm) flexible beading wire, .015
- beading needles, #12
- chainnose pliers
- crimping pliers
- roundnose pliers
- wire cutters

a

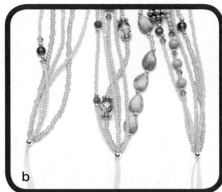

b

c

EDITOR'S NOTE:
To get a group of threads through a large-hole bead easily, lasso the entire bunch with a short piece of flexible beading wire. Go through the large-hole bead with the beading wire, and pull the group of threads through behind it.

d

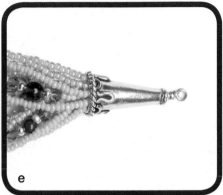

e

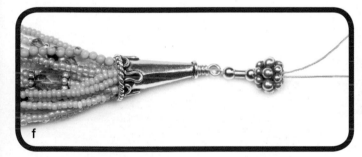

f

g

step*by*step

[1] Cut a 3-in. (7.6cm) piece of 20-gauge wire, and make a wrapped loop (Basics, p. 10) at one end.
[2] Cut eight 1-yd. (.9m) pieces of Power Pro or DandyLine. Holding the group of threads with the ends flush, center the wrapped loop on the group, and make a square knot (Basics) around the loop (photo a).
[3] On each of the 16 strands, pick up 7½ in. (19.1cm) of beads. I picked up a single color of seed beads on eight strands and a single color of seed beads interspersed with various patterns of crystals, turquoise, glass, coral, and silver beads on the other eight. As you finish each strand, attach a stop bead (Basics) to the end.

[4] Separate the strands into three groups. Remove the stop beads, and add or remove beads as necessary to make the beaded portion of the strands even. Over all the strands in each group, string a 3mm bead (photo b).
[5] Over all 16 strands, string a large-hole 4mm bead (photo c).
[6] Repeat steps 1–5 to make 16 similar strands for the second side.
[7] Over all 32 strands, string an 8mm bead, the focal bead, and an 8mm (photo d).
[8] String fringe on each thread tail below the focal bead: Pick up the desired beads, ending with a seed bead. Skip the seed bead, and go back through the next several beads. Secure the tail with a few half-hitch knots (Basics) between beads, and trim.

[9] On each side of the necklace, string a cone over the wire, covering the ends of the strands, and make a wrapped loop (photo e).
[10] Cut a 4-in. (10cm) piece of flexible beading wire. On one end of the wire, string an 8mm, a 3mm, a crimp bead, and a 3mm, and go through the wrapped loop at one end of the necklace. Go back through the beads just strung (photo f). Crimp the crimp bead (Basics), and trim the excess wire.
[11] On the other end of the beading wire, string a 3mm, a crimp bead, a 3mm, and half of the clasp. Go back through the last three or four beads (photo g), crimp the crimp bead, and trim. Cover the crimp beads with crimp covers if desired.
[12] Repeat steps 10 and 11 on the other end of the necklace. ●

Branched fringe wrap

Accent a multistrand necklace with pearl fringe.

designed by **Ludmila Raitzin**

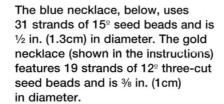

The blue necklace, below, uses 31 strands of 15° seed beads and is ½ in. (1.3cm) in diameter. The gold necklace (shown in the instructions) features 19 strands of 12° three-cut seed beads and is ⅜ in. (1cm) in diameter.

MATERIALS
necklace 20 in. (51cm)

- 2–3 16-in. (41cm) strands 3–5mm pearls
- 2 4mm round beads
- 7–10g size 11° Japanese cylinder beads
- 2 hanks size 15° seed beads or size 12° three-cut seed beads
- clasp
- 2 cones, 8–11mm large-opening diameter
- 6 in. (15cm) 22-gauge wire
- Fireline 6 lb. test or nylon beading thread, color to match seed beads
- DandyLine, .006 or .008
- beading needles, #10 and #12
- G-S Hypo Cement
- tape
- chainnose pliers
- roundnose pliers
- wire cutters

step*by*step

Seed bead strands

[1] Thread a needle on 24 in. (61cm) of Fireline or beading thread, and tape one end. Transfer 18 in. (46cm) of 15° seed beads or 12° three-cut seed beads onto the thread (**photo a** and Editor's Note, p. 26). Remove the needle, and tape the end.
[2] Repeat step 1 until you have enough strands to fill the large opening of the cones.
[3] Cut two 3-in. (7.6cm) pieces of wire. At one end of

each, make a wrapped loop (Basics, p. 10) large enough to accommodate the strands and small enough to fit into the cone.
[4] Remove the tape from one end of all the strands, and gather the ends. Bring the ends through a wrapped loop, and tie an overhand knot (Basics and **photo b**).
[5] Snug up the beads against the wrapped loop, and repeat step 4 on the other side. Glue the knots, and trim the thread close to the knots.

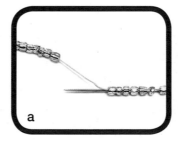

a

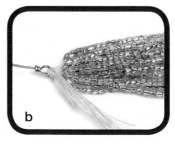

b

Branch fringe

[1] Thread a #10 needle on 31 in. (79cm) of DandyLine, and tape the tail 6 in. (15cm) from the end. String 22 in. (56cm) of cylinder beads. Remove the needle, and tape the end.

[2] Start a new length of Fireline or beading thread, and secure it to one end of the DandyLine strand with a surgeon's knot (Basics).

[3] Sew through seven cylinders on the DandyLine strand (figure, a–b). Pick up six cylinders, a pearl, and a cylinder (b–c). Skip the last cylinder, and sew back through the pearl and three cylinders (c–d).

[4] Pick up two cylinders, a pearl, and a cylinder (d–e).

[5] Skip the last cylinder, and sew back through the beads just picked up and the next two cylinders (e–f).

[6] Repeat step 4. Repeat step 5, ending by sewing through only one cylinder (f–g).

[7] Repeat steps 3–6 (g–h) along the strand of cylinders. Vary the thickness and length of the fringe as you work.

[8] Don't end the thread; tape it to the DandyLine. Tie the knotted ends of the fringe to a wrapped loop, and wrap the fringe around the seed bead strands (photo c). Add or remove beads as necessary on the fringe strand. Remove the tape, and tie the Dandy-Line and thread to the other wrapped loop. Glue the knots and trim the tails.

Finishing

[1] On one side of the necklace, string a cone and a 4mm bead (photo d).

[2] Pull the strands into the cone. Make the first half of a wrapped loop next to the 4mm.

[3] Slide one half of the clasp into the wrapped loop (photo e), and finish the wraps. Trim the excess wire.

[4] Repeat steps 1–3 on the other side of the necklace. ◗

EDITOR'S NOTE:
To transfer beads from a hank, separate one strand of beads from its hank. Tape one end. Tie the other end to a piece of thread with a square knot (Basics, p. 10). Slide a few beads at a time over the knot and onto the thread. Repeat for the remaining strands.

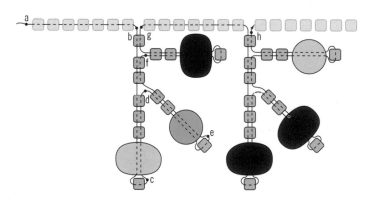

FIGURE

designed by
Ludmila Raitzin

Focal
bead fun

Set off a large focal bead with a spray of accent beads in a multistrand necklace.

As an alternative to Ludmila's design, we used glass and crystal beads and colored cord. You could also use leather, silk, or cotton cord and wood, bone, or other natural beads to complement the design.

MATERIALS

necklace 17 in. (43cm)

- 22mm focal bead
- **124** 5–6mm pearls with large holes, or crystals
- **2** 4mm accent beads
- lobster claw clasp
- **2** 15mm cones or end caps
- 12 in. (30cm) 20–22-gauge wire, half-hard
- 2-in. (5cm) length of chain to accommodate clasp
- nylon beading thread
- 41 yd. (37m) 20 lb. hemp cord
- beading needles, #12
- cyanoacrylate glue
- rubber bands
- scissors
- bead reamer (optional)
- chainnose pliers
- roundnose pliers
- wire cutters

step*by*step

[1] Cut 60 23-in. (58cm) and two 46-in. (1.2m) pieces of hemp cord. Fold the long strands in half and lay them out, loops opposite each other **(photo a)**. Lay the rest of the strands on top of the folded strands. Gather all the strands on one end, including the folded loop, and align the ends. Secure the strands with a rubber band ¾ in. (1.9cm) from the end **(photo b)**.

[2] Cut a 6-in. (15cm) piece of wire. Make the first half of a wrapped loop (Basics, p. 10) on one end. Slide the cord loop into the wire loop, and finish the wrapped loop **(photo c)**.

[3] Tie an 18-in. (46cm) piece of thread around the strands ⅛ in. (3mm) from the end. Wrap the thread around the end to secure the strands. Tie the tails with a square knot (Basics), thread a needle on the tails, and sew into the wraps. Trim the tails.

a

b

c

d

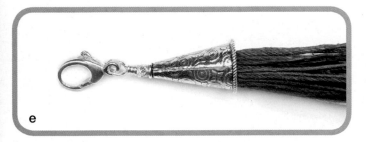

e

f

[4] Dot the cord ends with glue **(photo d)**, and allow them to dry. Remove the rubber band.

[5] Above the wrapped loop, string an end cap or cone and an accent bead. Make the first half of a wrapped loop, slide a lobster claw clasp into the loop, and finish the wraps **(photo e)**.

[6] Separate 17 strands of cord, including the loop of the unfinished end, and make an overhand knot (Basics) 4 in. (10cm) from the cone **(photo f)**. String a focal bead on one of the strands (or on more strands if the bead's hole allows it) and slide it up to the knot **(photo g)**.

[7] Make an overhand knot with all the strands so the focal bead is snug between the two knots **(photo h)**.

[8] Dot the end of each strand with glue, allow it to dry, and trim it diagonally.

String two 6mm pearls or crystals on each strand **(photo i)**. If the holes of the pearls are too small, use a bead reamer to enlarge them.

[9] Gather all the ends and secure them with a rubber band. Align each strand with the cord loop, trimming each strand to remove the glued end. Repeat steps 2–5 to complete the necklace, using chain instead of the clasp in step 5. ○

EDITOR'S NOTE:
Cord sometimes comes wrapped around cards and can be kinky when unwrapped. To take out the kinks, cut the strands to length, run warm water over them, and lay them out flat until they dry.

g

h

i

Crisscross.
earrings

Gold-filled and sterling small-link chains give dangle earrings a delicate look.

designed by **Melody MacDuffee**

step*by*step

[1] Cut two 2½-in. (6.4cm) pieces of 22-gauge wire, and straighten each piece. On one end of each, place an earring back or wrap with tape.

[2] Cut five 26-link pieces of both sterling and gold-filled chain.

[3] Cut both sterling and gold-filled chain in the following lengths: 25 links, 11 links, nine links, seven links, five links, and three links **(photo a)**.

[4] Cut a 17-link piece of chain in either gold-filled or sterling to match the earring findings. String an earring finding through the center link of the 17-link chain **(photo b)**.

[5] On one piece of wire, string one end of the 17-link chain, the 25-link sterling chain, and a gold-lined 11º seed bead.

String a 26-link sterling chain and a gold-lined 11º. Repeat four times.

String a 26-link gold-filled chain and a silver-lined 11º. Repeat four times.

String the 25-link gold-filled chain and the other end of the 17-link chain **(photo c)**.

Secure the wire end with tape or an earring back.

[6] On the second wire, string the other end link of the 25-link sterling chain and a silver-lined 11º.

String the first 26-link gold-filled chain, the three-link sterling chain, and a silver-lined 11º.

String the second 26-link gold-filled chain, the five-link sterling chain, and a silver-lined 11º.

String the third 26-link gold-filled chain, the seven-link sterling chain, and a silver-lined 11º.

String the fourth 26-link gold-filled chain, the nine-link sterling chain, and a silver-lined 11º.

String the fifth 26-link gold-filled chain, the 11-link sterling chain, and a silver-lined 11º **(photo d)**.

[7] Crossing the sterling 26-link chains behind the gold-filled chains, string the first 26-link sterling chain, the 11-link gold-filled chain, and a gold-lined 11º.

String the second 26-link sterling chain, the nine-link gold-filled chain, and a gold-lined 11º.

String the third 26-link sterling chain, the seven-link gold-filled chain, and a gold-lined 11º.

String the fourth 26-link sterling chain, the five-link gold-filled chain, and a gold-lined 11º.

String the fifth 26-link sterling chain, the three-link gold-filled chain, and a gold-lined 11º.

String the 25-link gold-filled chain **(photo e)**.

[8] Make a simple loop on each end of both wires so the tail touches the wire **(photo f)**. Position the earring-wire chain on the top of the loops.

[9] Make a second earring to match the first. ●

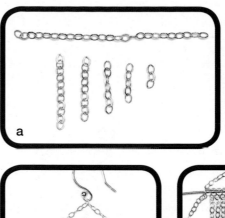

a

b

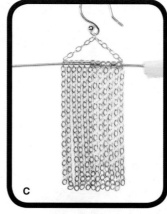

c

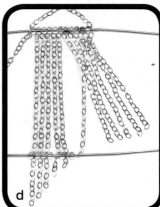

d

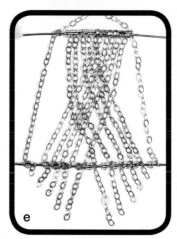

e

f

MATERIALS

earrings

- size 11º Japanese seed beads
  2g gold-lined crystal
  2g silver-lined crystal
- 10 in. (25cm) 22-gauge gold-filled or sterling wire, half-hard
- 27 in. (69cm) sterling chain (approximately 1.25mm per link or 20 links per inch)
- 27 in. (69cm) gold-filled chain (approximately 1.25mm per link or 20 links per inch)
- pair of earring findings
- tape or plastic earring backs
- roundnose pliers
- wire cutters

Valentine earrings

Pair crystals and sterling silver chain for a lovely earring set.

by **Anna Elizabeth Draeger**

Cut the chain into single heart links, and use the pieces as cute little charms to dangle from the earrings.

step*by*step

[1] Cut the heart-link chain in half, making sure each half has 31 links. Cut each half into two five-link segments, three three-link segments, and four single hearts.

[2] On one end of the wire, make a plain loop (Basics, p. 10). String a 4mm bicone crystal and make a plain loop. Trim the wire. Repeat using the remaining wire to make a second small-bead unit.

Repeat to make two medium-bead units, stringing a 4mm round crystal and a bicone.

a

b

c

d

e

f

MATERIALS

earrings

• Swarovski crystals
  2 6mm rondelles
  14 4mm bicones
  4 4mm rounds
• 10 in. (25cm) 22-gauge
  silver wire
• 10 in. (25cm) heart-link
  chain, 31 links per earring
  (Fire Mountain Gems,
  800-355-2131,
  firemountaingems.com)
• 2 1-in. (2.5cm) 22-gauge
  head pins
• 4 4–6mm jump rings
• pair of earring findings
• chainnose pliers
• roundnose pliers
• wire cutters

Repeat to make a large-bead unit, stringing a bicone, a 6mm rondelle, and a bicone (**photo a**).

[**3**] Open the loop of the round-bead end of a medium-bead unit, and attach a single heart. Close the loop. Repeat with the matching unit and the two small-bead units (**photo b**).

[**4**] String a bicone on a head pin, and make a plain loop. Open the loop and attach a three-link chain (**photo c**). Close the loop.

[**5**] Open a jump ring (Basics) and attach the two five-link chains. Close the jump ring (**photo d**).

[**6**] Open a loop of the large-bead unit. Attach a three-link chain, a medium-bead unit, and the remaining end link of a five-link chain. Close the loop. Repeat on the other

side of the large-bead unit (**photo e**).

[**7**] Open a jump ring, and attach the remaining end links of the three-link chains, a small-bead unit, the dangle, and the remaining small-bead unit. Close the jump ring (**photo f**).

[**8**] Open the loop of an earring finding. Attach the top jump ring of the earring, and close the loop.

[**9**] Repeat steps 2–8 to make a second earring. ❂

Dancing
bead clusters

Make a lavish bracelet with sparkling beads and silver charms.

designed by **Jane Hardenbergh**

MATERIALS
both projects
- chainnose pliers
- roundnose pliers
- wire cutters

blue-and-purple bracelet
7½ in. (19.1cm)
- 4mm crystals
  24 each of **2** colors, A and I
  32 each of **8** colors, B–H
  (for colors, see the December 2006 Resource Guide at BeadandButton.com)
- **76** 3mm silver beads
- **304** 2mm silver beads
- **190** 4mm spacers
- **38** silver charms
- toggle clasp with chain
- 9½ ft. (2.9m) 22-gauge wire
- 7 in. (18cm) chain, 6mm links (33 links total)
- **266** 1-in. (2.5cm) head pins
- **38** 6mm jump rings
- **2** 4mm jump rings

rainbow bracelet 8 in. (20cm)
- **224** 6mm Czech glass beads (16 each of 14 colors)
- **168** 5mm silver beads
- **196** 3mm silver beads
- **28** small silver heart charms (twopurplepandas.com)
- toggle clasp
- 7 ft. (2.1m) 22-gauge wire
- 7 in. (18cm) chain, 10mm links (27 links total)
- **196** 1-in. (2.5cm) head pins
- **28** 6mm jump rings
- **2** 4mm jump rings

step*by*step

Blue-and-purple bracelet

The key design trick in this bracelet is arranging the nine colors in a spectrum, starting with color A and ending with color I. Refer to **photo a** in steps 1–3.

[1] String beads on head pins as follows, and make a plain loop (Basics, p. 10) above each top bead. Make six of each dangle for colors A and I. Make eight of each dangle for colors B–H:
- 4mm bicone crystal
- 2mm bead, crystal, 2mm
- 4mm spacer, crystal, spacer, 2mm

[2] To make a jointed dangle, cut a 1-in. (2.5cm) piece of wire, and make a plain loop on one end. String a crystal, and make a loop in the same plane as the first.

On a head pin, string a 3mm bead, a 4mm spacer, and a 2mm. Make a plain loop. Open the loop, and attach it to a loop on the first component. Make a total of three jointed dangles each for colors A and I. Make four each for colors B–H.

[3] To make a charm dangle, cut a 2-in. (5cm) piece of wire, and make a plain loop on one end. String a 2mm, a 3mm, and a crystal, and make a second loop. Open the bottom loop, attach a charm, and close the loop. Make a total of three charm dangles each for colors A and I. Make four each for colors B–H.

[4] Open a 6mm jump ring (Basics), and string eight dangles as in **photo b**. Make a total of three jump ring units each for colors A and I. Make four each for colors B–H.

[5] Attach a color A jump ring unit to an end link of chain. Close the jump ring.

[6] Attach another A jump ring unit to the other side of the same chain link (**photo c**). Skip a link, and attach the remaining A jump ring unit to the next link.

[7] Attach a color B jump ring unit to the other side of the last link used in step 6. Skip a link, and attach two B jump ring units. Skip a link, and attach the fourth B jump ring unit. Continue attaching jump ring units to each side of every other link (**photo d**), ending with color H.

[8] Open a 4mm jump ring, and attach half of a clasp to an end chain link between the jump rings (**photo e**). Repeat on the other end.

Rainbow bracelet

[1] String beads on head pins as follows, and make a plain loop (Basics) above each top bead. Make four of each dangle for each color:
- 6mm bead
- 3mm bead, 6mm, 3mm
- 5mm bead, 6mm, 5mm

[2] To make a jointed dangle, cut a 1-in. (2.5cm) piece of wire, and make a plain loop on one end. String a 6mm, and make a loop in the same plane as the first.

On a head pin, string a 3mm, a 5mm, and a 3mm. Make a plain loop. Open the loop, and attach it to a loop on the first component. Make two jointed dangles for each color.

[3] To make a charm dangle, cut a 2-in. (5cm) piece of wire, and make a plain loop on one end. String a 3mm, a 5mm, and a 6mm, and make a second loop. Open the loop next to the 6mm, attach a charm, and close the loop.

Make two charm dangles for each color.

[4] Repeat step 4 of the blue-and-purple bracelet to make two jump ring units for each color.

[5] Attach two same-color jump ring units to every other link in the chain.

[6] Attach a clasp as in step 8 of the blue-and-purple bracelet. ●

Bewitching
bezels

Create bezels for coin-shaped gemstones in a modern necklace.

designed by **Vicky Nguyen**

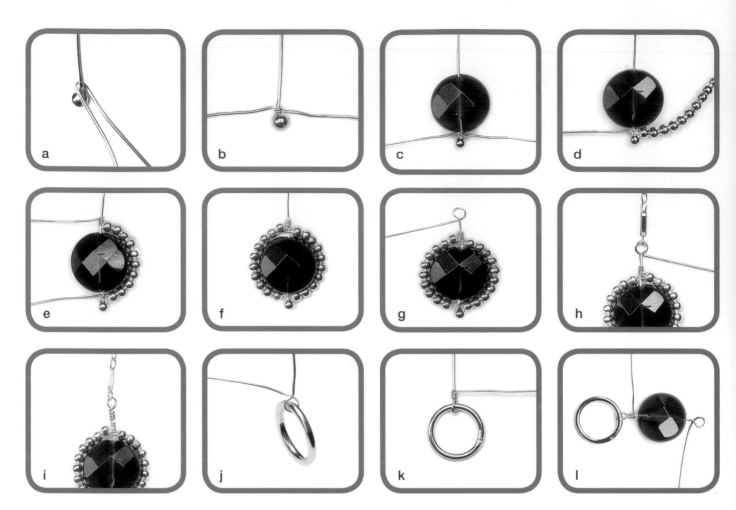

stepbystep

Necklace

Dangles

[1] Cut the fine-gauge chain as follows: two 1½-in. (3.8cm) pieces, two 2-in. (5cm) pieces, one 2½-in. (6.4cm) piece.

[2] Cut six 4-in. (10cm) pieces of 26-gauge wire.

[3] Fold a piece of wire in half, and place a head pin in the fold (photo a). Wrap each end around the head pin so the ends are going in opposite directions (photo b). String a coin-shaped bead on the head pin (photo c).

[4] String ten 2mm beads on one end of the 26-gauge wire (photo d), and wrap the wire twice around the head pin above the coin bead (photo e). Repeat with the other wire end. Trim the wire ends flush against the head pin (photo f).

[5] Make the first half of a wrapped loop (Basics, p. 10) with the head pin (photo g).

[6] Repeat steps 3–5 five times to make a total of six bezeled coins.

[7] To complete a dangle, attach the wrapped loop of one bezeled coin to an end link of a fine-gauge chain (photo h), and finish the wraps (photo i).

[8] Repeat step 7 four times to make a total of five dangles. You'll have one bezeled coin left over.

Assembly

[1] Cut a 6-in. (15cm) piece of wire, and make the first half of a wrapped loop 2½ in. (6.4cm) from one end. Attach the loop to a soldered jump ring (photo j), and finish the wraps (photo k). Do not trim the wire.

[2] String a coin bead on the long wire end, and make the first half of a wrapped loop (photo l). Attach the loop to a soldered jump ring, and finish the wraps (photo m).

[3] String ten 2mms on one wire end, and secure the tail with a few wraps (photo n).

[4] On the other wire end, string five 2mms, the longest dangle, and five 2mms. Secure the tail with a few wraps, and trim (photo o).

[5] On each soldered jump ring, repeat steps 1–4, attaching the remaining dangles from longest to shortest.

[6] Repeat steps 1–4 five times on each side without adding dangles. In step 2 of the last repeat, attach an end link

EDITOR'S NOTE:
This bezeling technique also works with beads of other shapes and sizes. Try round or oval beads, and be sure to adjust the number of 2mms you use for bezeling to suit the beads in your design.

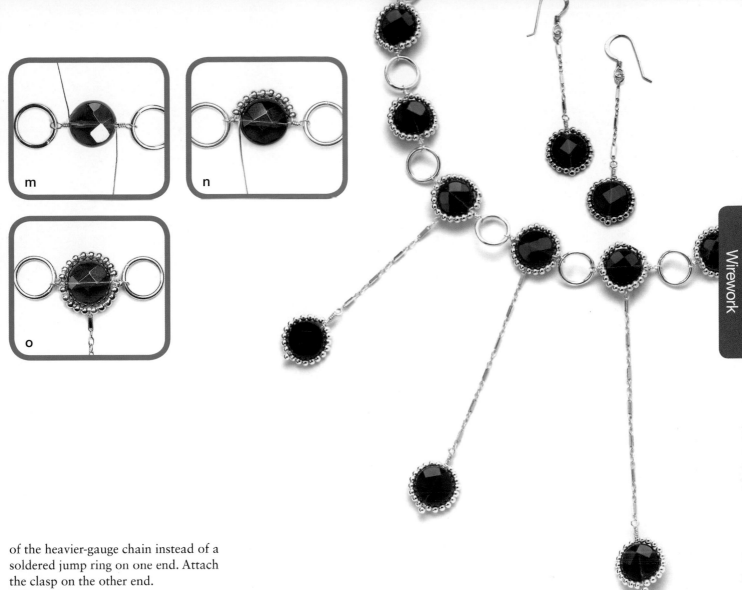

of the heavier-gauge chain instead of a soldered jump ring on one end. Attach the clasp on the other end.

[7] Attach the remaining bezeled coin to the available end link of the extender chain, finish the wraps, and trim.

Earrings

[1] Cut a 1-in. (2.5cm) piece of chain and a 4-in. (10cm) piece of wire.

[2] Make a bezeled coin as in steps 3–5 of "Dangles." Attach the loop to an end link of chain, and finish the wraps.

[3] Open a 3mm jump ring (Basics), and attach it to the top link of chain on the dangle. Close the jump ring.

[4] Open the loop of an earring finding, and attach the 3mm jump ring. Close the loop.

[5] Make a second earring to match the first. ●

MATERIALS
both projects
- chainnose pliers
- roundnose pliers
- wire cutters

necklace 18 in. (46cm)
- **21** 10mm coin-shaped beads (chalcedony beads available at The Bead Shop, beadshop.com)
- **420** 2mm round sterling silver or gold-filled beads
- clasp
- **8** ft. (2.4m) 26-gauge sterling silver or gold-filled wire
- **3** in. (7.6cm) sterling silver or gold-filled cable chain, 8mm links
- **10** in. (25cm) sterling silver or gold-filled rolo chain, 2mm links; or fancy bar-and-link chain, 1.3mm links

- **6** 2-in. (5cm) sterling silver or gold-filled decorative head pins
- **14** 10mm sterling silver or gold-filled soldered jump rings (beadshop.com)

earrings
- **2** 10mm coin-shaped beads (beadshop.com)
- **40** 2mm round sterling silver or gold-filled beads
- **8** in. (20cm) 26-gauge sterling silver or gold-filled wire
- **2** in. (5cm) sterling silver or gold-filled rolo chain, 2mm links; or fancy bar-and-link chain, 1.3mm links
- **2** 2-in. sterling silver or gold-filled decorative head pins
- **2** 3mm sterling silver or gold-filled jump rings
- pair of earring findings

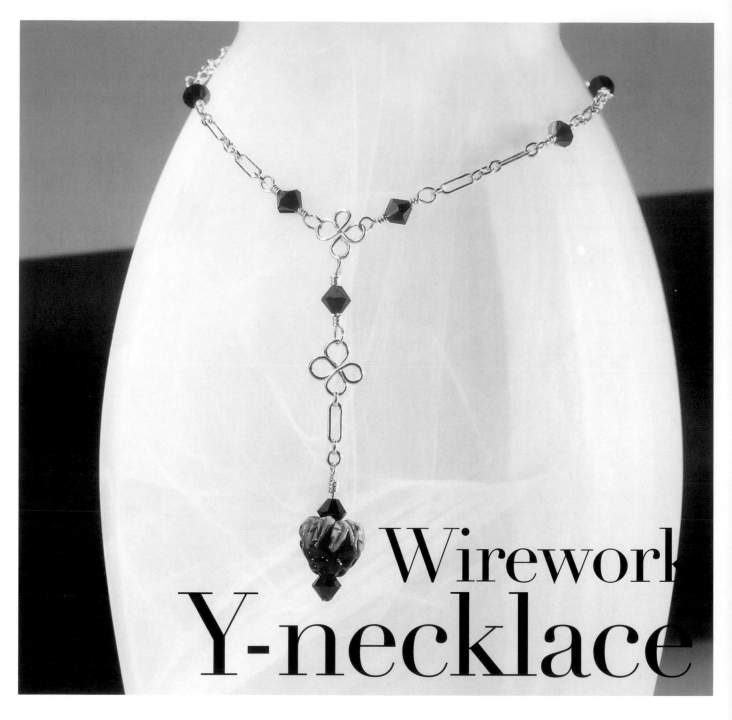

Wirework Y-necklace

Form flowers from wire, then add a lampworked strawberry focal bead and a crystal-accented clasp.

designed by **Tammy Powley**

step*by*step

Wire flowers

[1] Cut a 2-in. (5cm) piece of 20-gauge wire. Using roundnose pliers, make a simple loop on one end, working approximately ½ in. (1.3cm) from the pliers' tip.

Position the pliers next to the first loop, and make a second loop **(photo a)**. Make two more loops, each next to the previous loop, and trim any excess wire **(photo b)**. Repeat to make a total of five flower components.

[2] Set one flower component aside. Flatten the remaining flower components by placing each on a hard surface and firmly tapping it with a rawhide mallet a few times.

Components

[1] Cut eight 1-in. (2.5cm) pieces and one ⅜-in. (1cm) piece **(photo c)** of chain.

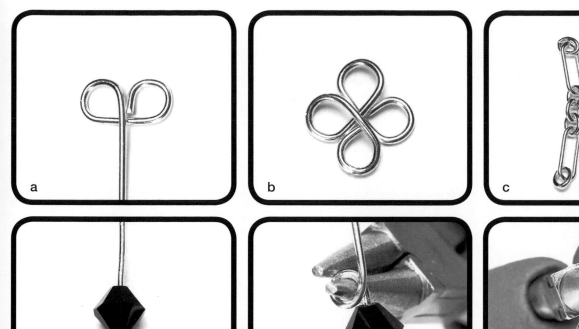

a

b

c

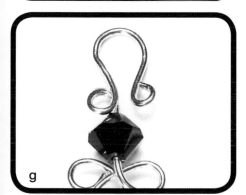

d

e

f

g

MATERIALS

necklace 16 in. (41cm)

- lampworked focal bead
- 15 6mm or 8mm Swarovski crystals, in each of 2 colors
- 2½ ft. (76cm) 20-gauge sterling silver wire, half-hard
- 9 in. (23cm) sterling silver bar-and-circle chain (CGM, cgmfindings.com)
- 2-in. (5cm) head pin
- rawhide mallet
- chainnose pliers
- nylon-jaw pliers
- roundnose pliers
- wire cutters

[2] Cut a 1-in. (2.5cm) piece of wire. On one end, make the first half of a wrapped loop (Basics, p. 10). String a 6mm or 8mm bicone crystal and make the first half of a wrapped loop on the other end. Repeat to make a total of 11 bicone units, using bicones in two colors.

[3] On a head pin, string a bicone, the focal bead, and a bicone. Make the first half of a wrapped loop.

Assembly

[1] Attach the focal-bead unit to one end of the ⅜-in.

(1cm) chain. Complete the wraps. Slide the other end of the chain onto a flower component. The component may open somewhat as you slide the chain onto it. If it does, use nylon-jaw pliers to close the component.

[2] Attach one loop of a bicone unit to the flower component on the petal opposite the chain. Attach the remaining loop to a second flower component. Complete the wraps.

[3] On each petal adjacent to where you just attached the bicone unit, attach one loop of a bicone unit.

[4] On each side, attach a 1-in. (2.5cm) chain, a bicone unit, a 1-in. (2.5cm) chain, a bicone unit, a flower component, a bicone unit, a 1-in. (2.5cm) chain, a bicone unit, and a 1-in. (2.5cm) chain. Complete the wraps.

Clasp

[1] Using a 2-in. (5cm) piece of 20-gauge wire, make the first three loops of a flower component; do not trim the tail. String a bicone on the tail (photo d).

[2] Using roundnose pliers, grasp the wire tail above the

bicone and make a loop (photo e).

[3] Grasp the tail above the loop, and bend the wire over the widest part of the pliers' jaw (photo f).

[4] Trim the wire about 1 in. (2.5cm) from the bend. Use your pliers to curl the end hook (photo g).

[5] Slide the hook component on one end of the necklace. Use nylon-jaw pliers to gently close the flower's three loops. Slide the remaining flower component on the other end of the necklace, and close the loops. ●

Wire-wrapped bracelet

Wrap assorted beads around a sterling silver form to make an upscale accessory in a flash. Make your bracelet with a single layer of beads, or wrap layers upon layers for a sculptural look.

designed by **Miachelle DePiano**

MATERIALS
bracelet 6½ in. (16.5cm)
- assorted 4–8mm beads
- 6 ft. (1.8m) 20- to 24-gauge sterling silver wire
- sterling silver bracelet form (Metalliferous, metalliferous.com)
- chainnose pliers
- nylon-jaw pliers (optional)
- wire cutters

step*by*step

To create a neat appearance at the ends, wrap the bracelet in two sections, working from each end toward the middle. As you wrap, your wire may kink. To smooth it out, flatten the kinks with nylon-jaw pliers.

[1] Cut the 20- to 24-gauge wire in half. With one piece, make a right-angle bend about ¼–½ in. (6–13mm) from one end.

[2] Place the bent end of the wire along the inside of the form at one end, pointing the tip of the wire away from the end of the form. Neatly wrap the long end of wire around the form (photo a) until the tail is covered.

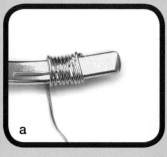

a

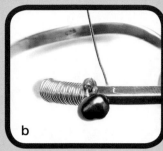

b

c

d

[3] Pick up one or two beads, and, holding the beads on the outer surface of the form, wrap the wire around the form (photo b). To anchor the beads, make another wrap (photo c). Repeat until you reach the middle of the bracelet, picking up beads as desired.

[4] To secure the wire, make a few more wraps without any beads. With chainnose pliers, tuck the tail under the beads on top of the bracelet (photo d). Trim, if needed.

[5] Repeat steps 1–4 on the other end of the bracelet.

[6] To make a sculptural bracelet, as the purple-and-blue bracelet (bottom right), add layers of beads using the following methods:

• Continue wrapping around the bracelet form as before, placing the new beads directly on top of the previous layer. To reduce the amount of exposed wire on the inside of the form, use the previous layer as an armature around which to wrap instead of wrapping around the form.

• If your bead holes will accommodate more than one pass of the wire, string a few beads, and go through a bead on the previous layer.

• String a few beads, go under a wire on a previous layer, do not wrap, and continue. ●

EDITOR'S NOTE:
Choose a bracelet form with a flat inner surface. Some forms are made with round wire, which makes it difficult to get the beads to stay in place.

Build loops upon loops of monochromatic crystals and beads for flashy earrings. You can also try one as a pendant!

MATERIALS
earrings
- bicone crystals
  2 8mm, color A
  2 6mm, color B
  32 4mm, color A
  24 4mm, color B
- 3mm fire-polished beads
  46 color C (to match color A)
  22 color D (to match color B)
  34 color E (accent color)
- size 11º seed or cylinder beads (all to match color A)
  5g color F, matte
  5g color G, metallic
  5g color H, transparent or silver-lined
- 13 in. (33cm) 22-gauge sterling silver wire, half-hard
- 4 yd. (3.7m) 28-gauge sterling silver wire, dead-soft
- **2** 2-in. (5cm) sterling silver head pins
- **2** 4–6mm soldered jump rings
- pair of earring findings
- chainnose pliers
- roundnose pliers
- wire cutters

Swinging crystal earrings

Wirework and crystals make for large, yet light, earrings.

designed by **Melody MacDuffee**

step*by*step

When complete, these earrings have a distinct front and back. To help you identify the front while you're working, bend the end loops of the U-shaped base so the openings face toward the back.

Outer round
[1] Cut two 6½-in. (16.5cm) pieces of wire. Set one piece aside for the second earring. Use roundnose pliers to form a simple loop on each end of the wire. Gently bend the wire into a U, making sure that the loops both face the same direction **(photo a)**.
[2] Cut a 1-yd. (.9m) piece of 28-gauge wire. Secure the wire by wrapping it tightly four or five times around the left side of the U-shaped base, next to the loop **(figure, point a)**.

[3] Pick up a color G 11º seed bead, a color B 4mm bicone crystal, and a G. Holding the beads in a small loop next to the base wire, wrap the working wire tightly around the base twice **(a–b** and **photo b)**.
[4] Pick up a color F 11º, a color A 4mm bicone, and an F, and wrap the working wire around the base twice as before **(b–c)**.
[5] Repeat steps 3 and 4 until you have 23 beaded loops around the outside of the base and have reached the end loop on the right side. Wrap the wire tightly around the base four or five times to match the other end **(c–d)**. Do not trim.

Inner round 1
[1] Continuing with the 28-gauge wire, pick up a color H 11º, a 3mm color C

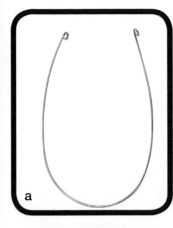

a

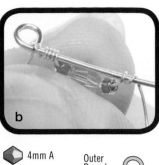

b

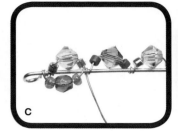

c

d

e

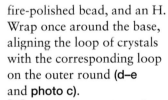

f

EDITOR'S NOTE:
If you're having trouble fitting all 23 loops on the outer round of the base wire, gently slide the existing loops along the wire to make room for the last few wraps.

Bead legend:
- 4mm A
- 4mm B
- 3mm C
- 3mm D
- 3mm E
- 11º F
- 11º G
- 11º H

Outer Round

Inner Round 1

Inner Round 2

Inner Round 3

Inner Round 4

FIGURE

fire-polished bead, and an H. Wrap once around the base, aligning the loop of crystals with the corresponding loop on the outer round (d–e and **photo c**).
[2] Pick up a G, a C, and a G, and wrap the wire around the base as before (e–f).
[3] Repeat steps 1 and 2 until you have completed 23 inner loops that line up with the outer loops (f–g). Tightly wrap the wire around the base several times to secure it at **point g**, and trim.

Inner round 2
[1] Cut 1 ft. (30cm) of 28-gauge wire. Secure the end with two or three wraps on the third inner loop, at **point h**.
[2] Pick up an H, a color E fire-polished bead, and an H. With the working wire, go through the next loop of the

first inner round, front to back, positioning the wire between the C and lower G (**photo d**). Squeeze the working wire at that point to establish the new loop.
[3] Repeat step 2 until you have 17 loops total (i–j). Wrap tightly at **point j** two or three times, and trim.

Inner round 3
[1] Cut 1 ft. (30cm) of 28-gauge wire. Secure the end at **point k** with two or three wraps as before.
[2] Pick up an F, a G, a color D fire-polished bead, a G, and an F. Secure the working wire to the previous round, as in step 2 of "Inner round 2" (k–l).

[3] Repeat step 2 to form 11 loops in total (l–m). Wrap tightly at **point m** two or three times, and trim.

Inner round 4
[1] Cut 1 ft. (30cm) of 28-gauge wire. Secure the end at **point n** with two or three wraps.
[2] Pick up an H, an A, and an H, skip over one or two Ds and secure the working wire (n–o). Repeat three times for a total of four evenly spaced loops at the bottom center of the base (o–p). Secure the end at **point p** with two or three wraps, and trim.

Assembly
[1] On a head pin, pick up an F, an 8mm bicone, an E, a G, a 6mm bicone, a G, an E, an A, an E, and an H. Make the first half of a wrapped loop (Basics, p. 10 and **photo e**). Attach the loop to a soldered jump ring, and finish the wraps.
[2] Open one loop of the base, attach the soldered jump ring, and close the loop. Repeat with the other loop, making sure the dangle hangs in the middle (**photo f**).
[3] Open the loop of an earring finding, attach the earring, and close the loop. Make a second earring to match the first. ●

Tiny dancers

Wire dance partners encircle a focal bead.

designed by **Karen Rakoski**

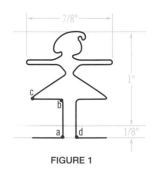

step*by*step

[1] Using your chainnose pliers, grip the wire 2 in. (5cm) from the end, and make a right-angle bend.

[2] With the 2-in. (5cm) end on the left, position your wire over the **figure 1** template so that the bend lines up with **point a**. Grasp the working end just below where it lines up with **point b**, and bend the wire over your pliers to match the figure (**photo a**).

[3] Lay your wire on the template, lining up **points a** and **b**. Grip the working wire with your pliers at **point c** to create another bend (**photo b**).

[4] Continue making bends, following the template and switching between roundnose and chainnose pliers as needed (see Editor's Note, p. 48), until you've created a female form

that's 1⅛ in. (2.9cm) tall and ⅞ in. (2.2cm) wide from arm-tip to arm-tip (**c–d**).

[5] At **point d**, use your chainnose pliers to make a right-angle bend. This bend is now the base of the next form (**figure 2, point a**). Line your wire up with the next template (**photo c**), and make a male form (**a–b**).

[6] Repeat steps 3–5 to make another female form and a male form, following **figures 1**

and 2. When laid flat, the forms should form a rough circle.

[7] Hold the forms so that all the bases touch in the center. Wrap the working wire around the base of the first form's legs (**photo d** and **figure 3, a–b**).

[8] Cross the working wire over the second form, and wrap tightly around its legs (**photo e** and **b–c**). Repeat to wrap the legs of the third form (**c–d**). On the final form, make sure that the wire tail is

FIGURE 1

FIGURE 2

EDITOR'S NOTE:
To use a single dancer, lengthen the arms enough to reach around the bead, intertwining them at the back.

a

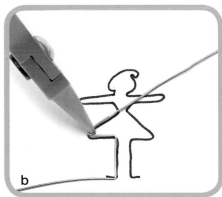

b

c

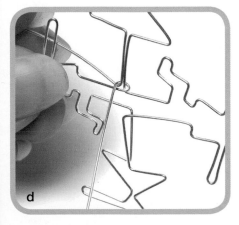

d

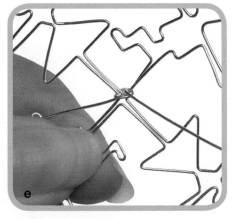

e

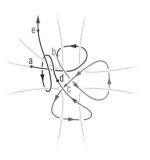

FIGURE 3

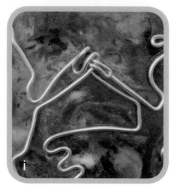

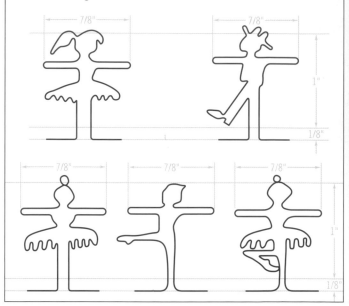

MAY WE CUT IN?

If you'd like, substitute these country or ballet dancers for the rock 'n' roll figures made in the instructions.

7/8"   7/8"   1"   1/8"

7/8"   7/8"   7/8"   1"   1/8"

wrapped alongside the legs within the final loop (d–e).

[9] Secure the tail by using it to wrap a tight loop around the working wire, close to the base. Leaving a ½-in. (1.3cm) tail, trim the tail, and align it parallel to the working wire.

[10] String your focal bead over both wire ends (photo f). If the hole of your bead is too big, use the long wire to pick up enough matching seed beads to fill the hole.

[11] Arrange the forms so that a male and a female are facing each other on each side of the bead, and gently bend them up. Make a wrapped loop (Basics, p. 10) above the bead, and trim the excess wire (photo g).

[12] Using your chainnose pliers, gently compress the ends of the female forms' hands. Bend up the tips, and insert them into the males' hands. Using your roundnose pliers, uniformly bend each female's hand over slightly to secure the connection (photo h), making sure not to tighten so much that you distort any of the forms.

[13] Once all the forms are initially joined, gently tighten the hand connections. If there's too much slack around the bead, fold the males' hands over as well (photo i). Adjust all the forms around the bead so that no parts will catch on anything. ◉

EDITOR'S NOTES:

• **You can achieve different curves by varying where you grip the wire along the jaws of your pliers. For gentle curves, use the larger end of your roundnose pliers. Use the tip when you want to make small rounded bends or circles. Choose chainnose pliers for flat areas and sharp angles.**

Concentrate on one bend at a time. Don't worry if it's not perfect. You can use chainnose pliers to gently flatten out any bend that doesn't match your template, and try again.

• **To match a differently sized bead, adjust the figures shown. Or create your own templates: Wrap a piece of paper around the width of your bead. Divide that measurement by four (if you'd like four figures) to determine the widest part of each figure. To accommodate the connections, add ⅛ in. (3mm) to the arms on each side of every figure. Add ⅛ in. (3mm) to the height of each figure at the feet for wrapping the base. Sketch out those measurements as a rough pattern, and draw your new character templates within those lines.**

Crystals &rings

Connect crystal
montees and jump
rings to make a
sparkling silver
Y-necklace and
matching earrings.

designed by **Stephen Parfitt**

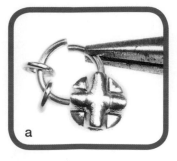

a

b

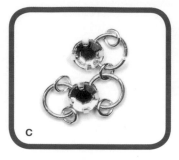

c

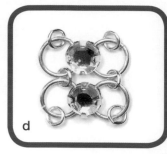

d

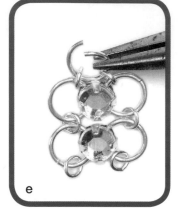

e

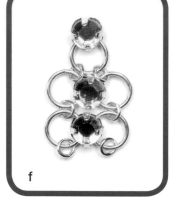

f

g

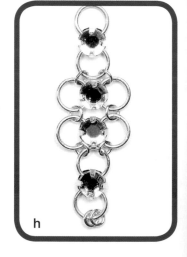

h

MATERIALS

both projects
- chainnose pliers
- flatnose or bentnose pliers
- roundnose pliers
- wire cutters

necklace 18 in. (46cm)
- 3 8mm bicone crystals
- 13 4.8mm four-hole Czech cross-channel montees (La Bead Oh, 217-544-8473)
- lobster claw clasp with jump ring
- 14 in. (36cm) chain, small links
- 3 1-in. (2.5cm) head pins
- 27 22-gauge jump rings, 6mm outside diameter
- 24-gauge jump ring, 4mm outside diameter (optional)
- 26 26-gauge soldered jump rings, 3mm outside diameter

earrings
- 2 8mm bicone crystals
- 8 4.8mm four-hole Czech cross-channel montees
- 2 1-in. (2.5cm) head pins
- 20 22gg 6mm jump rings, outside diameter
- 20 26gg 3mm soldered jump rings, outside diameter
- pair of earring findings

step*by*step

Necklace

[1] Open a 6mm jump ring (Basics, p. 10). Slide the open jump ring through two adjacent holes of a montee and through two soldered 3mm jump rings (photo a, back view shown). Close the jump ring. Repeat on the other side of the montee (photo b, back view shown).
[2] Open a 6mm jump ring, and slide it through a 3mm jump ring, two holes of a montee and a corresponding 3mm jump ring from the previous step (photo c). Close the 6mm jump ring.
[3] Repeat step 2 on the other side of the montee (photo d).
[4] Open a 6mm jump ring, and slide it through the 3mm jump rings on one end of the segment (photo e).
[5] Slide the open jump ring through two holes of a montee, and close the jump ring (photo f). Connect a 6mm jump ring to the other side of the montee (photo g).

[6] Repeat steps 4 and 5 on the other end of the segment, sliding two 3mm jump rings onto the second 6mm jump ring before closing it (photo h).
[7] Repeat steps 1–6 to make a second short segment.
[8] Repeat steps 1–3. Then repeat steps 2–4 to make a long segment that has three central montees. Close the end jump ring (photo i). Repeat step 6 (photo j).
[9] Open a 6mm jump ring and slide it through the end 3mm jump rings of both short segments and through one side of a montee. Close the ring (photo k). Use a 6mm jump ring to connect the montee to the end 3mm jump rings on the long segment (photo l).
[10] String a crystal on a head pin, and make a plain loop (Basics and photo m, left).
[11] Cut the head off a head pin. Make a plain loop at one end. String a crystal, and make a second loop in the same plane as the first (photo m,

right). Make a total of two crystal connectors.
[12] Cut the chain in half. Open a loop of a crystal connector, attach it to an end link of chain, and close the loop. Open the other loop, and attach it to the end of a short segment (photo n). Repeat on the other side.
[13] Open the loop of the crystal head pin unit, attach it to the bottom of the long segment, and close the loop (photo o). Open the loop of the clasp, and attach it to an end link of chain (photo p).

50

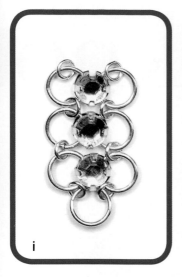

i

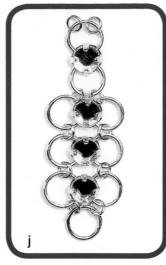

j

k

l

m

o

n

p

If your chain is not large enough for the clasp, attach a 4mm or 6mm jump ring to the other end link.

Earrings
[1] Repeat steps 1–3 of the necklace.
[2] Repeat steps 2–3 twice.
[3] Repeat step 4 on each end of the segment, and close the rings.
[4] Repeat step 10.

[5] Open the loop of the crystal head pin unit, connect it to an end 6mm jump ring on the component, and close the loop. Open the loop of an earring finding, connect it to the remaining 6mm jump ring, and close the loop.
[6] Make a second earring to match the first. ○

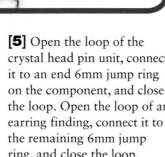

MATERIALS

bracelet 7 in. (18cm)

- 10–15mm furnace-glass bead
- **2** 6mm silver or gold-filled accent beads
- **4** 3mm silver or gold-filled accent beads
- clasp
- 12 in. (30cm) 22-gauge sterling silver or gold-filled wire, half-hard
- **71** 16-gauge sterling silver or gold-filled jump rings, 5.5mm inside diameter
- bentnose pliers
- chainnose pliers
- roundnose pliers
- wire cutters

a

b

c

step*by*step

Jump ring knots

[1] Close two jump rings and open six jump rings (Basics, p. 10).
[2] Slide the two closed jump rings on an open jump ring **(photo a)**. Close the jump ring.
[3] Slide an open jump ring on the pair of jump rings **(photo b)**. Close the jump ring. Place the jump ring cluster on

a work surface and position it as shown **(photo c)**.
[4] Slide a jump ring through the center hole of the cluster **(photo d)**. Close the jump ring.
[5] Repeat step 4, positioning the two jump rings just added as a pair.
[6] Slide a jump ring through the center hole of the cluster. Do not split the pairs of jump rings. Close the jump ring **(photo e)**.

[7] Repeat step 6 to add the last jump ring.
[8] Repeat steps 1–7 seven times to make a total of eight jump ring knots.

Assembly

[1] Open a jump ring. Slide it through one pair of jump rings on each of two knots **(photo f)**. Close the jump ring.
[2] Open a jump ring, and slide it through the pair of

bracelet

Jump ring knots linked by single jump rings form a supple bracelet. A furnace-glass bead attached with a wire loop creates a colorful charm.

designed by **Penney Acosta**

EDITOR'S NOTE:
If you're using a thin furnace-glass bead like the one in the gold bracelet, string the wire through the hole and make a loop and a set of wraps above it as for a top-drilled bead (Basics, p. 10).

d

e

f

jump rings opposite the connector jump ring just added **(photo g)** and a pair of jump rings on the next knot. Close the jump ring.
[3] Repeat step 2 to connect all the jump ring knots.
[4] Cut three 4-in. (10cm) pieces of 22-gauge wire.
[5] On one wire, make a wrapped loop at one end (Basics). String the furnace-glass bead, and make the first half of a wrapped loop.

[6] On one of the other wires, make the first half of a wrapped loop large enough to accommodate two jump rings. On the loop, string the pair of jump rings opposite the last jump ring connector. Finish the wraps. String a 3mm accent bead, a 6mm accent bead, and a 3mm on the wire. Make the first half of a wrapped loop, attach half of the clasp, and finish the wraps. Trim the excess wire.

[7] Repeat step 6 on the other end of the bracelet, making the second wrapped loop large enough to accommodate the clasp and the loop of the charm. Attach the charm to the second wrapped loop and finish the wraps. ●

g

53

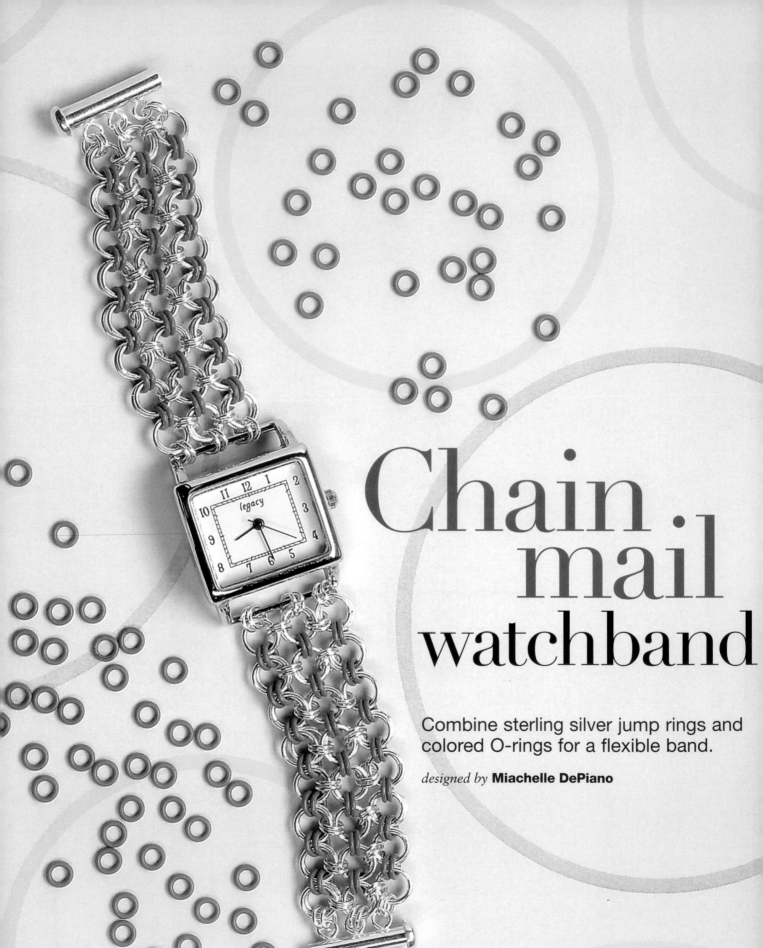

Chain mail watchband

Combine sterling silver jump rings and colored O-rings for a flexible band.

designed by **Miachelle DePiano**

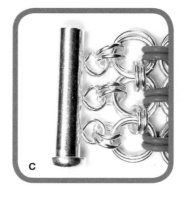

step*by*step

[1] Open 42 6.9mm A jump rings and 40 4.5mm B jump rings (Basics, p. 10). Construct a 2+2 chain, which is a simple sequence of pairs of As and O-rings, using 14 As and 12 O-rings **(photo a)**. Repeat to make a total of three chains.

[2] To attach two chains, slide two Bs through the first two pairs of As in each chain, and close them **(photo b)**. Repeat for the length of chain.

[3] Repeat step 2 to attach the third chain to the first two chains.

[4] Repeat steps 1–3 to make the second watchband panel.

[5] To attach a panel to half of a clasp, slide two Bs through each end pair of As and the corresponding clasp loop, and close them **(photo c)**. Repeat to attach the other end of the panel to the bar of a watch face **(photo d)**.

[6] Repeat step 5 with the other panel. ◉

MATERIALS

watch 6 in. (15cm)

- ribbon watch face, 1½ x 1 in. (3.8 x 2.5cm) (size can vary)
- slide clasp (bar or 3-strand)
- 84 19-gauge sterling silver jump rings, 6.9mm outside diameter, A (Lonnie's, lonniesinc.com)
- 80 21-gauge sterling silver jump rings, 4.5mm outside diameter, B (Lonnie's)
- 72 rubber O-rings, 4.8–5mm (Fire Mountain Gems, 800-355-2137, firemountaingems.com)
- bentnose pliers
- chainnose pliers

EDITOR'S NOTE:
To adjust the length of the watchband, add or omit three sets of jump rings per panel. This will increase or decrease the total length of the band by approximately ½ in. (1.3cm).

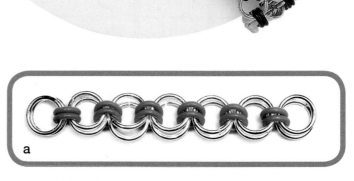

a

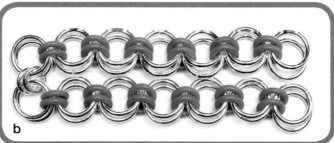

b

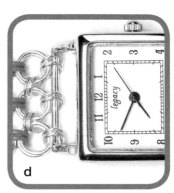

c

d

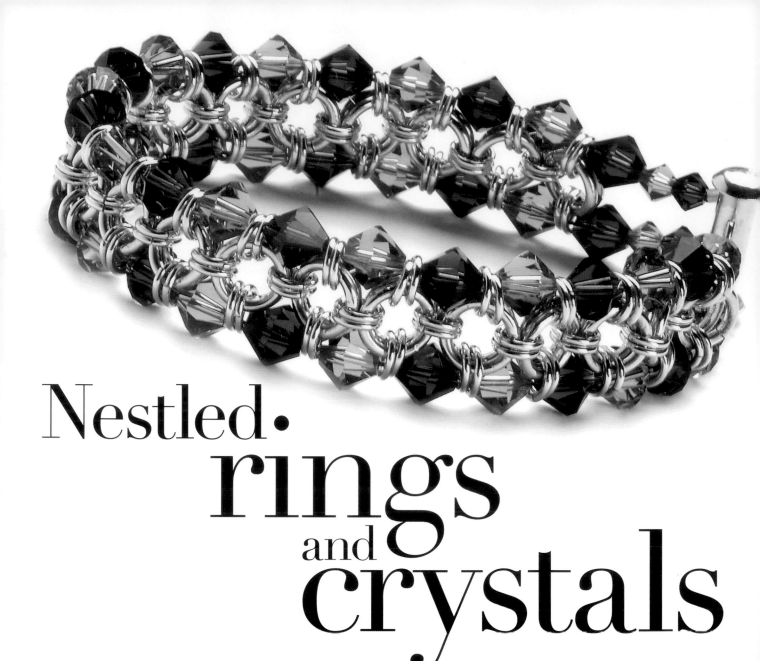

Nestled·
rings
and crystals

Feminize a core of easy chain mail with sparkling crystals.

designed by **Deanna Kittrell**

MATERIALS
bracelet 7½ in. (19.1cm)
- **44** 6mm bicone crystals or
  22 each of **2** colors: A, B
- **4–8** 4mm bicone crystals
- 1g size 15º Japanese seed beads (optional)
- 2-strand clasp
- jump rings (dsdesigns@surewest.net)
  42 16-gauge, 5mm inside diameter
  124 20-gauge, 3mm inside diameter
- **4** crimp beads
- flexible beading wire, .014
- bentnose pliers
- chainnose pliers
- crimping pliers
- wire cutters

a

b

c

d

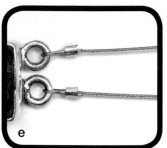

e

f

g

step*by*step

[1] Close all the 3mm jump rings and open all the 5mm jump rings (Basics, p. 10).
[2] Slide six 3mm jump rings on a 5mm jump ring **(photo a)**. Close the 5mm jump ring.
[3] Repeat the path with a second 5mm jump ring. Close the 5mm jump ring **(photo b)**.
[4] Pick up a 5mm jump ring, go through the two center 3mm jump rings from the previous cluster, and pick up six 3mm jump rings. Close the 5mm jump ring **(photo c)**.
[5] Repeat the path with a second 5mm jump ring **(photo d)**.
[6] Repeat steps 4 and 5 until you have 20 pairs of 5mm jump rings. When you add the last pair of 5mm jump rings, pick up only four 3mm jump rings in step 4.
[7] Cut two 12-in. (30cm) pieces of flexible beading wire. On each wire, string a crimp bead and the corresponding loop of half of

the clasp. Go back through the crimp beads. Crimp the crimp beads (Basics), and trim the tails **(photo e)**.
[8] On one wire, string one or two 4mm crystals, a color A 6mm crystal, and the first two 3mm jump rings along one edge of the chain **(photo f)**.
[9] String a color A 6mm crystal (or a color B 6mm crystal if using two colors), and the next two 3mm jump rings **(photo g)**.
[10] Continue adding 6mm crystals (alternating color A and B crystals if using two colors) until you reach the last two 3mm jump rings. String a 6mm crystal, one or two 4mm crystals, and a crimp bead. Secure the end of the wire with tape.
[11] On the second wire, repeat steps 8–10, but don't secure the end with tape. Remove the tape from the first wire. String the wires through the corresponding loops of the other half of the clasp. Go back through the crimp beads, but don't crimp them yet.

[12] Close the clasp, and check the tension. There should be space between the crystals so the chain does not bunch up when it's worn. Crimp the crimp beads, and trim the tails. ●

EDITOR'S NOTE:
To keep the spacing along the edges of the bracelet even, string a 15° Japanese seed bead between each 6mm crystal.

Circular

chain mail

Combine colored metal and brass or sterling silver jump rings to make a pair of chain mail earrings. Colored jump rings make it easy to see the interlocking pattern.

designed by **Sandy Amazeen**

earrings

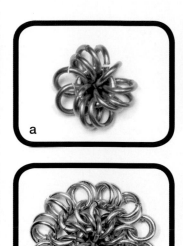

a

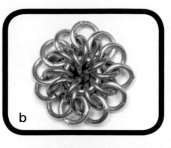

b

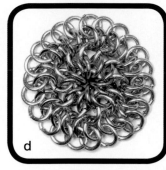

c

d

f

g

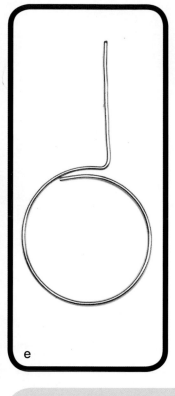

e

MATERIALS
earrings

- **2** 3mm accent beads
- 12 in. (30cm) 20-gauge brass wire
- **2** 18-gauge brass or sterling silver jump rings, 3mm inside diameter
- 20-gauge brass jump rings, 3mm inside diameter
  24 color A
  48 color B
  72 brass or sterling silver
- pair of earring findings
- 1-in. (2.5cm) dowel
- hammer
- steel block or anvil
- bentnose pliers
- chainnose pliers
- roundnose pliers
- wire cutters

EDITOR'S NOTE:
For more colors and gauges of jump rings, visit bluebuddhaboutique.com.

step*by*step

[1] Open an 18-gauge 3mm brass jump ring and close ten 20-gauge 3mm color A jump rings (Basics, p. 10).

[2] Slide the ten As on the 18-gauge jump ring. Close the 18-gauge jump ring. Open two more As, and attach them to the 18-gauge jump ring. Close the As **(photo a)**, making sure they do not go through any of the previous As.

[3] Open 12 20-gauge brass jump rings. Slide one open jump ring through two As from the previous step and close the jump ring. Continue around the As, sliding each brass jump ring through one A of the previous pair and the next jump ring. Position each brass jump ring on top of the previous one. To add the last brass jump ring, position it on top of the previous one, but below the first one, connecting one A from each pair **(photo b)**.

[4] Open 24 3mm color B jump rings, and slide two Bs through each brass jump ring added in step 3 **(photo c)**.

[5] Open 24 20-gauge brass jump rings. Connect each brass jump ring to a pair of Bs as in step 3 **(photo d)**.

[6] Cut a 6-in. (15cm) piece of 20-gauge brass wire. Bend the wire around a 1-in. (2.5cm) dowel. Make a right-angle bend on the top of the circle, leaving a ½-in. (1.3cm) overlap. Straighten the wire above the bend **(photo e)**. Put the wire frame on a steel block or anvil, and tap it with a hammer to harden it.

[7] Slide the entire outer round of jump rings onto the wire frame **(photo f)**.

[8] To maintain the frame's diameter, grasp the crossed wires with chainnose pliers, and wrap the short tail around the long tail twice, making the wraps next to the pliers **(photo g)**. Trim the short wire.

[9] String an accent bead and make a wrapped loop (Basics). Open the loop of an earring finding and attach it to the wrapped loop.

[10] Make a second earring to match the first. ●

Complement an oval or diamond-shaped double-drilled cubic zirconia with crystals to make a flashy adornment.

Delight in crystal rings

Combine crossweave technique, cubic zirconias, and crystals to make quick and easy rings.

designed by **May Brisebois**

MATERIALS
ring
- 9 x 11mm double-drilled oval or diamond-shaped cubic zirconia
- 3mm bicone crystals
  16 color A
  10 color B
- 1g size 11º seed beads, color B
- monofilament or flexible beading wire, .010
- G-S Hypo Cement
- wire cutters

stepbystep

Oval ring

[1] Center three color A crystals on 1 yd. (.9m) of monofilament or beading wire. Over both ends, string an oval cubic zirconia (**photo a**).

[2] Cross the ends through three As (**photo b**).

[3] On each end, pick up five As, and go through two As on the opposite side (**photo c**).

[4] On each end, pick up two color B crystals, and cross the ends through another B (**photo d**).

[5] On each end, pick up two 11º seed beads, and cross the ends through two 11ºs. Repeat until the ring band is ⅜ in. (1cm) short of the desired length.

[6] On each end, pick up two 11ºs, and cross the ends through a B (**photo e**).

[7] On each end, pick up two Bs, and cross the ends through the middle A on the opposite side of the cubic zirconia (**photo f**).

[8] Weave the ends back into the ring band. Tie a few half-hitch knots (Basics, p. 10) between the beads, and dot the knots with glue. When the glue dries, trim the tails.

EDITOR'S NOTE:
You can make a pendant simply by weaving both ends of the wire to one of the longer points of the diamond-shaped cubic zirconia and enclosing a soldered jump ring in a circle of 11º seed beads.

g

h

Diamond ring

[1] Center five color A crystals on 1 yd. (.9m) of monofilament or beading wire. Over both ends, string the diamond-shaped cubic zirconia (**photo g**).

[2] On each end, pick up three As and go back through the same holes on the cubic zirconia (**photo h**).

[3] On each end, pick up two As and cross the ends through another A (**photo i**).

[4] Follow steps 4–8 of the oval ring to finish. ⊙

i

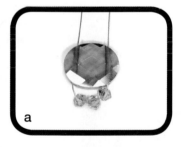

a

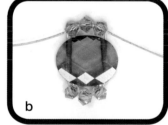

b

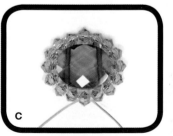

c

d

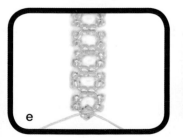

e

f

Crossweave technique

Elegant
pathways

Fire-polished beads mimic the color and sparkle of cut gemstones in a design stitched on the diagonal and accented with teardrop edging.

designed by **Chris Prussing**

step*by*step

Row 1

[1] Cut 2 yd. (1.8m) of Power Pro or Fireline, and thread a needle on each end.

[2] Pick up an 11º seed bead and center it on the thread. With the right-hand needle, pick up a color A 4mm fire-polished bead, a 15º, a teardrop bead, a 15º, and a color B 4mm fire-polished bead **(figure 1, a–b)**.

[3] With the left needle, pick up an A, an 11º, and an A **(d–e)**.

[4] Cross the needles through an 11º **(b–c and e–f)**.

[5] Following the pattern for the placement of the 4mms for rows 1 and 2 **(figure 2)**, continue stitching for the desired length of the necklace. With each stitch, the right needle picks up a 4mm, a 15º, a teardrop, a 15º, and a

4mm. The left needle picks up a 4mm, an 11º, and a 4mm. Then both needles cross through an 11º.

[6] Secure the thread with a concealed square knot, p. 64, in the last 11º picked up **(figure 1, point g)**. Sew through the beadwork, and tie a concealed square knot as indicated in **figure 1** by the double-triangle symbol. Trim the thread.

Row 2

[1] Cut 2 yd. (1.8m) of Power Pro or Fireline, and thread a needle on each end.

[2] Pick up an 11º and center it on the thread. With each needle, pick up four 15ºs. Cross the needles through an 11º **(figure 3, a–b and e–f)** to form a loop.

[3] Retrace the thread path through the loop, and tie a concealed square knot as indicated by the double-triangle symbol in the loop detail of **figure 3**.

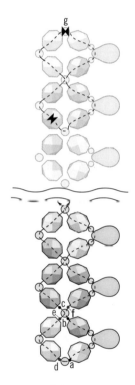

FIGURE 1

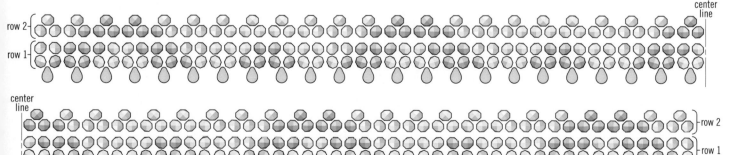

FIGURE 2

[4] With the right needle, pick up an 11º and an A. Sew through the 11º opposite the first teardrop in row 1 **(f–g)**. Pick up an A **(g–h)**.

[5] With the left needle, pick up an 11º, two 15ºs, an A, and two 15ºs **(b–c)**.

[6] Cross the needles through an 11º **(c–d and h–i)**.

[7] Continue stitching, following the color pattern. With each stitch, the right needle picks up a 4mm, sews through the next top 11º from row 1, and picks up a 4mm. The left needle picks up two 15ºs, a 4mm, and two 15ºs. Then both needles cross through an 11º.

[8] Repeat step 7 for the length of the necklace. Before completing the last cluster, pick up an 11º on each needle **(figure 4, a–b and e–f)**. Then cross the needles through an 11º **(b–c and f–g)**. Tie a concealed square knot in the last 11º picked up.

[9] With each needle, pick up four 15ºs **(c–d and g–h)**. Cross the needles through an 11º. Sew back through the beadwork as shown, and tie a concealed square knot as indicated **(figure 5)**. Trim the thread.

[10] Open a jump ring (Basics, p. 10). Slide it through half of a clasp and the beaded loop at one end of the necklace. Close the jump ring. Repeat on the other end. ◑

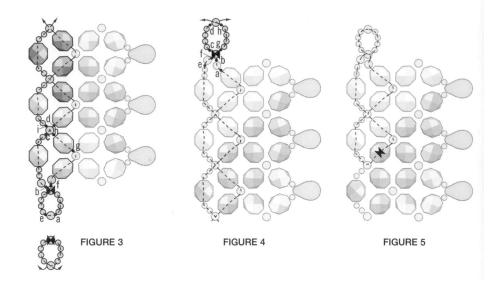

FIGURE 3   FIGURE 4   FIGURE 5

MATERIALS

necklace 18½ in. (47cm)

- **46** 6mm Czech teardrop beads
- 4mm Czech fire-polished beads
  88 color A
  124 color B
  110 color C
- Japanese seed beads
  2g size 11º
  2g size 15º
- clasp
- **2** 3mm jump rings
- Power Pro 10 lb. test, white; or Fireline 6 lb. test, crystal
- beading needles, #12
- bentnose pliers
- chainnose pliers

HOW TO TIE A CONCEALED SQUARE KNOT

Start with the thread that is exiting the bead where you'll conceal the knot.

Cross the right end over, then under, the left end. Cross the left end over, then under, the right end. Pass the right thread back through the bead.

Pull the knot inside the bead. Tighten.

Creative crossings

Stitch a necklace with pearl and crystal motifs.

designed by **Noriko Romanko**

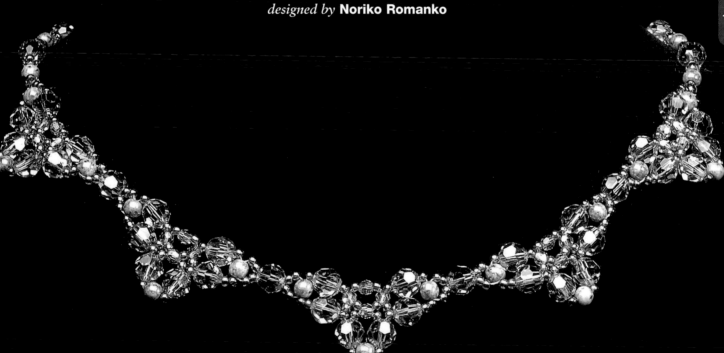

stepbystep

[1] Center a 4mm bead, crystal, or pearl on 2 yd. (1.8m) of cord. Thread a needle on each end of the cord.

[2] Using the left, or top, needle, pick up an 11º seed bead, a 6mm bead, and an 11º (figure 1, a–b). Using the right, or bottom, needle, pick up two 11ºs, a 6mm, and an 11º (d–e).

[3] Cross the needles through a 3mm bead (b–c and e–f).

[4] Continue working both needles as follows:
Top needle: Pick up an 11º, a 3mm, and an 11º (figure 2, a–b).
Bottom needle: Pick up an 11º, a 3mm, an 11º, a 6mm, an 11º, a 4mm, an 11º, a 6mm, and an 11º (c–d). Sew through the 3mm again in the same direction (d–e). Keep the tension tight so the beads form a loop next to the previous loop.

MATERIALS

necklace 17 in. (43cm)

- round crystals, pearls, or glass beads
  - 40–46 6mm or 5mm
  - 23–29 4mm
  - 36–44 3mm
- 2g size 11º seed beads
- clasp
- DandyLine .006
- beading needles, #10 or #12

FIGURE 1

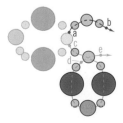

FIGURE 2

FIGURE 3

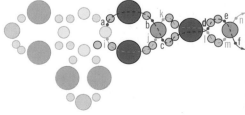

FIGURE 4

FIGURE 5

FIGURE 6

FIGURE 7

FIGURE 8

Crossweave technique

[5] Pick up an 11º with the bottom needle, and cross the needles through a 3mm (**figure 3, a–b** and **c–d**).
Top needle: Pick up an 11º, a 6mm, and an 11º (**figure 4, a–b**).
Bottom needle: Pick up an 11º, a 6mm, and two 11ºs (**i–j**).
Both needles: Cross through a 4mm (**b–c** and **j–k**). This completes one motif.
[6] Pick up two 11ºs on each needle. Hold the needles together, and pick up a 6mm (**c–d** and **k–l**). Pick up two 11ºs on each needle (**d–e** and **l–m**). Cross through a 4mm (**e–f** and **m–n**).
[7] Repeat steps 2–6 three times. Then repeat steps 2–5 for a total of five motifs.
[8] Using the bottom needle, sew through the two 11ºs and the 6mm of the last motif (**figure 5, a–b**). Pick up an 11º, and sew through the next 6mm, 11º, 4mm, 11º, and 6mm (**b–c**). Pick up an 11º, and sew through the next 6mm, two 11ºs, and the 4mm (**c–d**). Continue through the next two 11ºs, the 6mm, two 11ºs, and the next 4mm (**d–e**).
[9] Repeat step 8 across the remaining four motifs. End with your needle exiting the end 4mm on the first motif.
[10] Pick up two 11ºs and a 3mm. Then string the following pattern three times: an 11º, a 4mm, an 11º, a 3mm, an 11º, a 6mm, an 11º, and a 3mm. Tape or clamp the needle so the beads don't fall off.

[11] Repeat step 10 with the other needle on the other end of the necklace.
[12] Using the needle on the left side of the necklace, pick up an 11º, a 4mm, two 11ºs, a 3mm, and three 11ºs. Sew through the loop or jump ring on a clasp half, pick up three 11ºs, and sew through the 3mm in the same direction to form a loop (**figure 6, a–b**). Reinforce the loop with a second thread path. Pick up two 11ºs, and sew through the 4mm and 11º (**b–c**).
[13] Keep the tension fairly tight so the beads are snug but not stiff, and tie a half-hitch knot (Basics, p. 10). Sew back through the remaining strung beads to the first 3mm (**figure 7, point a**), tying a few half-hitch knots between beads. Pick up two 11ºs, and sew through the 4mm (**a–b**). Sew through the top two 11ºs (**b–c**). Tie a half-hitch knot, and sew back through the two new 11ºs and the 4mm (**c–d**).
[14] Using the other needle, repeat steps 12 and 13.
[15] To reinforce the top edge of the motifs, continue sewing through the beads as shown (**figure 8, a–b**). Then sew through the bottom 11ºs and the 6mm to the next 4mm (**b–c**). Repeat across the remaining motifs. Secure the tails in the beadwork. ◦

Linked
crystal
squares

Making connections is easy with crystals and seed beads.

designed by **Jordana Hollander**

step*by*step

Making the squares

You can make this project with either 11º cylinder or seed beads. When making the squares, the bead counts are the same regardless of which kind of 11º you're using.

[1] On 18 in. (46cm) of Fireline or conditioned thread (Basics, p. 10), pick up six 11ºs and a 4mm bicone crystal. Leaving a 6-in. (15cm) tail, go back through the 11ºs in the same direction (**figure 1, a–b**). Pick up six 11ºs, and go through all 12 11ºs again (**b–c**). Tie the tail and the working thread with a square knot (Basics).

[2] Pick up an 11º, a 4mm, and an 11º. Skip two 11ºs on the ring, and go through the next 11º (**figure 2, a–b**). Repeat around to add a total of four 4mms (**b–c**). Step up through the first 11º and 4mm added in this step (**c–d**).

[3] Pick up an 11º, a 4mm, and an 11º, and go through the next 4mm on the previous round (**figure 3, a–b**). Repeat around to add a total of four 4mms (**b–c**). Secure the working thread in the beadwork with a few half-hitch knots (Basics) between beads, and trim. Secure the tail the same way.

[4] Repeat steps 1–3 either 13 times for an 18-in. (46cm) necklace (for a total of 14 squares) or 16 times for a 21-in. (53cm) necklace (for a total of 17 squares).

Assembly

The bead counts for assembling the necklace are different depending upon whether you're using cylinder or seed beads. If you're using cylinders, as we did in the instructions and step-by-step photos, you'll use a pattern of five cylinders, one 4mm, and five cylinders. If you're using seed beads, substitute three seed beads each time the instructions say to pick up five cylinders.

[1] Center a clasp half on 2 yd. (1.8m) of Fireline or conditioned thread. Attach a needle at each end of the thread.

[2] On one needle, pick up five cylinders, a 4mm, and five cylinders. On the other needle, pick up five cylinders, go through the 4mm, and pick up five cylinders (**photo a**).

[3] Cross the needles through a corner 4mm on a square (**photo b**).

[4] Retrace the thread path with both needles for security.

[5] With each needle, sew through the next eight edge beads of the square, exiting the 4mm at the opposite corner.

[6] Repeat steps 2 and 3 (**photo c**) and 5 to connect all the squares.

[7] On one needle, pick up five cylinders, a 4mm, five cylinders, and the other clasp half. With the other needle, pick up five cylinders, go through the 4mm, and pick up five cylinders. Go through the loop of the clasp half, and continue through the beads picked up with the first needle and the 4mm on the last square. With the first needle, go back through the beads picked up with the second needle, and continue through the 4mm on the last square. Retrace the thread path, secure the tails with a few half-hitch knots between beads, and trim. ●

MATERIALS

necklace 18 in. or 21 in. (46cm or 53cm)

- **141** or **171** 4mm bicone crystals
- 2g size 11º Japanese cylinder or seed beads
- clasp
- nylon beading thread conditioned with beeswax or Thread Heaven, or Fireline 8 lb. test
- beading needles, #12

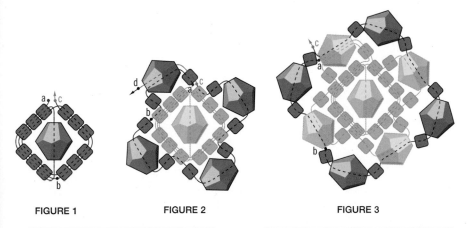

FIGURE 1   FIGURE 2   FIGURE 3

a

b

c

EDITOR'S NOTE:

This design adapts easily to a bracelet or earrings. To make a bracelet, simply follow the instructions, but make fewer squares (approximately six). To make earrings, make two squares, and attach each one to an earring finding the same way you would attach a clasp half.

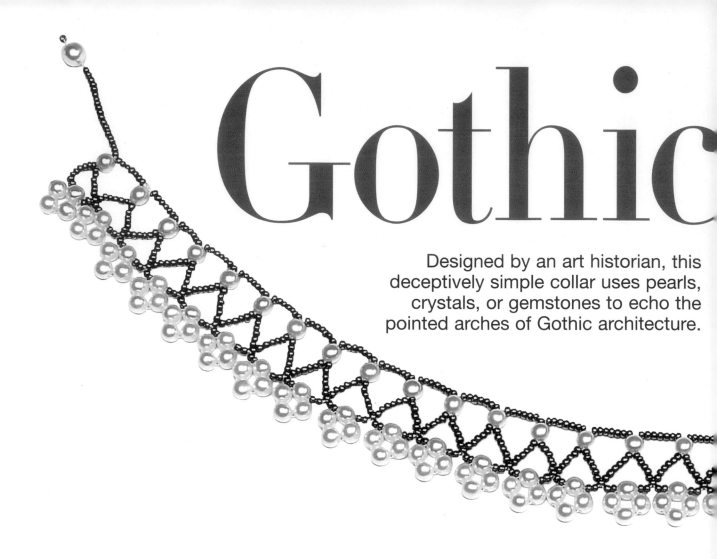

Gothic

Designed by an art historian, this deceptively simple collar uses pearls, crystals, or gemstones to echo the pointed arches of Gothic architecture.

MATERIALS

necklace 16–18 in.
(41–46cm)

- **170** (approximately) 4mm round pearls, crystals, or gemstones
- 10g size 11º seed beads
- 6mm bead for clasp
- Power Pro 10 lb. test
- beading needles, #12

step*by*step

[1] Thread a needle on 2 yd. (1.8m) of Power Pro. Leaving a 6-in. (15cm) tail, pick up 1 in. (2.5cm) of 11º seed beads (approximately 20 beads), the 6mm bead, and an 11º **(figure 1, a–b)**. Skip the last 11º, and sew back through the rest of the beads **(b–c)**.

[2] Pick up a 4mm bead, nine 11ºs, and four 4mms, and sew through the first of the four 4mms again **(figure 2, a–b)**.

[3] Pick up nine 11ºs, and sew back through the first 4mm picked up in the previous step **(b–c)**. Be sure the third 11º has a large enough hole for several thread passes.

[4] Pick up seven 11ºs, a 4mm, and six 11ºs, and sew back through the third 11º picked up in the previous step **(c–d)**. Pick up two 11ºs and four 4mms, and sew through the first of the four 4mms again **(d–e)**.

[5] Pick up nine 11ºs, and sew back through the first 4mm pickcd up in the previous step **(e–f)**.

[6] Repeat steps 4 and 5 until the necklace is approximately

EDITOR'S NOTE:

To make the upper and lower portions of the clasp loops consistent, use an even number of beads for each ring.

FIGURE 1

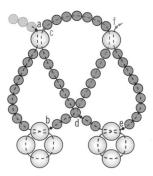

FIGURE 2

arches

designed by **Margaret Duffy**

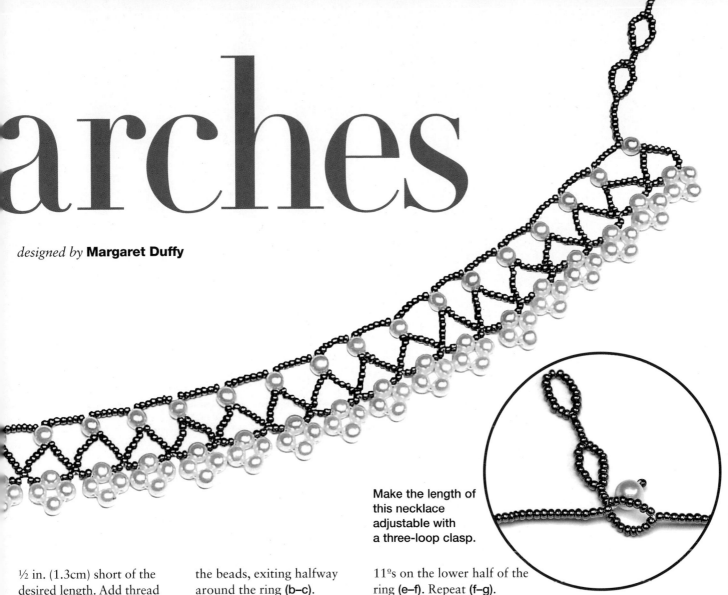

Make the length of
this necklace
adjustable with
a three-loop clasp.

½ in. (1.3cm) short of the
desired length. Add thread
(Basics, p. 10) as needed.
[7] Pick up nine 11ºs
(figure 3, a–b).
[8] Pick up enough 11ºs
to form a ring that will fit
over the 6mm at the other
end. Sew through the first
bead picked up to test the
fit. Add or remove beads if
necessary, then sew through

the beads, exiting halfway
around the ring **(b–c)**.
[9] Pick up four 11ºs plus
the number of 11ºs used
for the last ring, and sew
through the first half of the
ring **(c–d)**. Repeat to make
a third ring, but go back
through all the beads two or
three times **(d–e)**. Sew back
through the next four 11ºs,
and continue through the

11ºs on the lower half of the
ring **(e–f)**. Repeat **(f–g)**.
[10] Retrace the thread path
for the entire necklace as
shown **(g–h)**. Secure the
tails with a few half-hitch
knots (Basics) between beads,
and trim. ●

FIGURE 3

71

Have fun with this
adaptable pattern.
Make your bracelet
narrow or wide,
and embellish it to
your liking.

Flowering chain

Large beads stitch up quickly to make a lovely bracelet.

designed by **Yvanne Ham**

stepbystep

To experiment with colors for this bracelet, go to BeadAndButton.com to download a blank pattern by selecting April 2007 from Free Projects under the PROJECTS menu.

Wide bracelet
Side one

[1] On 2 yd. (1.8m) of Fireline or conditioned thread (Basics, p. 10), attach a stop bead (Basics) 6 in. (15cm) from the end.
[2] Pick up two color C 11º seed beads, a 4mm round bead, two Cs, a color A fire-polished bead, two color D 11ºs, and an A. Sew through the first C picked up, going in the same direction **(figure 1, a–b)**.
[3] Pick up a C, a 4mm round, two Cs, and an A, and sew back through the last D picked up in the previous stitch, going in the opposite direction **(b–c)**.
[4] Pick up a D, an A, two Cs, and a 4mm round, and sew back through the last C picked up in the previous stitch **(c–d)**.
[5] Pick up a C, a color B fire-polished bead, two Ds, and a B, and sew back through the last C picked up in the previous stitch **(d–e)**.
[6] Pick up a C, a 4mm round, two Cs, and a B, and sew back through the last D picked up in the previous stitch **(e–f)**.
[7] Pick up a D, a B, two Cs, and a 4mm round, and sew back through the last C picked up in the previous stitch **(f–g)**.
[8] Pick up a C, an A, two Ds, and an A, and sew back through the last C picked up in the previous stitch **(g–h)**.

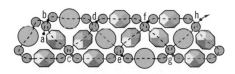

FIGURE 1

> **Mental mantra:**
> *For each stitch on the first side (except the first and last stitches), you'll pick up five beads – a small bead, a big bead, two small beads, and a big bead – prior to joining to the previous stitch. The exact bead sequence is not intuitive, however, so until you understand the pattern, Yvanne suggests repeating this to yourself as you're working: small, big, small, small, big, join.*

FIGURE 2

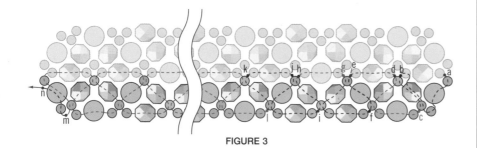

FIGURE 3

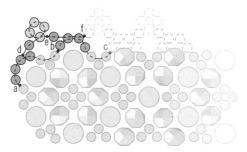

FIGURE 4

[9] Repeat steps 3–8 until the band is approximately ½ in. (1.3cm) short of the desired length. End with step 4, but pick up an extra C after you pick up the first five beads. Sew through the last C picked up in the previous stitch, going in the same direction (**figure 2, a–b**), then continue through the next A, two Ds, A, and C (**b–c**).

Side two
[1] Pick up a C, a 4mm round, two Cs, and an A, and sew through the last D added on the first side (**figure 3, a–b**).
[2] Pick up a D, and sew back through the A and the last C added in the previous stitch (**b–c**).
[3] Pick up a C, a 4mm round, two Cs, and an A, and

sew back through the D added in the previous stitch (**c–d**). Continue through the next three beads of the band (**d–e**).
[4] Pick up a C and a 4mm round, and sew back through the last C picked up in the previous step (**e–f**).
[5] Pick up a C, a B, two Ds, and a B, and sew back through the C picked up in the previous stitch (**f–g**). Continue through the next three beads of the band (**g–h**).
[6] Pick up a C and a B, and sew back through the last D picked up in the previous stitch (**h–i**).
[7] Pick up a D, a B, two Cs, and a 4mm round, and sew back through the C picked up in the previous stitch (**i–j**). Sew through the next three beads on the band (**j–k**).

[8] Pick up a D and an A, and sew back through the last C picked up in the previous stitch (**k–l**).
[9] Repeat steps 3–8 to the end of the band, ending with step 4 (**l–m**). Pick up a C, and sew back through the last 4mm round (**m–n**). Secure the thread with a few half-hitch knots (Basics) between beads, and trim. Remove the stop bead, and secure the beginning tail in the beadwork.

Embellishment
[1] Secure 1 yd. (.9m) of thread within the beadwork, and exit at **figure 4, point a**. Pick up four Cs, and sew through the next two Cs along the edge (**a–b**). Repeat (**b–c**) around the entire bracelet. To limit the embellishment to this

outline, as in the copper bracelet (bottom, p. 72), secure the thread, and trim.
[2] To add the picot edging, as in the blue bracelet, p. 72, sew through the beadwork to exit at **point d**. Pick up a C and four color E 11ºs, and sew through the first E picked up again (**d–e**). Pick up a C, and sew through the middle two Cs on the next set of four embellishment Cs (**e–f**). Repeat around the bracelet. Secure the thread, and trim.

Clasp
Design a toggle clasp of your own, or choose one of the following toggle bars and secure it with a bead loop.

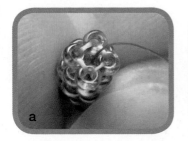

a

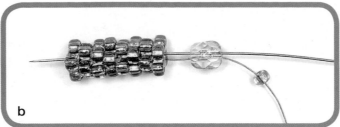

b

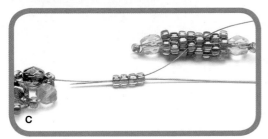

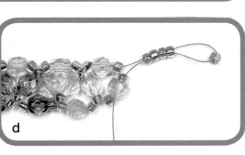

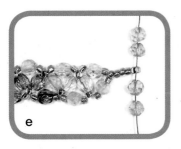

c

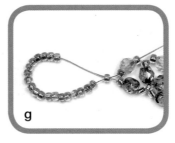

d

e

f

g

Peyote toggle bar

[1] On 1 yd. (.9m) of thread, attach a stop bead. Using Cs, work eight rows in flat, even-count peyote stitch (Basics) to make a strip that is ten beads wide and has four beads along each flat edge. Zip up (Basics) the strip to form a bar. To add an accent bead at each end of the bar, continue on to step 2. Otherwise, remove the stop bead, secure the tails, and trim.

[2] To add accent beads to the toggle bar, sew into the center of the bar, and exit one end (photo a).

[3] Pick up a fire-polished bead and an 11º, skip the 11º, and sew back through the fire-polished bead and the bar (photo b). Repeat on the other end of the bar. Remove the stop bead, secure the tails, and trim.

[4] Secure 1 ft. (30cm) of thread in the band, and exit at the center of one end. Pick up four 11ºs, sew diagonally through two center 11ºs on the bar, and sew back through the four 11ºs (photo c). Sew into the beadwork, retrace the thread path a few times, and secure the tail.

Bead-and-wire toggle bar

[1] Secure 1 ft. (30cm) of thread in the beadwork, and exit at the center of one end of the bracelet. To make the toggle stem, pick up five 11ºs, skip the last 11º, sew back through the first four 11ºs, and sew into the beadwork (photo d). Retrace the thread path a few times, secure the tail, and trim.

[2] On 3 in. (7.6cm) of wire, string two 4mm rounds, the last 11º of the toggle stem, and two 4mm rounds (photo e).

[3] Bend one end of the wire around the last 4mm, and wrap it around the wire between the last two beads (photo f). Trim. Repeat on the other end of the wire.

Clasp loop

[1] Secure 1 ft. (30cm) of thread in the beadwork, and exit at the middle of the end opposite the toggle bar.

[2] Pick up enough 11ºs to fit around the toggle bar, sew back through the first 11º picked up, and sew into the beadwork (photo g). Retrace the thread path a few times, secure the tail, and trim.

Narrow bracelet

Follow the instructions for side one of the wide bracelet, but alternate between three colors of fire-polished beads (colors A, B, and F) for the flower motifs. Embellish as in the wide bracelet, if desired, and add a clasp. ◐

Finish your bracelet with a peyote stitch toggle bar (copper band) or a bead-and-wire toggle bar (green band).

Slinky wrist wrap

Seed bead loops embellish a flexible netted tube.

by **Lynne Soto**

step*by*step

Base

[1] On a comfortable length of Fireline, leave a 10-in. (25cm) tail, and pick up three color A 11º seed beads. Sew through the 11ºs again to form a ring (**figure 1, a–b**).

[2] Pick up an A and sew through the next A (**b–c**). Repeat twice (**c–d**). Step up through the first A picked up in this step (**d–e**) to begin the next round.

[3] Pick up an A, a color B 11º, and an A, and sew through the next A on the previous round (**e–f**). Repeat twice (**f–g**). Step up through the first A and B picked up in this step (**g–h**). Snug up the beads to begin forming a tube.

[4] Working in tubular netting, repeat step 3, sewing through Bs instead of As in the previous rounds (**figure 2, a–b**), until the tube is the desired length. Add thread as needed (Basics, p. 10).

[5] To taper the end, pick up an A and go through the next B. Repeat twice. Step up through the next A. Pick up an A, and sew through the next A. Repeat twice and snug up the As. Sew back through the last three As added. Make a few half-hitch knots (Basics). If the thread is longer than 12 in. (30cm) do not cut it. If it is shorter than 12 in. (30cm), scw through the beadwork, and trim. Add 2 ft. (61cm) of thread.

Clasp

[1] Continuing with the working thread, pick up four 8ºs. Sew through the last three 8ºs twice to form a ring (figure 3, a–b).

[2] Pick up an 8º and sew through the next 8º (b–c). Repeat twice (c–d). Step up through the first 8º picked up in this step (d–e).

[3] Pick up two 8ºs, three color C 11ºs, and two 8ºs, and sew through the next 8º on the previous round (e–f). Repeat twice (f–g).

[4] Repeat step 3 twice, sewing through the same 8ºs for both repeats.

[5] Pick up two 8ºs, three Cs, and two 8ºs, and sew through the 8º across the open center.

[6] Sew through the first 8º picked up in step 1. Secure the thread with a few half-hitch knots, and trim.

[7] To make the loop, thread a needle on the 10-in. (25cm) tail and pick up enough 8ºs (approximately 20) to fit around the beaded button. Sew through the beadwork, retrace the thread path through the loop, make a few half-hitch knots, and trim.

Embellishment

[1] Secure 2 yd. (1.8m) of Fireline at one end of the netted tube with a few half-hitch knots, and leave a 6-in. (15cm) tail.

[2] Exit a B so your needle points toward the length of the bracelet. Pick up two 8ºs, three Cs, and two 8ºs, and sew through the next diagonal B (figure 4, a–b and photo).

[3] Repeat step 2 (b–c) along the length of tube, working on a diagonal to make the fringe spiral around the base. Secure the Fireline in the beadwork with a few half-hitch knots, and trim.

[4] Repeat steps 1–3 to add a second spiral fringe next to the first.

[5] Secure the tails with a few half-hitch knots, and trim. ◉

MATERIALS
bracelet 8 in. (20cm)
- 16g size 8º Japanese seed beads
- size 11º Japanese seed beads
  4g color A
  3g color B
  2g color C
- Fireline 6 lb. test
- beading needles, #12

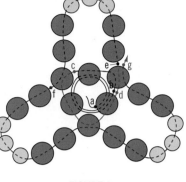

FIGURE 3

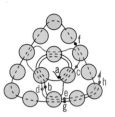

FIGURE 1

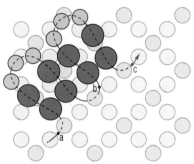

FIGURE 2

FIGURE 4

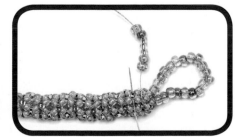

Quick holiday ornament

Get a head start on winter decorating with easy beaded snowflakes.

designed by **Sandra D. Halpenny**

[1] Using 1½ yd. (1.4m) of conditioned thread (Basics, p. 10), pick up 12 11º seed beads. Sew through the first bead again to form a ring. Leave an 8-in. (20cm) tail.
[2] Pick up three 11ºs, skip a bead, and sew through the next bead on the ring **(figure 1, a–b)**. Repeat around the ring, adding a total of six three-bead sets **(b–c)**. Sew through two beads on the first set to step up **(c–d)**.
[3] Pick up three 11ºs. Sew through the bead your thread is exiting in the same direction, and sew through the next bead on the previous round **(figure 2, a–b)**. Pick up five 11ºs, and sew back through the first bead picked up and two beads of the next three-bead set **(b–c)**. Repeat around the ring **(c–d)**. Step up as shown **(d–e)**.
[4] Flip the beadwork so your thread is exiting the right side of the 11º. Pick up six 11ºs and a 4mm bicone crystal. Sew under the thread bridge between the top two beads on the next spike and back through the crystal **(figure 3, a–b)**. Pick up six 11ºs, and sew through the top

bead of the next spike and back through the last 11º **(b–c)**.
[5] Pick up five 11ºs and a crystal. Sew under the thread bridge between the top two beads on the next spike and back through the crystal **(c–d)**. Pick up six 11ºs, and sew through the top bead of the next spike and back through the last 11º **(d–e)**. Repeat three times **(e–f)**.
[6] Pick up five 11ºs and a crystal. Sew under the thread bridge between the top two beads on the next spike and back through the crystal **(f–g)**. Pick up five 11ºs. Sew through the 11º on the first loop, the top bead of the spike below, and all the 11ºs on the first loop **(g–h)**.
[7] Pick up an 11º, and sew through the first three beads on the next loop **(figure 4, a–b)**. Pick up six 11ºs, and sew through the last three beads on the next loop **(b–c)**. Repeat one round, and step up through the first 11º added on this round **(c–d)**.
[8] Pick up five 11ºs, and sew through the bead your thread is exiting in the same direction and the 11º first picked up **(figure 5, a–b)**.

[9] Pick up nine 11ºs and a crystal. Sew under the thread bridge between the top two beads on the next spike, and back through the crystal **(b–c)**.
[10] Pick up seven 11ºs, and sew back through the fourth 11º **(c–d)**. Pick up an 11º, and sew through the last two 11ºs on the previous loop **(d–e)**. Retrace the thread path through the crystal, and sew through the next two 11ºs **(e–f)**.
[11] Pick up eight 11ºs, and sew through the bead above the next crystal **(f–g)**. Pick up four 11ºs. Sew through the eighth bead on the last loop, the 11º above the crystal, and the first 11º of the new loop **(g–h)**.
[12] Repeat steps 9–11 four times **(h–i)**.
[13] Repeat steps 9 and 10 **(i–j)**. Pick up seven 11ºs, and sew through the 11ºs on the first loop **(j–k)**. Secure the threads in the beadwork with a few half-hitch knots (Basics) between beads, and trim.
[14] Dip the finished snowflake in floor polish. Blot the excess polish with a paper towel. Press the snowflake flat on a piece of waxed paper and let dry. ●

FIGURE 1

FIGURE 2

FIGURE 3

FIGURE 4

FIGURE 5

MATERIALS

one ornament

- **12** 4mm bicone crystals
- 3g size 11º Japanese seed beads
- Fireline 6–8 lb. test or DandyLine .006
- beading needles #12
- Future floor polish
- waxed paper

designed by **Jan Zicarelli**

Sparkling Waves

step*by*step

[1] On 2 yd. (1.8m) of conditioned thread (Basics, p. 10), pick up four cylinder beads, leaving a 1-yd. (.9m) tail. Working in ladder stitch (Basics), sew back through the four beads, and pull them snug so you have two side-by-side columns **(figure 1, a–b)**.

[2] Pick up two cylinders, and sew back through the last pair of cylinders. Sew back through the cylinders just added **(b–c)**. Continue adding pairs of cylinders until your band is the desired length and the number of rows is divisible by three. Add one more row. To reinforce the band, zigzag back through its entire length. Secure the thread with a few half-hitch knots (Basics) between beads, and trim.

[3] Thread a needle on the 1-yd. (.9m) tail, and pick up one 3mm fire-polished bead, four cylinders, and a 3mm. Sew through the second pair of cylinders on

the ladder. Sew through the next pair of cylinders in the opposite direction **(figure 2, a–b)**. Repeat for the length of the bracelet. Exit from the last row on the ladder.

[4] Pick up one 3mm and two cylinders, and go through the last two cylinders of the previous stitch **(c–d)**. Sew back through the two new cylinders. To reinforce the ladder, zigzag back through the cylinders **(d–e)** for the entire length of the second half of the band.

[5] To add the interior waves, exit between the two end cylinders at one end of a ladder, and tie a half-hitch knot. Pick up one 15º seed bead, a 3mm, a 15º, a 3mm, and a 15º, and wrap the working thread around the thread bridge between the fourth pair of cylinders **(figure 3)**. Repeat along the length of the band, encircling the thread bridge between every fourth pair of cylinders.

[6] Sew through to the other side of the band, exit between the two end cylinders, and repeat step 5 to add waves to the other ladder section.

[7] To add the edge waves, exit an exterior corner cylinder, and anchor the thread by wrapping it around the thread bridge between the first and second cylinder. Pick up a 15º, a 3mm, a 15º, a 3mm, and a 15º, and sew under the thread bridge between the third and fourth cylinders **(figure 4)**. Repeat along the edge, encircling every third thread bridge.

[8] Stitch through to the other side of the band, and repeat step 7 to add waves to the other edge. Secure the tail, and trim.

[9] To add the clasp, secure a length of thread near one end of the band. Sew through the beadwork to exit between a cylinder and a 3mm at the end of the band. Sew through the first loop of one clasp half, and sew back through the

FIGURE 1

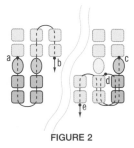

FIGURE 2

FIGURE 3

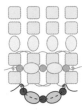

FIGURE 4

FIGURE 5

bracelet

Ladder-stitched cylinder beads form the base of a bracelet accented with waves of fire-polished beads.

inner cylinder. Retrace the thread path five or six times. Sew through the 3mm and a cylinder. Secure the second loop the same way **(figure 5)**. Secure the working thread in the beadwork with a few half-hitch knots between the beads, and trim. Repeat to add the other clasp half to the other end. ⦿

MATERIALS

bracelet 6¾ in. (17.1cm)

- **199** 3mm oval fire-polished beads, crystal
- 7g size 8º Japanese cylinder beads
- 2g size 15º seed beads
- 2-strand slide clasp
- nylon beading thread, conditioned with beeswax or Thread Heaven
- beading needles, #12

EDITOR'S NOTE:
Using colored thread with light-colored crystal beads will enhance the wave effect.

Ladder stitch

Spiky beaded beads

Embellish a simple ladder stitch base with crystals to make spiky beads, then unite them with a strand of gemstones, crystals, or glass beads for a necklace that perfectly highlights a favorite pendant.

by **Julia Gerlach**

MATERIALS

both projects
- Fireline 6 lb. test, or nylon beading thread, conditioned with beeswax or Thread Heaven
- flexible beading wire, .018
- beading needles, #10
- crimping pliers
- wire cutters

blue-and-salmon necklace 18 in. (46cm)
- glass pendant (James Yaun of TC Glass Arts, tcglassarts.com)
- 16-in. (41cm) strand 5mm kyanite beads
- **150** 3mm bicone crystals
- **4** 3mm gold beads
- 5g size 11º seed beads, in each of **3** colors: A, B, C

- **25** 1.5mm gold beads
- clasp
- **2** crimp beads

green-and-purple necklace 18 in. (46cm)
- glass pendant
- **32** 5mm bicone crystals
- **150** 3mm bicone crystals
- **67** 3mm silver beads
- **20** size 2º (7mm) dichroic-lined seed beads (Kandra's Beads, 800-454-7079, kandrasbeads.com)
- 5g size 11º seed beads, in each of **3** colors: A, B, C
- clasp
- **2** crimp beads

step*by*step

Beaded beads

[1] Thread a needle on 1 yd. (.9m) of conditioned thread or Fireline (Basics, p. 10), and, leaving a 6-in. (15cm) tail, pick up six color A 11º seed beads. Sew through all six beads again, and pull tight so you have two stacks of three beads sitting side by side (**figure 1, a–b**).

[2] Pick up three As, sew back through the previous stack of three As, and continue through the three As just added (**b–c**). Continue stitching a three-bead ladder (Basics) until you have five stacks of three beads (**c–d**).

[3] Bring the ends together, sew through the first stack of As, and continue through the last stack of As to join the ladder into a tube (**figure 2**).

[4] Sew through the first A of the next stack (**figure 3, a–b**).

[5] Pick up a color B 11º, a 3mm crystal, and a color C 11º (**b–c**). Skip the C, and sew back through the 3mm (**c–d**). Pick up a B, and, going in the same direction, sew back through the A your thread exited to begin this picot and the next A in the ladder (**d–e**).

[6] Repeat step 5 to add picots over the other As in the ladder row.

[7] Repeat steps 4–6 until you've made a picot over every A on the tube.

[8] Sew into the beadwork, secure the thread tail with a few half-hitch knots (Basics) between beads, and trim. Secure the other tail.

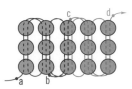

FIGURE 1

FIGURE 2

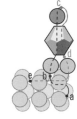

FIGURE 3

a

b

c

d

[9] Repeat steps 1–8 to make a total of ten beaded beads.

Blue-and-salmon necklace

[1] Cut a 24-in. (61cm) piece of flexible beading wire. Center a 5mm kyanite bead, three 1.5mm beads, and a 5mm (photo a). Center the pendant over the 1.5mms.

[2] On one half of the necklace, string a beaded bead (photo b).

[3] String a 5mm, a 1.5mm, a 5mm, a 1.5mm, a 5mm, and a beaded bead (photo c).

[4] Repeat step 3 three times (photo d).

[5] String five 5mms and a 1.5mm three times, and then string three 5mms (photo e).

[6] String a 3mm bead, a crimp bead, a 3mm, and half of the clasp. Go back through the 3mms, the crimp bead, and the last three 5mms (photo f), and crimp the crimp bead (Basics). Trim the excess wire.

[7] Repeat steps 2–6 on the other half of the necklace.

Green-and-purple necklace

[1] Cut a 24-in. (61cm) piece of flexible beading wire. Center a 5mm crystal, three 3mm beads, and a 5mm. Center the pendant over the 3mms.

[2] On one half of the necklace, string a beaded bead.

[3] String a 3mm, a 5mm, a 3mm, a 2º seed bead, a 3mm, a 5mm, a 3mm, and a beaded bead.

[4] Repeat step 3 three times.

[5] String a 3mm, a 5mm, a 3mm, and a 2º six times, and then string a 3mm and a 5mm.

[6] String a 3mm, a crimp bead, a 3mm, and half of the clasp. Go back through the last six beads, and crimp the crimp bead (Basics). Trim the excess wire.

[7] Repeat steps 2–6 on the other half of the necklace. ○

e

f

Ladder stitch

Geometric lace

by **Lynne Soto**

Seed beads enhance two bracelets inspired by Norwegian Hardanger lace.

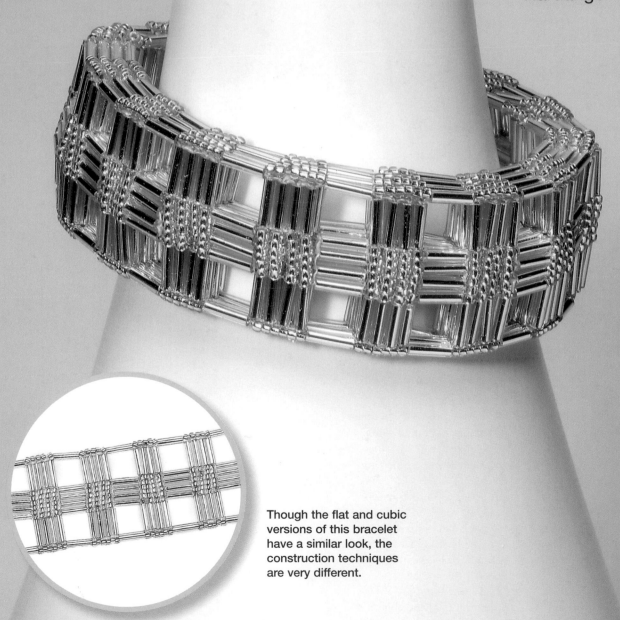

Though the flat and cubic versions of this bracelet have a similar look, the construction techniques are very different.

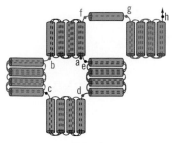

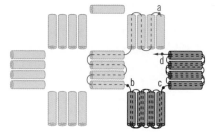

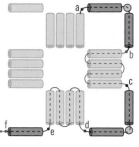

FIGURE 1   **FIGURE 2**   **FIGURE 3**

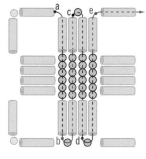

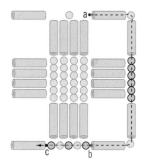

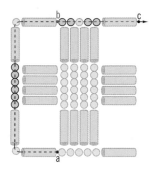

FIGURE 4   **FIGURE 5**   **FIGURE 6**

step*by*step

Flat bracelet

Bracelet base

[1] Thread a needle on 2 yd. (1.8m) of conditioned thread (Basics, p. 10), leaving a 6-in. (15cm) tail.

[2] Working in ladder stitch (Basics), make a four-bead ladder using size 2 bugle beads (figure 1, a–b). Repeat three times to make three separate segments (b–c, c–d, and d–e). Snug up each segment to the previous one.

[3] Sew through the first bugle of the first ladder segment to form a square (e–f and photo a).

[4] Pick up a bugle and snug it up to the first ladder segment (f–g).

[5] Sew a four-bugle ladder (g–h).

[6] Sew back through the ladder segment made in step 5 and the fourth ladder segment made in step 2 (figure 2, a–b).

[7] Sew two four-bugle ladder segments (b–c and c–d). Sew through the end bugle of the ladder segment made in step 5.

[8] Repeat steps 4–7 until your bracelet is the desired length. Add thread as needed (Basics). To change the bracelet length, add or omit ladder segments in groups of three.

[9] Pick up a bugle, a 15º seed bead, and a bugle (figure 3, a–b). Sew through the end ladder segment (b–c). Pick up a bugle, a 15º, and a bugle (c–d).

[10] Sew through the next ladder segment (d–e). Pick up a bugle (e–f).

[11] Repeat step 10 for the length of the bracelet. Sew through the last ladder segment on this side.

[12] Repeat step 9 to add the corner bugles and 15ºs to the other end.

Open center-square embellishment

[1] Sew through the first bugle of the next ladder segment, pick up six 15ºs, and sew through the bugle across the open square (figure 4, a–b).

[2] Pick up a 15º, sew through the next bugle, pick up six 15ºs, and sew through the bugle across the open square (b–c).

[3] Repeat step 2 for the remaining open center squares (c–d and d–e). Sew through the next edge bugle.

[4] Repeat steps 1–3 for the length of the bracelet.

Edge embellishment

[1] Sew through the corner bugles and 15º, pick up six 15ºs, and sew through the corner bugles and 15º (figure 5, a–b).

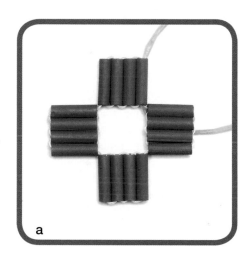

a

[2] Pick up a 15º, sew through the next 15º, pick up a 15º, sew through the next 15º, and pick up a 15º (b–c). Sew through the next edge bugle.

[3] Repeat step 2 for the length of the bracelet.

[4] Repeat step 1 to turn the corner (figure 6, a–b).

[5] To add 15ºs to the other edge, pick up two 15ºs, sew through the 15º, pick up two 15ºs, and sew through the edge bugles (b–c). Secure the thread with a few half-hitch knots (Basics) and secure the tail in the beadwork.

Ladder stitch

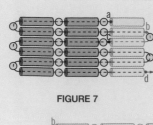

FIGURE 7

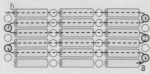

FIGURE 8

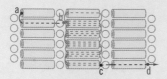

FIGURE 9

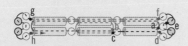

FIGURE 10

Toggle bar

[1] Thread a needle on 1 yd. (.9m) of thread, leaving a 6-in. (15cm) tail. Working in ladder stitch, make a six-bugle ladder.

[2] Pick up a 15º, a bugle, a 15º, a bugle, a 15º, a bugle, a 15º, a bugle, and a 15º. Sew through the next bugle on the ladder **(figure 7, a–b)**. Pick up a 15º and sew through the next bugle **(b–c)**.

[3] Repeat step 2 twice **(c–d)**. Sew back through the bugles and 15ºs to snug up the beads and add 15ºs to the spaces on the ends **(figure 8, a–b)**.

[4] Sew through the adjacent bugle and 15º **(figure 9, a–b)**. Reinforce the middle row of bugles, using ladder stitch **(b–c)**. Sew through the next 15º and bugle **(c–d)**.

[5] Fold the beadwork in half, sewing through rows 1 and 6 to connect the sides **(figure 10, a–b)**. Sew through the middle bugles **(b–c)**, the next 15º and bugle **(c–d)**, and an end 15º.

[6] Pick up a 15º and sew through the next 15º **(d–e)**. Repeat **(e–f)**. Sew across the row **(f–g)**.

[7] Repeat step 6 **(g–h)** on the other edge. Secure the thread with a few half-hitch knots, and trim.

MATERIALS

flat bracelet 7 in. (18cm)
- 5g size 2 (6mm) Japanese bugle beads
- 3g size 15º Japanese seed beads
- Nymo D, conditioned with beeswax or Thread Heaven
- beading needles, #12

cubic bracelet 7 in. (18cm)
- 20g size 2 (6mm) Japanese bugle beads
- 10g size 15º Japanese seed beads
- Nymo B, conditioned with beeswax or Thread Heaven
- beading needles, #12

Bracelet ends and toggle loop

[1] On 2 yd. (1.8m) of thread, leave a 6-in. (15cm) tail, and sew through the corner bugles and 15º.

[2] To attach the toggle bar (see "Toggle bar," left), pick up three 15ºs, sew through the middle bugle of the bar, and pick up three 15ºs. Sew through the corner bugles and 15º. Make a half-hitch knot and reinforce the bar thread path. Secure the thread with a few half-hitch knots, and trim.

[3] Repeat step 2 on the other end of the bracelet.

[4] To make the loop half of the clasp, pick up enough 15ºs (approximately 30) to fit around the bar and sew through the opposite bugle. Make a half-hitch knot and reinforce the loop thread path. Secure the thread with a few half-hitch knots, and trim.

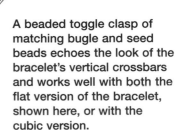

A beaded toggle clasp of matching bugle and seed beads echoes the look of the bracelet's vertical crossbars and works well with both the flat version of the bracelet, shown here, or with the cubic version.

Cubic bracelet

Cube units

[1] Thread a needle on 30 in. (76cm) of conditioned thread (Basics), leaving a 6-in. (15cm) tail. Pick up two bugle beads. Work in ladder stitch (Basics) until you have 16 bugles **(photo b)**.

[2] Fold the 16-bugle ladder into four-bugle segments, and sew through the bugles to hold the first and second, second and third, and third and fourth segments together **(photos c, d, and e)** to form a cube.

[3] Secure the tails with a few half-hitch knots (Basics), and trim.

[4] Repeat steps 1–3 to make 39 cubes. To change the bracelet length, add or omit cubes in groups of three.

Bracelet assembly

[1] Thread a needle on 2 yd. (1.8m) of thread, leaving a 6-in. (15cm) tail.

[2] Sew clockwise through a corner bugle of two cubes **(figure 11, a–b)**. Pick up a bugle, a 15º seed bead, and a bugle **(b–c)**, and sew through the bugle of cube 1 in this step **(c–d)**. Snug up the bugles, 15º, and cubes to form a square **(photo f)**.

[3] Step up through the second row of cube 1 in the opposite direction **(figure 12, a–b)**. Sewing counterclockwise, pick up a bugle, a 15º, and a bugle **(b–c)**. Sew through the second row of cubes 2 and 1 **(c–d)**.

[4] Step up through the third row of cube 1, and sew clockwise through the third row of cube 2 **(figure 13, a–b)**. Pick up a bugle, a 15º, and a bugle **(b–c)**, and sew through the first bugle in this step **(c–d)**.

[5] Step up through the fourth row of cube 1 **(figure 14, a–b)**. Pick up a bugle, a 15º, and a bugle **(b–c)**, and sew counterclockwise through the fourth row of cube 2 **(c–d)**. Sew through the fourth row again **(d–e)**.

[6] Zigzag through the top bugles of cube 2 **(e–f)**. Zigzag down the side of cube 2 **(f–g)**, sewing through the four bugles.

FIGURE 11

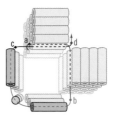

FIGURE 12

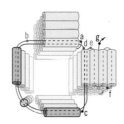

FIGURE 13

FIGURE 14

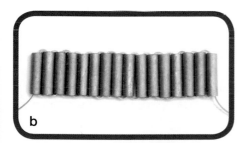

b

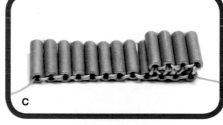

c

d

e

f

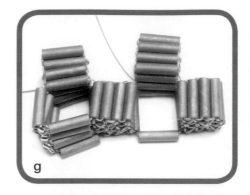

g

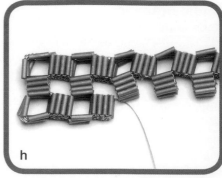

h

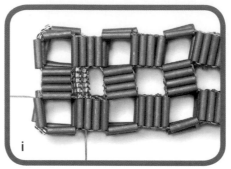

i

j

[7] Position two more cubes as shown in **figure 15**, and sew through the bottom corner bugle of the two new cubes, as in step 2. Pick up a bugle and sew through the bottom corner bugle of cubes 2 and 3 **(photo g)**.

[8] Repeat steps 3–7 for the length of the bracelet, but continue sewing through three cubes and picking up a bugle to form a square. Add thread as needed (Basics).

[9] When you reach the desired length of your bracelet, repeat step 2 to form the end corners.

[10] Add the remaining cubes, bugles, and 15ºs to make the other edge **(photo h)** and the fourth corner. Secure the tail with a few half-hitch knots, sew through the beadwork, and trim.

Center-square embellishment

[1] Secure 2 yd. (1.8m) of thread at one end of the base, leaving a 6-in. (15cm) tail. Sew through the corner bugles, 15º **(figure 16, a–b)**, and end bugle as shown.

[2] Pick up six 15ºs and sew through the bugle across the open square **(b–c)**.

[3] Sew through the next bugle **(c–d)**. Pick up six 15ºs and sew through the bugle across the open square **(d–e and photo i)**.

[4] Repeat step 3 twice **(e–f)**. Flip the bracelet, step up to the second row, and continue adding 15ºs to the remaining three rows inside the open square.

[5] Sew through the top bugles of the adjoining cubes as shown **(figure 17, a–b)** to position your needle to fill the next open center square.

[6] Repeat steps 2–5 to add 15ºs in all the open center squares. Secure the tails, and trim.

The gentle curve built into the cubic version of the bracelet creates a perfect fit.

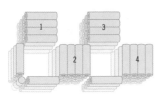

FIGURE 15

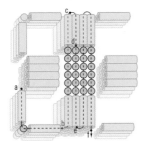

FIGURE 16

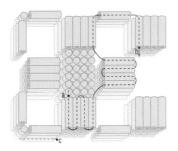

FIGURE 17

FIGURE 18

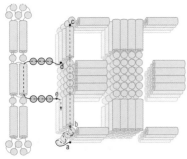

FIGURE 19

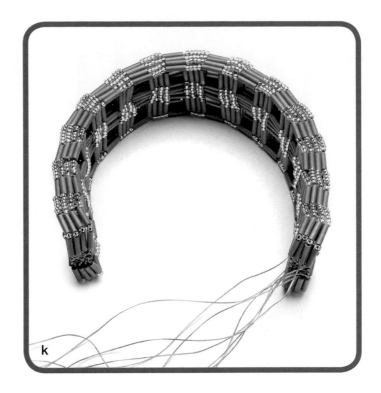

k

Edge embellishment
[1] Leaving a 6-in. (15cm) tail, secure 18 in. (46cm) of thread at one end of the bracelet, and sew through the beadwork to exit at **figure 17, point c.**
[2] Pick up four 15ºs and sew through the next bugle. Continue along the edge to the end of the band. Do not tie the thread or trim the tail.
[3] Repeat steps 1 and 2 for the remaining rows, but pick up five 15ºs for the second row and six 15ºs for the third and fourth rows **(photo j).**
[4] Repeat steps 1–3 on the other edge.
[5] Pull the eight threads to create a curve in the band that snugs up the 15ºs between the bugles **(photo k)**. Secure each tail with a few half-hitch knots, and trim.

Bracelet ends and toggle loop
[1] Thread a needle on 2 yd. (1.8m) of thread, leaving a 6-in. (15cm) tail.
[2] Sew through the corner bugles and 15º of the top row **(figure 18, a–b).**
[3] Pick up five 15ºs, and sew through the opposite bugles and 15º **(b–c).**
[4] Step down to the next row and repeat steps 2 and 3 for all four rows,

sewing through the respective corner bugles and 15ºs.
[5] Exit at a corner 15º and zigzag through the corner 15ºs to snug them up **(figure 19, a–b)**. Sew through the end bugles and 15ºs to the other corner **(b–c)**, and repeat the zigzag connection between the corner 15ºs. Sew through the beadwork to exit the second row of bugles at **point d.**
[6] To attach the toggle bar (see "Toggle bar," p. 86), pick up three 15ºs, sew through the middle bugle of the toggle bar, and pick up three 15ºs **(d–e)**. Sew through the corner bugles and 15º.
[7] Step up to the third row and repeat step 5. Secure the thread with a few half-hitch knots, and trim.
[8] Repeat steps 1–5 on the other end of the bracelet.
[9] To make the loop half of the clasp, pick up enough 15ºs (approximately 30) to fit around the toggle bar. Sew through the opposite bugle.
[10] Step up to the third row and repeat step 9. Secure the thread with a few half-hitch knots, and trim. ●

Ladder stitch

Structured

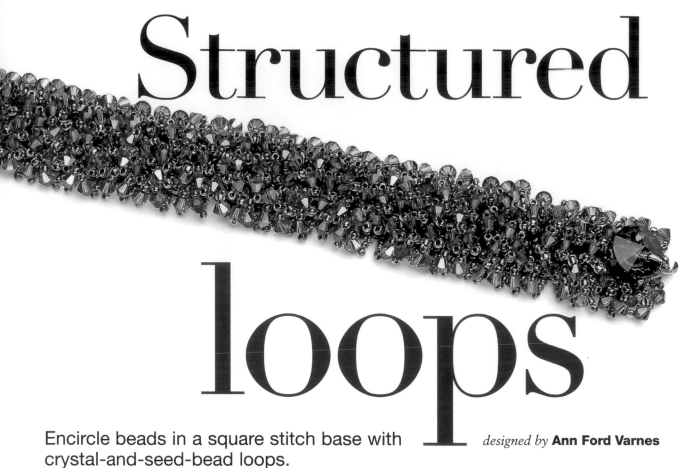

loops

Encircle beads in a square stitch base with crystal-and-seed-bead loops.

designed by **Ann Ford Varnes**

MATERIALS
bracelet 7 in. (18cm)
- **200** 4mm bicone crystals
- 40g size 6º seed beads
- 30g size 11º seed beads
- ½-in. (1.3cm) button for clasp
- conditioned nylon beading thread, or Fireline 6 lb. test
- beading needles, #10

step*by*step

[1] On 3 yd. (2.7m) of conditioned thread (Basics, p. 10), pick up a stop bead (Basics) and five 6º seed beads. Leaving a 6-in. (15cm) tail, work in square stitch (Basics), adding thread as needed (Basics). Work until the band is two rows short of the desired length. (My bracelet is 40 rows long.) Secure the tails in the beadwork with half-hitch knots (Basics), and trim.

[2] Start a new 3-yd. (2.7m) thread, and leave an 18-in. (46cm) tail. Secure the thread in the beadwork, and exit the first 6º in the last row **(figure 1, point a)**. Pick up three 11ºs, a 4mm bicone crystal, and three 11ºs. Sew back through the first two 6ºs in the row **(a–b)**, making a loop around the first 6º.

[3] Continue adding loops as in step 2. At the end of the row, sew through the end 6º in the next row **(figure 2, a–b)**.

[4] Add loops to each row of the base until you reach the third row from the end of the band. Modify the next two rows by adding loops to the first and last 6ºs only. Add loops to all the 6ºs in the last row as before **(figure 3 and photo a)**.

[5] Sew through the 6ºs to exit from the center of the open area. Attach the button to the open area of the base, using several thread paths **(photo b)**. Secure the thread, and trim.

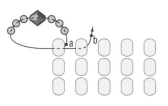

FIGURE 1

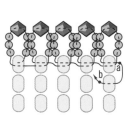

FIGURE 2

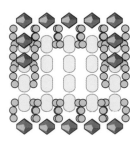

FIGURE 3

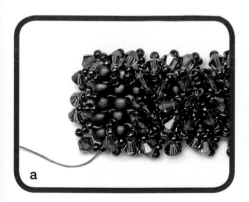

a

b

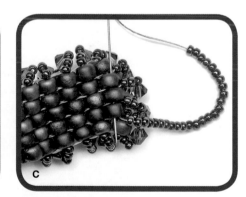

c

[6] Thread a needle on the tail, and sew through the first four 6ºs in the first row. Pick up enough 11ºs to fit around the button, and sew through the second, third, and fourth 6ºs in the first row (photo c). Retrace the thread path two times to reinforce the loop. Secure the tail, and trim. ●

EDITOR'S NOTE:
Vary the number of beads in your base row of 6º seed beads to make a wider or narrower bracelet.

Bugle bead embellishment

Tiers of bugle beads enhance a square stitch band in a casual necklace that's perfect for everyday wear.

It's easy to customize the look of this necklace with a handful of accent beads. See the Editor's Note, p. 95, to learn how to add this embellishment.

A square stitch band is the starting point for a lovely necklace.

designed by **June Wiseman**

MATERIALS

necklace 15½ in. (39.4cm)

- 4g Japanese size 1 (3mm) bugle beads
- seed beads
  10g size 11º
  3g size 14º or 15º
- nylon beading thread conditioned with beeswax or Thread Heaven
- beading needles, #10 or #12

a

b

c

d

step*by*step

Band

[1] Thread a needle on a comfortable length of conditioned thread (Basics, p. 10), and, leaving a 6-in. (15cm) tail, pick up a stop bead (Basics) and three 11º seed beads **(figure 1, a–b)**.

[2] Working in square stitch (Basics), pick up an 11º, and sew back through the last 11º picked up in the previous row and the 11º just added **(b–c)**. Pick up an 11º, and go through the middle bead in the previous row and the bead just added **(c–d)**. Pick up an 11º, and go through the first bead in the previous row and the bead just added **(d–e)**.

[3] Continue as above, making three square stitches per row, until the band is ½ in. (1.3cm) short of the desired length. The number of rows should be divisible by six for the embellishments to work out evenly. Remove the stop bead, secure both tails with a few half-hitch knots (Basics) between beads, and trim.

Embellishment

[1] Secure 1 yd. (.9m) of thread near one end, sew through the beadwork to exit an edge bead, and pick up a 14º, a bugle bead, an 11º, a 14º, an 11º, a bugle, and a 14º. Skip a row of square stitch, and sew into the edge bead of the next row **(figure 2, a–b)**. Sew through the next edge 11º **(b–c)**, and repeat **(c–d)**. Continue across until you reach the end. Secure the tails, and trim.

[2] Secure 1 yd. (.9m) of thread at one end, exit the first bugle on that end, and pick up a bugle, an 11º, a 14º, an 11º, and a bugle. Sew up through the next bugle and through the 14º and 11º above it **(figure 3, a–b)**. Sew down through the next 11º, 14º, and bugle **(b–c)**, and

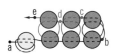

FIGURE 1

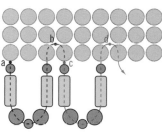

FIGURE 2

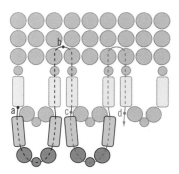

FIGURE 3

repeat (c–d). Continue across. Secure the tails, and trim.

[3] Secure 1 yd. (.9m) of thread at one end, exit the top edge bead, pick up three 14ºs, and sew into the next 11º (figure 4, a–b). Sew through the next 11º, and repeat across to the end. Secure the tails, and trim.

Clasp

[1] On 1 yd. (.9m) of thread, pick up a stop bead and ten 11ºs. Working in flat, even-count peyote (Basics), stitch a panel of ten rows (figure 5). Each straight edge should have five beads.

[2] Remove the stop bead, and zip up (Basics) the peyote edges to form a tube. Retrace the thread path, and secure the tails.

[3] Secure 1 yd. (.9m) of thread at one end of the necklace, and exit an edge 11º. Pick up four 11ºs, and sew diagonally through two middle 11ºs on the tube (photo a).

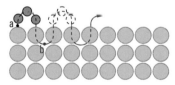

FIGURE 4

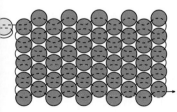

FIGURE 5

[4] Pick up an 11º, and sew through the two middle 11ºs of the four picked up in step 3. Pick up an 11º, and sew into the other edge bead at the end of the necklace (photo b). Retrace the thread path, and secure the tail.

[5] Secure 1 yd. (.9m) of thread at the other end of the necklace, and exit an edge bead. Pick up enough 11ºs to fit around the tube, and sew back through the third 11º picked up (photo c). Pick up two 11ºs, and sew into the other edge bead at the end of the necklace (photo d). Retrace the thread path, and secure the tail. ●

EDITOR'S NOTE:
If you want to glam it up a little, add crystal swags to your necklace, as shown on p. 93: Over the center ten loops of embellishment, make five swags, each consisting of a bugle bead, a 14º seed bead, three 11ºs, a 4mm bicone crystal, three 11ºs, a 14º, and a bugle. Make one more swag between the second and fourth swags with a bugle, a 14º, five 11ºs, a 6mm bicone crystal, five 11ºs, a 14º, and a bugle.

Square stitch

Beads
cubed

Multiply these bead cubes to add color and sparkle to a rubber-tubing bracelet.

designed by **Marissa McConnell**

MATERIALS
bracelet 7½ in. (19.1cm)
- Japanese seed beads (**4** size 8°s and **24** size 11°s per cube)
- **2** or more spacers that fit snugly over rubber tubing
- 1 in. (2.5cm) 18-gauge wire, full-hard
- nylon beading thread conditioned with beeswax
- 7–9 in. (18–23cm) 2mm black rubber tubing
- beading needles, #12
- cocktail straw
- Zap-a-Gap glue
- wire cutters

step*by*step

Beaded beads

[1] Thread a needle on 2 ft. (61cm) of thread conditioned with beeswax (Basics, p. 10). Leaving a 6-in. (15cm) tail, pick up eight 11º seed beads, and sew through the beads again to form a ring. Sew through the first two 11ºs again to position the needle away from the tail (**figure 1, a–b**).

[2] Working in right-angle weave (Basics), pick up six 11ºs, sew through the pair of 11ºs on the ring (**b–c**), and tighten the new 11ºs into a ring. Sew through the next four beads on the new ring (**c–d**).

[3] Repeat step 2 (**d–e**).

[4] Fold the three rings to form an open-ended U, and pick up two 11ºs. Sew through the end pair of 11ºs of the first ring (**figure 2, a–b**). Pick up two 11ºs and sew through the end pair of 11ºs of the third ring (**b–c**). Tighten the thread to form a cube.

[5] Slide the cube onto the cocktail straw. Sew through the top four pairs of 11ºs. Sew through the first pair again (**figure 3, a–b**). Secure the thread with a half-hitch knot (Basics).

[6] Sew through the first top 11º of the next pair (**figure 4, a–b**). Pick up an 8º and go under the thread bridge between the bottom pair of 11ºs (**b–c**). Sew back through the 8º and the second 11º of the top pair (**c–d**). Snug up the thread and turn the cube a quarter turn to the left.

[7] Repeat step 6 three times to add an 8º to the center of each side of the cube.

[8] Secure the thread with half-hitch knots, sew through the beadwork, and trim.

[9] Thread a needle on the tail. To reinforce the bottom of the cube, sew through the bottom four pairs of 11ºs as in step 5, and tighten the thread. Secure the thread with half-hitch knots, and trim the excess thread.

[10] Repeat steps 1–9, to make as many cubes as desired.

Assembly

[1] Measure your wrist to determine the length of the bracelet. Allow for a little slack in the measurement so the bracelet will slide over your hand. Cut the 2mm black rubber tubing to that length.

[2] Cut a 1-in. (2.5cm) piece of 18-gauge wire or a wire that will fit tightly inside the tubing.

[3] Glue half of the wire inside the tubing and let the glue dry (**photo**).

[4] Slide the spacers and beaded cubes onto the tubing. Close the bracelet by sliding the wire into the tubing. Glue the wire into the tubing for extra security, and position the cubes over the connection. ●

EDITOR'S NOTE:

To hold the beads in place, use spacers that fit snugly over the tubing. You can then add or interchange other cubes. To permanently close the bracelet, glue the end spacers in place over the join in the tubing.

FIGURE 1

FIGURE 2
SIDE VIEW

FIGURE 3
TOP VIEW

FIGURE 4
SIDE VIEW

Embellishing only
three sides of the base
creates a domed bead.

Bedecked
baubles

A base of right-angle weave provides a sturdy
starting point for sparkling crystal embellishments.

designed by **Mia Gofar**

a

step*by*step

Base

[1] On 2 yd. (1.8m) of Fireline, pick up four 4mm color A fire-polished beads, and leave an 8-in. (20cm) tail. Working in right-angle weave (Basics, p. 10), sew back through the first three As (figure 1, a–b).

[2] Pick up three As, and continue in right-angle weave (b–c). Repeat for the next stitch (c–d).

[3] Sew through the next three As of the last stitch (figure 2, a–b), and begin a second row of right-angle weave off the first. Pick up three As, and sew back through the bead the thread is exiting (b–c). Continue through the next three As (c–d). Complete the row as shown (d–e).

[4] Work a third row of right-angle weave off the second row (figure 3, a–b).

[5] Fold the beadwork in half, and work a fourth row of right-angle weave, connecting the first and third rows (figure 4, a–b).

[6] Retrace the thread path to reinforce the four As on each end. Exit an end bead (photo a). Don't trim the working thread.

[7] Make a total of three right-angle weave bases.

Embellishment

[1] Pick up a 4mm color B bicone crystal, an 11º seed bead, and a 4mm B. Sew through the opposite A (figure 5, a–b). Repeat twice down the vertical column of right-angle weave stitches.

[2] Pick up a 4mm color C bicone and sew through the 11º from the previous stitch (figure 6, a–b). Pick up a 4mm C and sew through the opposite A (b–c). Repeat to complete the column.

[3] Pick up an 11º and sew through the next end A (photo b).

[4] Repeat steps 1–3 twice to complete two more columns.

[5] Sew through the horizontal rows of As, adding an 11º between the columns as in step 3.

[6] Retrace the thread path, tying a few half-hitch knots (Basics) between beads. Trim the working thread, and secure the tail in the same manner.

[7] Repeat steps 1–6 to embellish the remaining bases.

Assembly

[1] On 22 in. (56cm) of flexible beading wire, string a crimp bead and lobster claw clasp. Go back through the crimp bead, and crimp it (Basics). Trim the excess wire.

[2] String five 4mm Cs, six 4mm color E bicones, five 4mm Cs, seven 4mm Es, three 4mm Cs, a 6mm color B bicone or rondelle, a 5mm color D bicone, an 8mm color C bicone, an 8mm color B bicone or round, an 8mm C bicone, a 5mm D, a 6mm B, a beaded bead, a 6mm B, a 5mm D, an 8mm C, an 8mm B, an 8mm C, a 5mm D, and a 6mm B.

[3] String an embellished bead, and then string the remaining crystals to mirror the first half of the necklace.

[4] String a crimp bead and 2 in. (5cm) of chain. Go back through the crimp bead and crimp it. Trim the excess wire. Use crimp covers to cover the crimps if desired.

[5] On a head pin, string an 8mm C round crystal and a 4mm B. Make the first half of a wrapped loop (Basics). Attach the dangle to the chain, and finish the wraps (photo c). ●

MATERIALS
necklace 17 in. (43cm)

- 8mm round crystal, color C
- 4 8mm round or bicone crystals, color B
- 8 6mm bicone crystals or rondelles, color B
- bicone crystals
  8 8mm, color C
  8 5mm, color D
  80 4mm, color C
  55 4mm, color B
  26 4mm, color E
- 84 4mm round fire-polished beads, color A
- 1g size 11º Japanese seed beads
- lobster claw clasp
- 2-in. (5cm) chain to accommodate lobster claw clasp
- 2-in. (5cm) 22-gauge head pin
- 2 crimp beads
- 2 crimp covers (optional)
- Fireline 6 lb. test
- 22 in. (56cm) flexible beading wire, .014
- beading needles, #12
- chainnose pliers
- crimping pliers
- roundnose pliers
- wire cutters

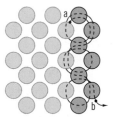

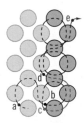

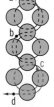

FIGURE 1   FIGURE 2   FIGURE 3   FIGURE 4   FIGURE 5   FIGURE 6

EDITOR'S NOTE:
Make an embellished bead with 3mm crystals and fire-polished beads instead of 4mms and with 15º seed beads instead of 11ºs. You can also embellish all four sides of the base.

Weave in the round

A variation of the right-angle weave stitch lets you create a circular shape that you can embellish with crystals and seed beads.

designed by **Barb Switzer**

Pendant
Base

[1] On 2 yd. (1.8m) of Fireline, pick up an 8º seed bead, two 11ºs, a cylinder bead, a 4mm bicone crystal, a cylinder, and two 11ºs **(figure 1, a–b)**, leaving an 8-in. (20cm) tail. Sew back through the 8º, two 11ºs, and the cylinder **(b–c)**, pulling the beads into a ring.

[2] Pick up a 4mm, a cylinder, and three 11ºs. Sew back through the two 11ºs and the cylinder from the previous step **(c–d)**. Then sew through the 4mm, the cylinder, and the first two 11ºs just added **(d–e)**.

[3] Pick up an 8º, two 11ºs, a cylinder, and a 4mm. Sew back through the cylinder and the two 11ºs from the previous step **(e–f)**. Then sew through the 8º, two 11ºs, and the cylinder just added **(f–g)**.

[4] Repeat steps 2 and 3 until you have 15 rings. To complete the base, pick up a 4mm, and sew through the cylinder and the two 11ºs from the first ring **(figure 2, a–b)**. Then, pick up an 11º, and sew through the two 11ºs and the cylinder from the last ring. Sew through the 4mm just added **(b–c)**.

Embellishment

[1] Pick up a 15º, an 11º, a 3mm bicone crystal, an 11º, and a 15º **(figure 3, a–b)**. Sew through the 11º opposite the 4mm. Pick up a 15º and an 11º, and sew through the 3mm **(b–c)**. Pick up an 11º and a 15º, and sew through the 4mm again **(c–d)**. Flip the base over, and repeat on the back. Exit the next 4mm on the base.

[2] Pick up a 15º, a cylinder, and a 15º **(d–e)**. Sew back through the cylinder, pick up a 15º, and sew through the next 4mm (e–f).

[3] Repeat steps 1 and 2 around the ring. On every other ring, sew through the 8º opposite the 4mm instead of a 11º. When you complete the circle, sew through the first three beads picked up in this step (figure 4, a–b).

[4] Pick up a 3mm, a 15º, and a 3mm. Sew through the next 15º (b–c). Repeat around the base.

[5] Reinforce the outer edge with a second thread path, and exit a 15º.

[6] Pick up an 11º and 15 15ºs. Sew back through the 11º and into the 15º on the outer edge to make a loop. Reinforce the loop with a second thread path. Secure the working thread with a few half-hitch knots (Basics, p. 10) between beads, and trim. Secure the tail in the same manner.

Necklace

[1] Center the pendant and two cylinders on 20 in. (51cm) of flexible beading wire. Secure one end of the wire.

[2] String a 4mm, a 3mm, a cylinder, an 11º, and a cylinder. Repeat, adding three 11ºs instead of one.

[3] String a 4mm, a 3mm, and a 4mm. String a cylinder, five 11ºs, and a cylinder.

[4] Repeat step 3 six times, altering the number of 11ºs added each time, as follows: seven 11ºs, nine 11ºs, 11 11ºs, 11 11ºs, nine 11ºs, and seven 11ºs. String a 3mm, a crimp bead, a 4mm, and half of a clasp. Go back through the 4mm and the crimp bead. Crimp the crimp bead (Basics), and trim the tail.

[5] Remove the tape, and repeat steps 2–4 on the other side of the pendant with the other half of the clasp. ●

MATERIALS

pendant
- bicone crystals
  16 4mm
  64 3mm
- Japanese seed beads
  16 size 8º
  1g size 11º
  1g cylinder beads
  2g size 15º or 14º
- Fireline 6 lb. test
- beading needles, #13

necklace 16 in. (41cm)
- bicone crystals
  34 4mm
  20 3mm
- Japanese seed beads
  5g size 11º
  3g size 11º cylinder beads
- clasp
- **2** crimp beads
- flexible beading wire, .014
- crimping pliers
- wire cutters

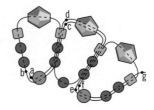

FIGURE 1

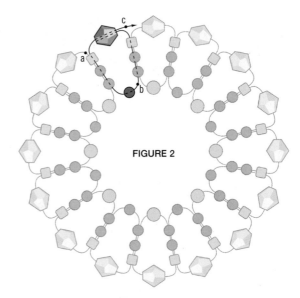

FIGURE 2

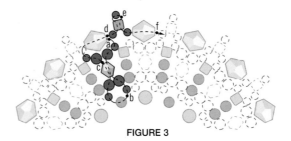

FIGURE 3

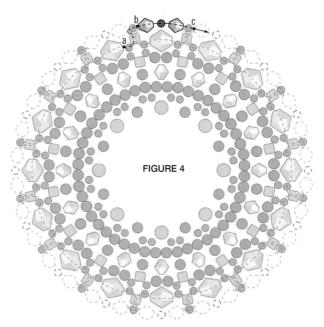

FIGURE 4

Cosmic crystals

Stitch sparkling right-angle weave saucers that are out of this world.

designed by **Deborah Staehle**

MATERIALS

earrings
- 4mm bicone crystals
  20 color A
  16 color B
- **2** 2-in. (5cm) head pins
- pair of earring findings
- Fireline 6 lb. test
- beading needles, #12
- G-S Hypo Cement
- chainnose pliers
- roundnose pliers
- wire cutters

a

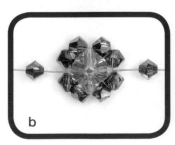

b

step*by*step

[1] On 1 yd. (.9m) of Fireline, pick up two color A and two color B crystals. Sew through all the crystals to form a ring. Exit the second B **(figure 1, a–b)**.

[2] Pick up two As and a B. Sew through the B the thread is exiting and continue through the next two As and the new B **(figure 2, a–b)**.

[3] Pick up a B and two As. Sew through the B the thread is exiting, and exit the new B **(figure 3, a–b)**.

[4] Pick up two As. Sew through the first B from step 1 and the B from step 3. Exit the two new As **(figure 4, a–b)**.

[5] To start the second layer, pick up two Bs, and sew through the two As from step 4 **(figure 5, a–b)**. Sew through the two new Bs and the two As from step 3 **(b–c)**.

[6] Pick up a B, and sew through the previous B and the two As from step 3. Exit the new B **(c–d)**. Pick up a B, sew through the two As from step 2 and the previous B. Exit the new B **(d–e)**.

[7] Sew through the next two As from step 1 and the first B added in step 5. Exit the last B added **(e–f)**. The tails should be next to each other.

[8] Tie the tails into a square knot (Basics, p. 10). Dot the knot with glue, let the glue dry, and trim the tails. Make a second crystal bead.

[9] On a head pin, string an A, a crystal bead, and an A **(photo a)**. Make the first half of a wrapped loop (Basics). Slide the earring finding into the loop, and finish the wraps.

[10] Make a second earring to match the first. ◉

EDITOR'S NOTES:
• **For a bracelet, make three crystal beads and string them horizontally (photo b) on flexible beading wire. String assorted beads and spacers between the crystal beads to reach the desired length.**

• **Deborah also uses a crossweave approach to create these earrings; contact her (see p. 245) for instructions.**

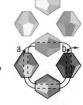

FIGURE 1   FIGURE 2

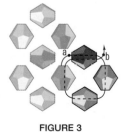

FIGURE 3

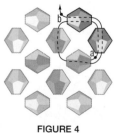

FIGURE 4

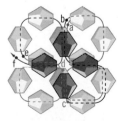

FIGURE 5

Stripes
forever

Teardrop-shaped fringe beads accent a striped bracelet with row-by-row color changes.

designed by **Phyllis Dintenfass**

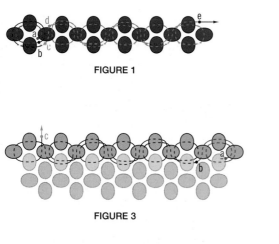

FIGURE 1

FIGURE 2

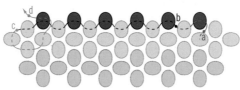

FIGURE 3

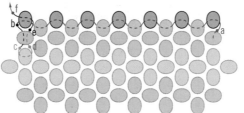

FIGURE 4

FIGURE 5

FIGURE 6

MATERIALS
bracelet 7 in. (18cm)

- **33–36** 3mm drop beads, color A
- **8–9** size 8º Japanese seed beads (optional)
- size 11º Japanese seed beads
  5g color A
  4g color B
- button for clasp (optional)
- Fireline 6 lb. test
- beading needles, #12
- drinking straw (optional)

step*by*step

Band

[1] On 2 yd. (1.8m) of Fireline, pick up four color A 11º seed beads **(figure 1, a–b)**, and leave a 24-in. (61cm) tail. Sew back through the four As **(b–c)** and continue through the next A to form a ring **(c–d)**. Snug up the beads.

[2] Work five stitches of right-angle weave (Basics, p. 10), using As **(d–e)**, for a total of six clusters.

[3] Pick up a color B 11º, and sew through the end A cluster **(figure 2, a–b)**. Pick up a B and sew through the next A **(b–c)**. Continue across the row, adding Bs between the As **(c–d)**. Pick up a B, sew through the end A in the previous row, and sew back through the B just added **(d–e)**. Flip the beadwork after every row to be in position to work the next row.

[4] Pick up three Bs, and sew through the last B added in step 3 and the three Bs just added **(figure 3, a–b)**. Continue working in right-angle weave across the row **(b–c)**.

[5] Pick up an A and sew through the next B **(figure 4, a–b)**. Continue across the row, adding As between the Bs **(b–c)**. Sew through the end cluster of Bs in the previous row and the last A added in this step **(c–d)**.

[6] Pick up three As, and sew through the last A added in the previous step and the three As just added **(figure 5, a–b)**. Continue across the row **(b–c)**. Sew through the adjacent end B in the previous row and the end A of the last stitch **(c–d)**.

[7] Repeat steps 3–6, ending with steps 3 and 4, to sew seven alternating A and B stripes. End with a B stripe. Also make the following change: In step 3, after adding each row of single Bs **(figure 6, a–b)**, secure the thread by sewing through the end A below the B just added **(b–c)**, the top B of the last cluster in the previous B stripe **(c–d)**,

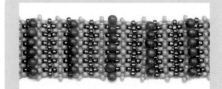

EDITOR'S NOTE:
In the original bracelet, the middle row of drops is off-center. To make it symmetrical, modify the center stripe of the band (step 12) by replacing the middle As in the cluster with drops (photo). Use seven, rather than six, drops across the stripe. Begin the stripe by repeating step 5 of the band. To sew the clusters, pick up As and drops in the following order: a drop, an A, and a drop. For the remaining five clusters, alternate picking up a drop and an A, and an A and a drop.

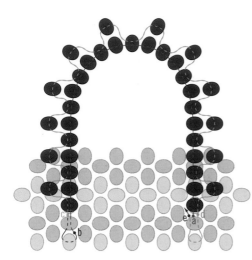

FIGURE 7

back through the A (d–e), and back through the B just added (e–f).

[8] Repeat steps 5 and 6, but in step 6 pick up As and 3mm drop beads in the following order: an A, a drop, and an A. For the remaining five clusters, alternate picking up an A and a drop, and a drop and an A.

[9] Stitch a stripe of Bs, a stripe of As, and a stripe of Bs.

[10] Repeat step 8.

[11] Stitch a stripe of Bs, a stripe of As, and a stripe of Bs.

[12] Repeat step 5, but use drops instead of As. Repeat step 6.

[13] Repeat steps 11 and 12 twice.

[14] Repeat step 7 to sew seven alternating stripes of As and Bs. Check the fit of your bracelet. The ends of the band should meet when you wrap it around your wrist. To increase the length, add alternating stripes of As and Bs to both ends to reach the desired length. Secure the tail with a few half-hitch knots (Basics) between beads, and trim.

Button clasp

If you plan to use a button for the clasp, you can either work it in as you stitch the base, positioning it approximately half the length of the button away from the end, or add it after the base is completed. To add it afterward, sew through the beadwork to exit where the button needs to be attached. Pick up five or six 11ºs and the shank of the button, and sew into a nearby bead. Retrace the thread path several times, secure the tail, and trim. Proceed to "Clasp loop" to complete the bracelet.

Toggle clasp

[1] To make a toggle bar, string a stop bead (Basics) on 1 yd. (.9m) of Fireline, and leave a 6-in. (15cm) tail.

[2] Pick up 12 As, and, working in flat, even-count peyote stitch (Basics), sew a strip with three As on each side.

[3] In the next row, replace four to six As in the center of the row with drops. Continue working in peyote stitch until the strip has seven As on each side.

[4] Zip up the strip (Basics) to form a tube. To stiffen the tube, cut a drinking straw to the length of the toggle bar. Cut the straw lengthwise, roll it tightly, and slide it inside the tube.

[5] To taper the ends of the tube, sew through the beadwork to exit an edge bead. Pick up an A, sew through the next A, and exit the following A. Continue around until you've added seven As. Sew through all the As added in this step to snug them up. Repeat at the other end of the tube.

[6] Sew through the beadwork and exit the fourth A from the end in the row opposite the drops.

[7] Sew two right-angle weave stitches to form a tab. Attach the toggle bar to the bracelet by sewing into the second stripe from the end as in the photo (top, left). Reinforce the tab, secure the thread with a few half-hitch knots, and trim.

Clasp loop

[1] To form the loop, thread a needle on the tail and sew through the beadwork to exit at **figure 7, point a**. Pick up enough As (approximately 25) to fit around the toggle bar or button. Sew through the base to **point b**.

[2] Anchor the thread by sewing through the adjacent B and back through the A just exited (b–c).

[3] Go back through the last A in the loop and embellish the loop with peyote stitch, using As (c–d).

[4] Sew into the base A where you began the loop and back through the adjacent B (d–e). Sew back through the loop to reinforce the stitching. Secure the thread with a few half-hitch knots, and trim. ●

Lacy ruffles and pearls

Pinch beads stitched in right-angle weave form the base of this bracelet.

designed by **Dottie Hoeschen**

Pearls now come in a variety of colors, so have fun selecting matching or contrasting seed beads for the ruffles.

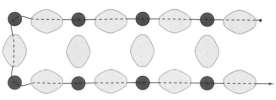

FIGURE 1

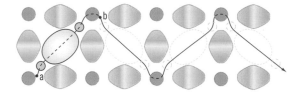

FIGURE 2

EDITOR'S NOTE:
If you use side-drilled pearls, they may twist within the pinch-bead ring. To support the beads, stitch a 6º bead on the back of the bracelet in the same method as for the pearls. This will fill in the space behind the pearls.

MATERIALS
bracelet 7¼ in. (18.4cm)
- **68–90** 5mm pinch beads
- **22–26** 4–6mm freshwater pearls
- seed beads
  48 or more size 8º
  7g size 11º
- clasp
- nylon beading thread
- beading needles, #10 or #12

step*by*step

[1] Measure your wrist, and subtract the length of the clasp plus 1 in. (2.5cm) to determine the length of the band.

[2] Thread a needle with a comfortable length of thread, and, leaving a 10-in. (25cm) tail, pick up four pinch beads. Sew through the first three beads, and tighten the thread to form a ring. Working in right-angle weave (Basics, p. 10), stitch the base with pinch beads to the length determined in step 1. Stitch an even number of rings.

[3] Pick up an 8º seed bead, and sew through the next pinch bead. Repeat around the edge of the bracelet, including the corners **(figure 1)**.

[4] To add the pearls, exit a corner 8º. Pick up an 11º, a pearl, and an 11º. Sew through the 8º at the opposite corner of the ring **(figure 2, a–b)**. Repeat for the length of the band. If you are using smaller pearls, you may need to pick up two 11ºs on each side of the pearl to cover the thread.

[5] To add the ruffle, exit a corner 8º. Pick up ten 11ºs, skip an 8º on the base, and sew through the next 8º **(figure 3, a–b)**. Repeat along the length of the band. Sew through the end pinch bead, and repeat on the other edge of the band.

[6] To form the second layer, sew through the end pinch bead and the adjacent 8º **(figure 4, a–b)**.

[7] Pick up six 11ºs, and sew through the next 8º on the base **(b–c)**. Repeat along the length of the band.

[8] Repeat steps 6 and 7 on the other edge.

[9] To add the clasp, exit at a corner 8º. Pick up three 11ºs, an 8º, two 11ºs, one clasp half, and two 11ºs **(figure 5, a–b)**. Sew back through the 8º, pick up three 11ºs, and sew into the other corner 8º **(b–c)**. Secure the working thread in the beadwork with a few half-hitch knots (Basics) between beads, and trim. Repeat on the other end of the band. ●

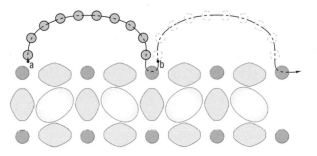

FIGURE 3

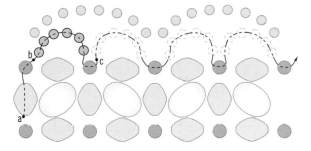

FIGURE 4

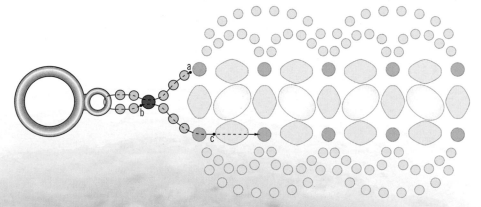

FIGURE 5

Dramatic looped band

Create a scalloped edge to change the shape of this bracelet.

designed by **Connie Blachut**

step*by*step

Base

[1] On 3 yd. (2.7m) of Fireline, pick up eight 8º seed beads, leaving a 10-in. (25cm) tail. Sew through the first four 8ºs again **(figure 1, a–b)**.

[2] Pick up six 8ºs, sew back through the last two 8ºs your thread is exiting **(b–c)**, and continue through four new 8ºs **(c–d)**.

[3] Pick up six 8ºs, and sew back through the last two 8ºs your thread is exiting **(d–e)**. Continue through all six new 8ºs **(e–f)**.

[4] To begin the next row, pick up six 8ºs, sew back through the two 8ºs your thread is exiting, and continue through the first two new 8ºs **(f–g)**.

[5] Pick up four 8ºs, and sew through the middle two 8ºs on the previous row and the last two 8ºs you exited on the previous stitch **(g–h)**. Continue through the four new 8ºs **(h–i)**, and sew through the last two 8ºs on the previous row **(i–j)**.

[6] Pick up four 8ºs, and sew through the last four beads you just exited. Continue through the four new 8ºs **(j–k)**.

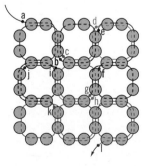

FIGURE 1

MATERIALS

bracelet 7½ in. (19.1cm)

- **30** 4–5mm pearls or crystals
- seed beads
  30g size 8º
  20g size 11º
- two-strand clasp
- Fireline 6 or 8 lb. test
- beading needles, #12

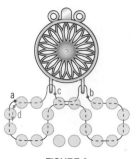

FIGURE 2

FIGURE 4

a

b

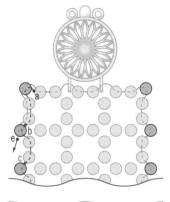

FIGURE 3

FIGURE 5

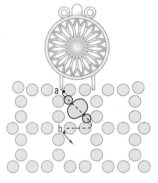

FIGURE 6

[7] To work the next row, flip your work over, and repeat steps 4–6 (k–l).
[8] Repeat steps 4–7 until you reach the desired length. Make your bracelet so the number of rows is divisible by 3. Set the thread aside.
[9] Pick up the tail, and sew through the first row of beads as shown in **figure 2, a–b**. Sew through one loop of the clasp and through the next two 8ºs (**b–c** and **photo a**). Sew through the other loop of the clasp and the next two 8ºs (**c–d**). Secure the tail with half-hitch knots (Basics, p. 10) between a few beads, and trim.
[10] Repeat on the other end with the working thread, but before securing the thread, exit at **figure 3, point a**. Pick up an 8º, and sew through the next two 8ºs along the side of the base (**a–b**). Pick up an 8º, and sew through the next two 8ºs (**b–c**). Continue around the base, reinforcing the clasp loops instead of adding 8ºs when you reach the ends (**c–d**). Exit at **point e**.

Scalloped edge
[1] Secure 2 yd. (1.8m) of Fireline in the beadwork, and exit at **figure 4, point a**.

[2] Pick up six 11ºs. Sew back through four 8ºs (**a–b**). Push the first loop onto the top of the bracelet.
[3] Pick up six 11ºs, skip one of the 8ºs on the side, and sew through the next four 8ºs (**figure 5, a–b**). Push the next loop on top of the first, making sure the loops form a spiral from the front of the bracelet to the back as you add loops.
[4] Repeat step 3 seven times for a total of nine loops, which make up the first scallop. To make the next scallop, position the first loop to lie on top of the bracelet (**photo b**). Repeat along the edge to make ten scallops. Repeat on the other edge. Secure the tails in the beadwork, and trim.

Center
[1] Secure 1 yd. (.9m) of Fireline in the beadwork, exiting at **figure 6, point a**.
[2] Pick up an 11º, a pearl, and an 11º. Sew through the next two center 8ºs in the same direction so the new beads lie across the center stitch diagonally (**a–b**). Repeat along the center row of the base.
[3] Secure the tails in the beadwork, and trim. ●

EDITOR'S NOTE:
Some 11º seed beads are a little larger than others, and if you use a hex-cut bead or another shape, you may have to change the amount of beads you use for each loop of the scalloped edge.

A metalsmith's
match

This beaded bracelet simulates granulation, the ancient art of fusing tiny metal spheres into intricate patterns.

designed by **Shelley Nybakke**

Use right-angle weave and layers of tiny metal beads to make this impressively sturdy bangle look granulated.

MATERIALS

two-tone bangle bracelet
- 50g size 11º metal seed beads, color A (thebeadparlor.com)
- 10g size 11º Japanese glass or metal seed beads, color B
- Fireline 10 lb. and 6 lb. test
- beading needles, #10

step*by*step

Metal seed beads can have sharp edges, so use doubled Fireline throughout. Start with 10 lb. test, and switch to 6 lb. test when you use the glass seed beads. Or, if you're using all metal beads, switch to 6 lb. test on the final layer, so your thread isn't as visible.

Base layer

[1] Center a needle on a length of doubled Fireline 10 lb. test. Leaving a 6-in. (15cm) tail, attach a stop bead (Basics, p. 10).
[2] Pick up four color A 11º seed beads, and form a ring by sewing through the first bead. Working in right-angle weave

(Basics), create a row that is six four-bead units wide.
[3] Continue in right-angle weave until you have a band that is six four-bead units wide and 70 rows long. To join the ends, pick up an A. Sew through the corresponding A in the first row, pick up an A, and sew through the A you just exited in row 70. Continue through the first A picked up in this step and the next edge A in row 1 (**figure 1**). Continue stitching in right-angle weave, adding one A per stitch, until the join is complete (**figure 2**).

Second layer

[1] To build the foundation for the second layer, exit an edge 11º at **figure 3, point a**,

and sew through the 11º adjacent to it (**a–b**).
[2] Pick up an A, and sew through the next 11º in the row (**b–c**), pulling the thread tight until the A clicks into place. Continue to the end of the row (**c–d**), adding a total of five As. Sew through two edge 11ºs to begin the next row (**d–e**).
[3] Repeat step 2 (**photo a**) until you've added second-layer foundation beads to the length of the bangle.
[4] Sew through the bead-work to exit one of the 11ºs added in step 3. Pick up an A, and sew through a foundation 11º parallel to the 11º your thread is exiting (**figure 4, a–b**).
[5] Pick up an A, and sew back through all four 11ºs, pulling tight (**b–c** and **photo b**).
[6] Continue in modified right-angle weave to finish the row, adding one bead at a time and sewing through the foundation layer to complete each stitch (**c–d**).
[7] To complete the second layer, repeat steps 4–6 for the length of the bangle.

Third layer

The third foundation layer is sewn lengthwise to strengthen the band.

[1] Secure a length of Fireline 6 lb. test in the bead-work and exit a second-layer A at **figure 5, point a**.

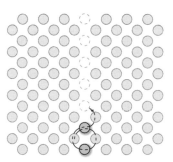

FIGURE 1

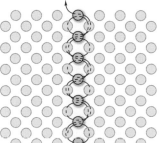

FIGURE 2

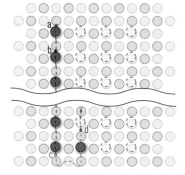

FIGURE 3

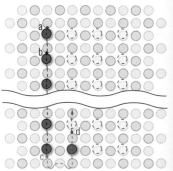

FIGURE 4

FIGURE 5

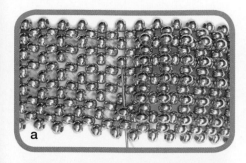

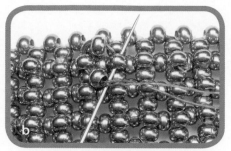

[2] Pick up a color B 11º and sew through the next second-layer A along the length of the bangle **(a–b)**, pulling tightly to click the B into place.

[3] Repeat step 2, adding Bs until you reach the end of the column **(b–c)**.

[4] Stitch through to the next parallel column, and repeat steps 2 and 3 **(c–d)** to make a total of four B foundation columns circling the bracelet **(photo c)**.

[5] Sew through the beadwork to exit a foundation B. Pick up a B, and working in modified right-angle weave, fill in the third layer as in steps 4–6 of the second layer **(photo d)**. Repeat for the

length of the bangle, sewing a layer that is three four-bead units wide.

Fourth layer

This layer's foundation is added widthwise, as in the second layer.

[1] Secure a length of Fireline 6 lb. test in the beadwork and exit a third-layer B.

[2] Pick up an A, and sew through the next third-layer B across the width of the bangle, pulling tightly to click the A into place. Repeat to add another A.

[3] To complete the fourth foundation layer, repeat step 2, adding two As to each row **(photo e)**.

[4] Sew through the beadwork to exit a foundation A. Working in right-angle weave, as in steps 4–6 of the second layer, fill in the remaining beads, using As in the center and Bs on each edge to achieve the striped pattern **(photo f)**. Repeat for the length of the bangle to make a layer that is two four-bead units wide. Secure the ends, and trim the tails. **◉**

EDITOR'S NOTE:
Smoke-colored Fireline works particularly well with metal beads, because its dark gray color recedes into the beadwork, appearing as a patina rather than as an obtrusive white thread.

Updating the
daisy
chain

Embellish daisy chains for a charming bracelet.

designed by **Julie Walker**

Green- and brown-toned beads give the bracelet above an earthy, casual look. The blue-toned version below gets its sparkle from silver disks and faceted beads with an AB finish.

MATERIALS
green bracelet (above)
6½ in. (16.5cm)
- 14–16 6mm top-drilled beads
- 30–34 4mm oval beads
- 15–17 3mm round beads
- Japanese seed beads
  5–7g size 8º
  5–7g size 11º
- 2-strand clasp
- Fireline 6 lb. test
- beading needles, #11

step*by*step

Daisy chain

[1] On 1 yd. (.9m) of Fireline, attach a stop bead (Basics, p. 10), leaving a 12-in. (30cm) tail.

[2] Pick up two 11º sccd beads, three 8º seed beads, two 11ºs, and three 8ºs. Sew back through all the beads, exiting from the first 11º **(figure 1, a–b)**.

[3] Pick up an 11º, a 4mm bead, and an 11º, and sew through the upper 11º on the opposite side of the ring **(b–c)**.

[4] To make the connecting tab between the daisy loops, pick up an 11º, and sew through the next 11º on the ring. Pick up an 11º, sew through the 11º just added, and snug up the beads **(c–d)**.

[5] Pick up ten 11ºs, and sew back through the second 11º added in step 4 **(d–e)**.

[6] Pick up a 4mm, and sew through the fifth 11º added in step 5 **(e–f)**.

[7] Repeat step 4 to make a tab.

[8] Pick up three 8ºs, two 11ºs, and three 8ºs, and sew through the lower 11º on the tab.

[9] Repeat steps 3–8 until the band is the desired length minus the length of the clasp.

[10] Repeat step 4, leaving the remaining Fireline for attaching the clasp.

[11] On 2 yd. (1.8m) of Fireline, make a second daisy chain, as in steps 1–10, but start by picking up 12 11ºs for the first loop. Stitch the same number of daisy loops, ending with a tab.

Assembly

[1] Lay the two daisy chains parallel to each other.

[2] With the working thread from the second daisy chain, sew back through the two 11ºs on the left half of the tab and lower section of the last daisy loop, exiting at **figure 2, point a**.

[3] Pick up an 11º, a 3mm bead, and an 11º. Sew through the corresponding 11ºs on the first daisy chain **(a–b)**.

[4] Sew through the two 11ºs on the left half of the tab. Pick up an 11º, and sew back through the 3mm **(b–c)**.

[5] Pick up an 11º, and sew through the corresponding 11ºs on the second daisy chain. Sew through the lower half of the next loop, exiting from the upper 11º of the next tab **(c–d)**.

[6] Pick up an 11º, a 3mm, and an 11º, and sew through the corresponding 11ºs on the first daisy chain **(d–e)**.

[7] Pick up two 11ºs, an 8º, an 11º, a 6mm bead, an 11º, an 8º, and two 11ºs, and sew through the left half of the tab **(e–f)**.

[8] Pick up an 11º, sew through the 3mm, pick up an 11º, and sew through the corresponding 11ºs of the second daisy chain **(f–g)**.

[9] Pick up two 11ºs, an 8º, an 11º, a 6mm, an 11º, an 8º, and two 11ºs **(g–h)**. Sew through the tab beads as shown **(h–i)**.

[10] Repeat steps 2–9 for the length of the band.

Clasp

[1] To add the clasp, thread a needle on the tail of the first chain, and exit the upper right corner of the tab. Pick up an 8º and an 11º, and sew through a clasp loop. Go back through the 11º, pick up an 8º, and sew through the two 11ºs on the right half of the tab **(figure 3, a–b)**. Retrace the thread path.

[2] Stitch through to the end tab on the other band **(b–c)**.

[3] Repeat the thread path in step 1 to connect the other daisy chain to the clasp. Secure the working thread in the beadwork with a few half-hitch knots (Basics) between beads, and trim.

[4] To add the other clasp half, remove the stop beads and repeat step 4 of the daisy chain to stitch a tab on the end of each chain. Repeat steps 1–3 of the clasp. ○

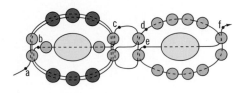

FIGURE 1

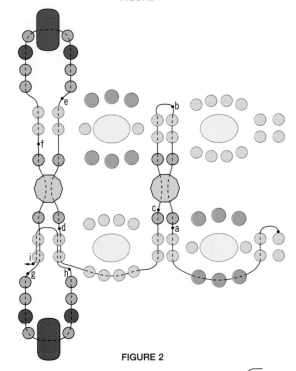

FIGURE 2

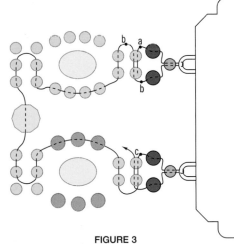

FIGURE 3

EDITOR'S NOTES:

• You may choose to reinforce each loop of the chain by going back through the ring before adding the center bead.

• To stitch the blue bracelet, left, increase the number of seed beads in the ring to accommodate the larger 8mm beads.

Delicate vines

Bicone crystals and seed beads pair up in this easy-to-stitch design.

designed by **Karen Price**

Different-sized seed beads provide textural contrast in the loops that encircle the bicone crystals.

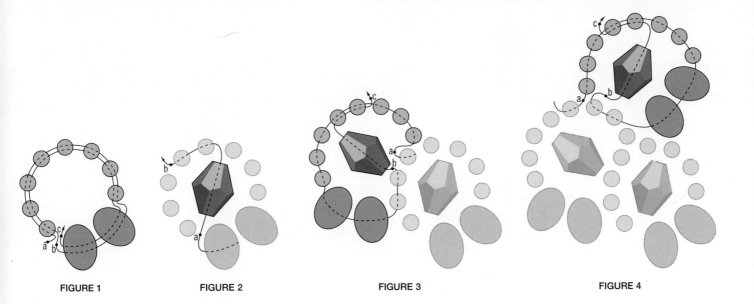

FIGURE 1   FIGURE 2   FIGURE 3   FIGURE 4

step*by*step

Necklace

[1] On 2 ft. (61cm) of conditioned thread (Basics, p. 10), leave a 10-in. (25cm) tail, and pick up eight 11º seed beads and two 6º seed beads **(figure 1, a–b)**. Sew through the beads to form a ring **(b–c)**, and tie a surgeon's knot (Basics).

[2] Pick up a 4mm bicone crystal, and sew through the fifth and then the fourth 11º of the ring **(figure 2, a–b)**.

[3] Pick up eight 11ºs and two 6ºs, and sew through the second and third 11ºs of the previous ring **(figure 3, a–b)**.

[4] Pick up a 4mm and sew through the fifth and then the fourth 11º just added **(b–c)**.

[5] Repeat steps 3 **(figure 4, a–b)** and 4 **(b–c)** until your necklace is ½ in. (1.3cm)

short of the desired length. Add thread as needed (Basics).

[6] Secure the tail with a few half-hitch knots (Basics) between beads, and trim.

Toggle bar and loop

[1] To make the beaded toggle bar, pick up ten 11ºs and stitch eight rows in flat, even-count peyote (Basics). You will have a strip ten beads wide, with four beads along each straight edge. Zip up (Basics) the strip to form a tube.

[2] Retrace the thread path to reinforce the join. Exit an end 11º.

[3] Pick up an 11º, a 6º, and an 11º. Sew back through the tube beadwork to the other end.

[4] Repeat step 3, but after adding the end beads, sew into the tube and exit at the center of the bar between two beads.

[5] To attach the tube to the necklace, pick up three 11ºs and sew counter-clockwise through the last ring of the necklace to anchor the thread. Sew back through the three 11ºs picked up in this step, the toggle bar, and the three 11ºs. Secure the thread in the ring with a few half-hitch knots, and trim.

[6] To add the loop for the toggle bar, thread a needle on the tail and pick up enough 11ºs (approximately 24) to fit around the toggle bar. Sew back through the first two 11ºs just added, make a half-hitch knot, and retrace the thread path to reinforce the loop. Secure the thread with a few half-hitch knots, and trim. ◗

MATERIALS
necklace 15 in. (38cm)
- **62** 4mm bicone crystals
- 9g size 6º Japanese seed beads
- 5g size 11º Japanese seed beads
- nylon beading thread, conditioned with beeswax or Thread Heaven
- beading needles, #12

Russian snake stitch

Japanese cylinder beads frame round crystals or fire-polished beads in an easy variation of a daisy chain.

designed by **Ny Wetmore**

step*by*step

Snake stitch band

[1] Center a needle on 2–4 yd. (1.8–3.7m) of conditioned thread (Basics, p. 10). Working with doubled thread, pick up eight color A cylinder beads and eight color B cylinder beads, leaving a 6-in. (15cm) tail. Go through all the beads again **(figure 1, a–b)**, tighten them into a ring, and tie a surgeon's knot (Basics).

[2] Sew through five As, pick up a 4mm fire-polished bead or crystal, and sew through the three Bs next to the knot **(b–c)**.

[3] Pick up five Bs and eight As, and sew through the three Bs you just went through on the previous ring **(figure 2, a–b)**.

[4] Pick up a 4mm, and sew through the three As before the color change **(b–c)**.

[5] Pick up five As and eight Bs, and sew through the three As you just went through on the previous ring **(c–d)**.

[6] Pick up a 4mm, and sew through the three Bs before the color change **(d–e)**.

[7] Repeat steps 3–6 until the bracelet is the desired length. Do not cut the thread.

Clasp button

[1] To make the button end of the clasp, pick up an A and four 4mms. Sew through the first two 4mms again. Pull the thread snug to form a square **(figure 3, a–b)**.

[2] Pick up four 4mms, slide them against the first square, and sew through the first two of these 4mms again. Pull the thread snug to form a square **(photo a and b–c)**.

FIGURE 1

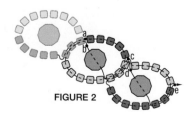

FIGURE 2

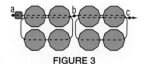

FIGURE 3

a

MATERIALS

bracelet 7½ in. (19.1cm)

- **32** 4mm round crystals or Czech fire-polished beads
- Japanese cylinder beads
  3g color A
  3g color B
- nylon beading thread conditioned with beeswax or Thread Heaven
- beading needles, #12

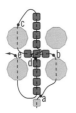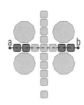

FIGURE 4

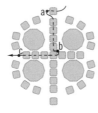

FIGURE 5

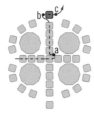

FIGURE 6

FIGURE 7

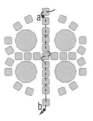

FIGURE 8

[3] Flip the second square so it lies on top of the first square, and sew back through the A picked up in step 1. Continue through a few beads of the bracelet band, make a half-hitch knot (Basics), and sew back through the A. Holding the cluster of 4mms so the base A is at the bottom, sew through a 4mm as shown in **figure 4, a–b**.

[4] Pick up three As, and sew through the 4mm diagonally across from the first 4mm you sewed through **(b–c)**.

[5] Pick up four As, sew through the middle A from step 4 **(c–d)**, pick up four As, and sew through the 4mm adjacent to where you started **(photo b** and **d–e)**.

[6] Turn the bead cluster a quarter turn to the right. Repeat steps 4 and 5 on the remaining three sides.

[7] To reinforce the bead cluster, stitch around the middle row of As, adding two As at each corner **(figure 5, a–b)**.

[8] Exit at a middle cylinder **(figure 6, point a)**. Sew up through the next four As **(a–b)**. Pick up an A **(b–c)**.

[9] Sew through the next four As on the opposite side **(figure 7, a–b)**, and sew through the middle row **(b–c)**, exiting the middle cylinder on the next side.

FIGURE 9

[10] To reinforce the button, stitch across the top and continue down through all the As on the other side and the A between the clasp and the base **(figure 8, a–b)**. Do not cut the tail.

Embellishments and clasp loop

[1] Thread a needle on the 1-yd. (.9m) tail and exit at **figure 9, point a**. To make the picot embellishments, go through a cylinder next to the knot. Pick up three cylinders in the same color as the cylinders in this section. Skip a cylinder, and sew through the next cylinder **(a–b)**. Repeat for the length of the band, stitching two picots on each ring.

[2] On the last ring, make two picots, and sew through the next three cylinders.

[3] Pick up enough cylinders to make a loop around the button and sew through the next cylinder **(figure 10, a–b)**. Secure the thread with a half-hitch knot. Retrace the thread path, and exit at **point b** in the direction of the non-embellished edge.

[4] Continue adding picot embellishments along the other edge of the band.

[5] To connect the picots, sew through the cylinders, and exit at the middle cylinder of the first picot. Pick up two cylinders that match the picot color, and sew through the last two cylinders of the next picot **(figure 11, a–b)**.

[6] Repeat step 5 along both edges. To finish, tie a few half-hitch knots between beads, secure the tails in the beadwork, and trim. **o**

FIGURE 10

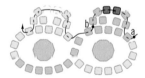

FIGURE 11

Pearl pizzazz bangle

Wear them individually or stacked for added interest.

by **Anna Elizabeth Draeger**

step*by*step

[1] On 4 yd. (3.7m) of Fireline, pick up one 8º seed bead and seven 8º cylinder beads. Repeat the pattern nine times, and center the beads on the Fireline. Sew through the first seed bead and the first cylinder strung to form a ring **(photo a)**.

[2] Work in tubular peyote stitch (Basics, p. 10) by picking up a cylinder, skipping a cylinder, and sewing through the next cylinder. Continue in peyote, but when you reach the seed bead, pick up a seed bead instead of a cylinder **(photo b)**. When the row is complete, step up through the first bead in the new round, and set aside the working thread. These first three rounds of peyote are the inside center rounds, which become the base from which the rest of the bangle is worked.

[3] Pick up the tail and step up through two cylinders, working in the opposite direction of the working thread. Complete a round of peyote stitch using only cylinders, stepping up through the first bead in the new round. Repeat on the other side **(photo c)**.

[4] Work a round of peyote using cylinders and substituting 4mm pearls for the seed beads **(photo d)**. This will force the rounds to flare out a little. Repeat on the other side **(photo e)**.

[5] Work a round of peyote using only cylinders. Repeat on the other side **(photo f)**.

[6] The last round gets added to one side only and becomes the outside center round. Work a round of peyote, but substitute a cylinder, a seed bead, and a cylinder for each 4mm pearl. For another variation, you can substitute a 3mm round bead or crystal for one of the three consecutive cylinders added in step 6 **(photo g)**. Zip up (Basics) the last round stitched with the last round on the other side **(photo h)**. Make sure to sew through all three beads (cylinder, seed bead, cylinder) when you reach the pearl. Secure the tails in the beadwork, and trim. ●

MATERIALS
bangle 2½ in. (6.4cm) inner diameter
- **20** 4mm Swarovski pearls
- **10** 3mm round crystals (optional)
- **20** size 8º seed beads
- **16g** size 8º Japanese cylinder beads
- Fireline 6 lb. test
- beading needles, #12

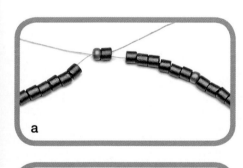

a

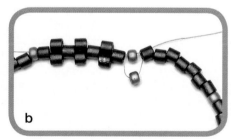

b

c

d

e

f

g

h

Electrifying

zigzag stripes

Triangular points create dimensional accents.

designed by **Jennifer Creasey**

step*by*step

[1] On 2 yd. (1.8m) of conditioned thread (Basics, p. 10), attach a stop bead (Basics) leaving a 2-ft. (61cm) tail.

[2] Beginning at the lower left-hand corner of the pattern, pick up 12 color A and two color B Japanese cylinder beads, and stitch the main panel in flat, even-count peyote stitch (Basics).

[3] Taper each end of the panel as follows: with the thread exiting **figure 1, point a,** turn as shown **(a–b).** Sew back through the bead at **point a** and the last bead added **(b–c).** Work six peyote stitches **(c–d),** turn **(d–e),** and sew back through the edge bead and the last bead picked up **(e–f).** Work five peyote stitches **(f–g),** turn **(g–h),** and sew back through the edge bead and the last bead picked up. Work two more rows of

peyote stitch, decreasing to four beads and then to three beads. Do not trim the tails.

[4] To add the points, secure 1 yd. (.9m) of thread in the beadwork with a few half-hitch knots (Basics). Stitch across the band, and exit the edge cylinder as indicated by the arrow shown on the pattern.

[5] Add the points in brick stitch (Basics), picking up the appropriate-color cylinders for each stitch.

[6] Stitch diagonally across the band to the next point on the other side of the band. Continue adding points for the length of the band.

[7] To add the clasp, thread a needle on the tail on one end, turn as you did at the end of each tapered row, and exit at **figure 2, point a.**

[8] Pick up an A, an accent bead, and an A, and sew through the loop on one clasp half. Pick up an A, sew

back through the accent bead, pick up an A, and sew through the third cylinder on the end row **(a–b).** Retrace the thread path a few times, secure the tail with a few half-hitch knots between beads, and trim. Remove the stop bead and repeat on the other end with the other tail and clasp half. ○

MATERIALS
bracelet 7 in. (18cm)
- 2 2–3mm accent beads
- Japanese cylinder beads
  3g color A
  3g color B
  2g color C
  2g color D
  2g color E
- clasp
- nylon beading thread conditioned with beeswax or Thread Heaven
- beading needles, #12

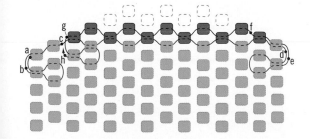

FIGURE 1

FIGURE 2

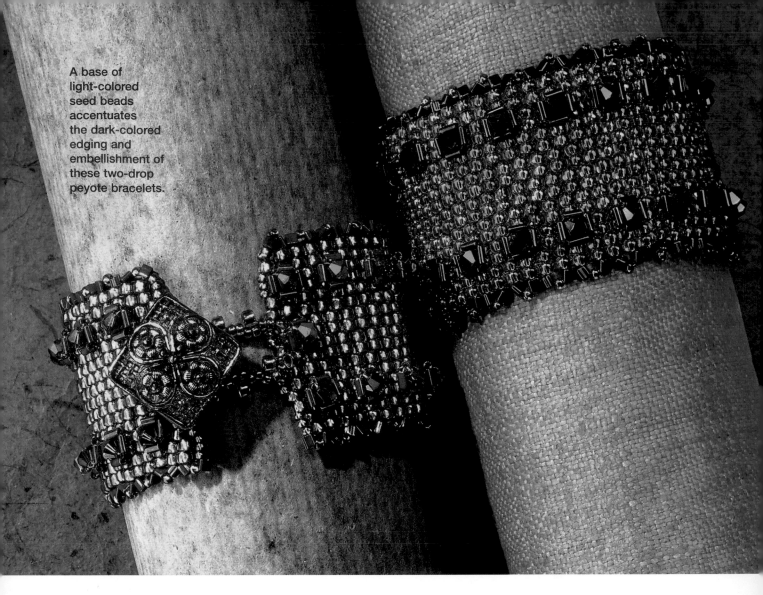

A base of light-colored seed beads accentuates the dark-colored edging and embellishment of these two-drop peyote bracelets.

Crystal-studded band

Go over the top with surface embellishments.

designed by **Julie Walker**

MATERIALS
bracelet 7 in. (18cm)
- **35–45** 4mm bicone crystals or fire-polished beads
- 5g size 1 (3mm) bugle beads
- Japanese seed beads
  25–30g size 8º
  10g size 11º
  5g size 11º triangle
- ½–¾-in. (1.3–1.9cm) button with shank
- Fireline 6 lb. test
- beading needles, #12

EDITOR'S NOTE:
For a secure connection between the base and the button, the 11º seed beads used to connect them should fit through the shank of the button. If the 11ºs will not fit, use 15ºs instead. Because they will be hidden by the button, the seed beads don't have to match the bracelet.

step*by*step

Base

[1] On 2 yd. (1.8m) of Fireline, attach a stop bead (Basics, p. 10), leaving a 12–15-in. (30–38cm) tail.

[2] Pick up 16 8º seed beads (**figure 1, a–b**). Pick up two 8ºs, skip the last two 8ºs, and sew through the next two (**b–c**). Work across the row in two-drop peyote stitch (Basics and **c–d**). Continue working four stitches per row in two-drop peyote until the band is ½ in. (1.3cm) short of the desired length. Add new thread (Basics) as needed.

[3] Work one row of four stitches using three 11ºs per stitch (**figure 2**).

[4] Sew through the beadwork to exit at the center of the base, three rows from one end (**figure 3, point a**). Pick up three 11ºs, the button, and three 11ºs, and sew into the base a few rows down (**a–b**). Sew through the beadwork (**b–c**), and retrace the thread path a few times. Secure the tail with a few half-hitch knots (Basics) between beads, and trim.

[5] Remove the stop bead from the other end, and repeat step 3.

[6] Sew through the beadwork to exit at **figure 4, point a**. Using an even number of beads, pick up enough 11ºs to make a loop around the button, and sew into the base two beads over (**a–b**). Sew through the beadwork (**b–c**), and, working with 8ºs, stitch a row of peyote around the loop, sewing through and skipping two 11ºs for each 8º (**c–d**). Sew into the

base, secure the tail with a few half-hitch knots between beads, and trim.

Embellishment

[1] Secure 1 yd. (.9m) of Fireline near one end of the band, and exit at **figure 5, point a**.

[2] Pick up a bugle bead, and sew through the two-drop stitch below the one your thread is exiting (**a–b**). Pick up a bugle, and sew through the previous two-drop stitch (**b–c**).

[3] Pick up a bugle, and sew back through the two-drop stitch you just went through in the same direction (**figure 6, a–b**). Pick up a crystal or fire-polished bead, and sew through the next two-drop stitch (**b–c**). Pick up a bugle, and sew back through the two-drop stitch you just went through (**c–d**).

[4] Sew through the bugles to snug them up (**figure 7, a–b**). Sew through the two-drop stitch of the base (**b–c**). Sew through the next two pairs of 8ºs as shown (**c–d**).

[5] Repeat steps 2–4 along the entire length of the bracelet. Add new thread as needed.

[6] Zigzag through to the other side of the band, and repeat steps 2–5. Secure the tail, and trim.

[7] Secure 1 yd. (.9m) of Fireline at one end of the band, and exit an end edge bead. Pick up a triangle bead, an 11º, and a triangle. Sew into the next pair of beads along the edge, and exit the following edge pair (**photo**). Continue making a three-bead picot along the entire edge.

[8] Zigzag to the other edge, and repeat the picot edging. Secure the tail, and trim. ●

FIGURE 1

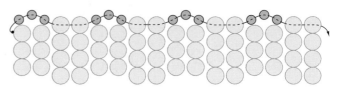

FIGURE 2

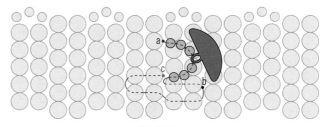

FIGURE 3

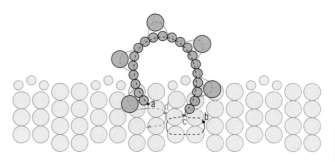

FIGURE 4

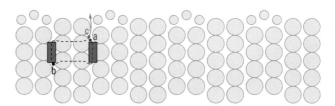

FIGURE 5

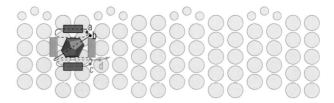

FIGURE 6

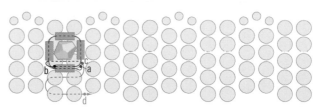

FIGURE 7

Peyote stitch

129

Playful
segmented
bracelet

Seed beads encircle acrylic tubing filled with silver beads.

designed by **Carol Alo**

Clear acrylic tubing takes on a creative function as the base of this bracelet and as a charm.

step*by*step

Bracelet base

[1] Measure your wrist, subtract the length of the clasp and the two cones, and cut one piece of acrylic tubing to that length.

[2] Cut a piece of flexible beading wire 6 in. (15cm) longer than the tubing, and insert it into the tube.

[3] String enough color A 11º seed beads on the wire to fill the tubing **(photo a)**.

[4] On one end of the wire, string a cone, a 4mm bicone crystal or fire-polished bead, a cylinder bead, a crimp bead, a cylinder, and half of the clasp. Go back through the beads and cone, tighten the wire, crimp the crimp bead (Basics, p. 10), and trim the excess wire **(photo b)**.

[5] Repeat step 4 on the other end of the wire.

Embellishment

To display the stitches, the tubing in **photos c–i** does not contain seed beads.

Segment 1 (photo c)

[1] On 1 yd. (.9m) of conditioned thread, leaving a 6-in. (15cm) tail, pick up 12 cylinders, and tie them into a ring around the tubing with a square knot (Basics). Sew through the beads again and exit the first cylinder.

[2] Pick up three cylinders, skip the next three cylinders, and sew through the following cylinder. Repeat twice. Sew through the first three cylinders added in this step. Snug the beads against the tubing as you add each round.

[3] Pick up a cylinder and sew through the next three cylinders. Repeat twice. Sew through the first cylinder.

[4] Working in modified peyote stitch (Basics), repeat steps 2 and 3 three times, alternating a round of three cylinders per stitch with a round of one cylinder per stitch. Sew through the first cylinder added in the last round.

Segment 2 (photo d)

[1] Pick up an A, a color B 11º, an A, three color C 11ºs, an A, a B, and an A **(figure 1, a–b)**.

[2] Sew through the next cylinder on the previous round and back through the last three 11ºs **(b–c)**.

[3] Pick up three Cs, an A, a B, and an A **(c–d)**. Repeat step 2 **(d–e)**.

[4] Pick up three Cs **(e–f)**. Sew through the first stack of 11ºs and the cylinder beneath them, and then sew back through the first three 11ºs.

[5] Repeat steps 1–4, anchoring the beads by sewing under the thread bridge next to the A below **(figure 2, a–b)**.

[6] With the thread exiting an A, pick up an A, a B, an A, and a cylinder **(figure 3, a–b)**. Sew back through the stack of six 11ºs. Cross to the next stack of 11ºs through the

a

b

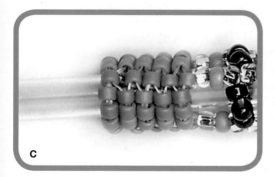

c

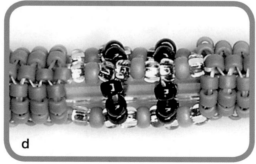

d

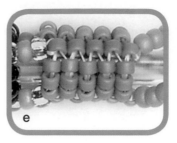

e

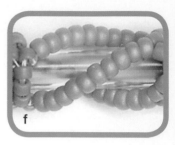

f

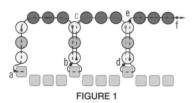

FIGURE 1

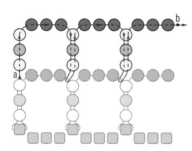

FIGURE 2

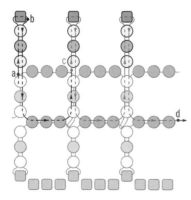

FIGURE 3

first connecting rung of Cs. Sew through the top three 11ºs of the next stack (b–c).

[7] Repeat step 6 twice (c–d). At the end of the second repeat, sew through six 11ºs and the first cylinder added in step 6.

Segment 3 (photo e)

[1] Pick up three cylinders and sew through the cylinder on top of the next stack of 11ºs. Repeat twice.

[2] Repeat steps 2–4 of segment 1 to work eight rounds of modified peyote stitch, alternating a round of three cylinders per stitch with a round of one cylinder per stitch.

Segment 4 (photo f)

[1] Pick up ten Bs, five cylinders, and ten Bs. Sew through the next cylinder on the previous round. Sew back through the last ten Bs.

[2] Pick up four cylinders and ten Bs. Sew through the next cylinder on the previous round. Sew back through the last ten Bs.

[3] Pick up three cylinders, and sew through the first stack of Bs and the cylinder beneath it. Sew back through the same stack of Bs, exiting at the top of the stack.

Segment 5 (photo g)

[1] Repeat steps 2–4 of segment 1 to work ten

rounds of modified peyote stitch, alternating a round of three cylinders per stitch with a round of one cylinder per stitch.

[2] Work the last round of modified peyote using one B per stitch. Sew through the first B added in this step.

Segment 6 (photo h)

[1] Work one round of modified peyote using three Cs per stitch, stepping up through the first three Cs.

[2] Work one round using one B per stitch. Step up through the first B.

[3] Work three rounds, alternating a round of three Cs per stitch with a round of one B per stitch.

[4] Work one round of one C per stitch.

[5] Work one round of three Bs per stitch.

[6] Work one round of one B per stitch. Step up through the first B added in this round.

[7] Work five rounds, alternating a round of three Cs per stitch with a round of one B per stitch.

[8] Work one round of one A per stitch. Sew through the next three Cs and one A.

Segment 7 (photo i)

[1] Pick up 25 cylinders, an A, three Cs, an A, and 25 cylinders, and sew through

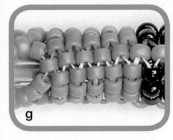

g

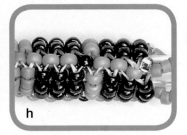

h

i

the next A on the previous round. Sew back through the second set of 25 cylinders.
[2] Pick up three Cs, an A, and 25 cylinders, and sew through the next A on the previous round. Sew back through the 25 cylinders.
[3] Pick up three Cs, sew through the first A added on this round, and twist the three strands of Cs around the tube.

Completing the stitching
[1] Starting at the other end of the bracelet, repeat segments 1–6.
[2] When completing the last row of segment 6, sew through the Cs added in the previous round, and connect the two sections by sewing through the As added in the last ring of segment 7. Retrace the thread path of this connecting round.
[3] Secure the thread tails with a few half-hitch knots (Basics), stitch through the beadwork, and trim.

Charm
[1] Cut a 1-in. (2.5cm) piece of acrylic tubing.
[2] Type a one- or two-word message for the scroll in 9-point type in your favorite font. Print and trim the text. Roll the message around a head pin and insert it into the tubing. Remove the head pin from the tubing.

[3] On the head pin, string an 11º, a 4mm, a spacer, the message tubing, a spacer, and an 11º (photo, below).
[4] Make the first half of a wrapped loop (Basics), attach it to the clasp, and finish the wraps. Trim the excess wire. ◐

MATERIALS
bracelet 7 in. (18cm)
- **3** 4mm bicone crystals or fire-polished beads
- **1g** each of size 11º Japanese seed beads
  silver, color A
  color B
  color C
- **1g** Japanese cylinder beads
- **2** 5mm spacers
- clasp
- **2** ¼-in. (6mm) cones
- **2**-in. (5cm) head pin
- **2** crimp beads
- nylon beading thread conditioned with beeswax or Thread Heaven
- flexible beading wire, .018
- beading needles, #13
- **10 in.** (25cm) clear acrylic tubing, ⅛-in. (3mm) inside diameter, ⁵⁄₃₂-in. (4mm) outside diameter (American Science & Surplus Store, sciplus.com)
- chainnose pliers
- crimping pliers
- roundnose pliers
- wire cutters

Entangled ivy-like layers are built on a simple, sturdy peyote band (above). Create a covered button clasp (below) to perfectly finish off this textural bracelet.

Leafy inspiration

Peyote stitch variations lay fertile ground for leafy free-form beadwork.

designed by **Linda Frechen**

stepbystep

Components
Base
[1] On a comfortable length of Fireline, pick up 80 8º triangle beads. To adjust the length of the bracelet, add or omit an even number of beads until the base is ½ in. (1.3cm) short of the desired length.
[2] Work in flat, even-count peyote stitch (Basics, p. 10) to complete a total of eight rows, for a strip that has four beads on each straight edge. Secure the tails with a few half-hitch knots (Basics) between beads, and trim.

Peyote arches
[1] Secure a new length of Fireline in the beadwork, and exit the third up-bead on one side **(figure 1, point a)**. Pick up 12 to 16 8ºs, skip seven up-beads, and sew through the three beads **(a–b)**.
[2] Make three more arches along the edge **(b–c)**. Sew through to the other side of the peyote base. Repeat to create arches on the other edge **(d–e)**.

MATERIALS
bracelet 7½ in. (19.1cm)
- 2g size 6º seed beads, berry color
- 16g size 8º triangle beads, deep gray/green
- size 11º seed beads
  16g deep green, color A
  27g leaf green, color B
  2g berry color, color C
- 4g size 11º Japanese cylinder beads, light-yellow green
- 5g size 15º seed beads, leaf green
- 16 in. (41cm) 26-gauge craft wire
- Fireline 4 lb. test
- beading needles, #12
- bamboo skewer
- ⅝ in. (1.6cm) cover-button kit (available at most fabric stores)
- 2-in. (5cm) cotton fabric square
- 1-in. (2.5cm) felt square
- chainnose pliers
- roundnose pliers
- wire cutters

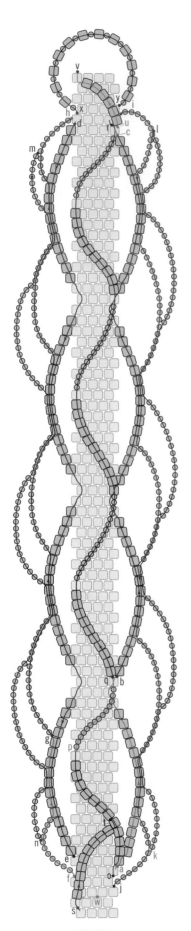

FIGURE 1

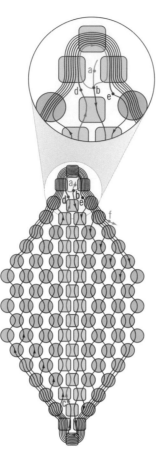

FIGURE 2

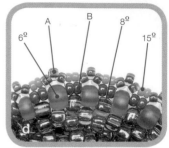

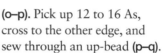

[3] Using color A 11º seed beads, make an arch between the base and the last 8º arch **(f–g)**. Connect all the 8º arches with 11º arches **(g–h)**. Sew through to the other side, and repeat **(i–j)**.

[4] Using As, add another row of 11º arches as desired **(photo a, k–l, and m–n)**.

[5] Work three to six rows of peyote as desired along the 11º arches, using As and color B 11ºs **(photo b)**. Secure the tails, and trim.

Base bridges

[1] Secure a new thread near one end of the bracelet, and exit at **point o**.

[2] Pick up 10 to 14 8ºs, cross diagonally to the other edge, and sew through an up-bead

(o–p). Pick up 12 to 16 As, cross to the other edge, and sew through an up-bead **(p–q)**.

[3] Repeat step 2 to create alternating bridges of 8ºs and 11ºs that zigzag across the base **(q–r)**.

[4] Add dimension to the 8º bridges by working three rows of peyote stitch using 8ºs. Switch to As for several rows (using two-drop peyote to fill the spaces, if needed), and finish by stitching several rows with 15ºs.

[5] To embellish the 11º bridges, work three rows of peyote stitch using As, then switch to 15ºs for six rows. Secure the peyote flap you just created to the base by stitching through the last row of beads and the 8ºs below them **(photo c)**.

[6] At each end of the base, add a bridge using eight to 12 8ºs **(s–t and u–v)**. To embellish these bridges, add rows of peyote as follows **(photo d)**:

Rows 1–2: Use 8ºs.
Row 3: Use 6ºs.
Row 4: Use two Bs so the Bs fall between the 6ºs.
Row 5: Use three As to form a decorative picot over the 6ºs.
Row 6: Use two 15ºs to fill in between the As.

Leaves

[1] On 2 ft. (61cm) of Fireline, pick up three cylinder beads. Pull them into a ring **(figure 2, a–b)** and tie a square knot (Basics).

[2] Pick up 18 cylinders, skip the last three, and sew back through the next cylinder **(b–c)**. Tighten the thread so that the last three beads form a picot to match the first three.

[3] Picking up one cylinder per stitch, work in flat peyote stitch to the end **(c–d)**, and sew through the three end beads **(d–e)**.

[4] Using Bs **(photo e)**, work six decreasing rows on each side of the strip of cylinders, alternating sides **(e–f)**. Tighten the thread to form the leaf. Secure the tails, and trim. Repeat to make 12 to 15 leaves.

Beaded wire tendril

[1] Wrap one end of a 16-in. (41cm) piece of 26-gauge

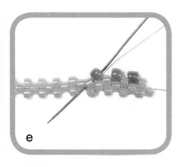

e

f

g

h

i

j

k

l

wire around a bamboo skewer a few times to secure it. String at least 9 in. (23cm) of 15ºs on the wire. The beaded wire needs to be long enough to intertwine with the leaves for the length of the bracelet. Add 15ºs to increase the length, or make several shorter pieces of beaded wire. **[2]** Wrap the beaded wire around the skewer to create a spiral **(photo f)**. Slide the beaded wire off the skewer, and make a small wrapped loop (Basics) on each end.

Closure button
[1] Trim cotton fabric to fit the pattern provided in the cover-button kit. Set the fabric inside the mold.
[2] To make attaching beads to the button easier, cut a felt pad to fit the button top. Set the felt into the mold on top of the fabric. Create a cover button following the kit's instructions.
[3] Leaving a 6-in. (15cm) tail, secure a comfortable length of Fireline in the center of the cover button, using an overhand knot (Basics). Pick up a color C 11º and a 15º. Sew back through the C into the fabric,

and exit one-half bead space away. Repeat, working out from the center **(photo g)** to cover the button with short fringe. Secure the tails, and trim.

Assembly
[1] Determine the placement of the leaves by draping sets of three over the base. Use the bridges on the base to support the leaves and add dimension. Sew the lower point of each leaf to the base **(photo h)**, and retrace the thread paths for support.
[2] Secure a few of the unattached leaf tips, keeping some unattached until later.
[3] To add the berries, sew through the base to exit where the ends of a group of leaves meet. Pick up a 6º, an A, and a 15º. Sew back through the A and the 6º and into the beadwork. Repeat to add one or two berries **(photo i)**. Position the berries close together so they cover the ends of the leaves. Attach

sets of berries in a few other spots, as desired.
[4] Arrange the beaded wire tendril over the top of the base so it twines across the bracelet and under some leaves. Straighten some spirals and leave others tightly coiled. Hide one wrapped loop under a leaf at one end and the other loop at the opposite end. Stitch the wrapped loops to the beadwork **(photo j)**. Sew through the beadwork and attach the tendril in other spots by sewing over the wire and back into the base. Use shorter beaded tendrils to fill in other areas, if desired. Secure the remaining leaf tips.
[5] Secure a new length of Fireline (Basics) in the ½-in. (1.3cm) space at the end of the base reserved for the button, and exit an 8º in the center **(figure 1, point w)**. Pick up seven Bs and the shank of the button. Sew back into the base **(photo k)**. Retrace the thread path several times, secure the tail, and trim.

[6] Secure a new length of Fireline to the other end of the bracelet, and exit the third up-bead **(point x)**. Pick up an alternating pattern of a B and an 8º until you have a loop large enough to fit over the button, and end with a B **(x–y)**. Sew through an 8º on the opposite edge of the bracelet **(photo l)** and retrace the thread path several times. Secure the tail, and trim. ●

EDITOR'S NOTE:
Our illustrations and bead counts are specific, but, as in any free-form design, you can adjust your bead counts, components, placement, and colors.

Peyote stitch

Linda Gettings purchased
curvy straws at the grocery
store and beaded around
them to make this eye-
catching necklace.

Bead around the bend

Work tubular peyote stitch around curvy drinking straws to create a lightweight necklace with pizzazz.

designed by **Linda Gettings**

step*by*step

Peyote stitch straws

[1] Cut two straws to the desired length (photo a). File the rough edges before you begin stitching.

[2] On 2 yd. (1.8m) of thread or Fireline, leave a 6-in. (15cm) tail, and pick up enough 11º seed or cylinder beads to fit around a straw. Tie the beads into a ring with a square knot (Basics, p. 10), and sew through the next bead.

[3] Holding the ring of beads in place on the straw, work in tubular peyote stitch (Basics) in your chosen colors.

To make thick bands of color, as in the orange necklace, work three to seven rows per color in a random pattern. To make a color gradation, as in the blue necklace, p. 140, work two rows of each color from dark to light, and then work the colors in reverse. Add thread (Basics) as needed.

To keep the beadwork smooth, you may need to decrease along the inside edge of the curves by stitching through previous rows for a few rounds until the beadwork on the outside edge of the curve catches up to the inside edge.

[4] Cinch each end of the peyote tube around the straw by sewing through the beads of the end row (photo b). Secure the thread with a few half-hitch knots (Basics) between beads, and trim.
[5] Repeat steps 2–4 with the second straw.

FYI: Use relatively stiff beading wire for this project. If your wire is too flexible, it may get stuck in the bends of the straw.

Assembly, necklace with clasp (orange necklace)
[1] Lay out the beads you will use for the neck strap and any others you want to string between the straws and the pendant.
[2] To determine what length of flexible beading wire to cut, temporarily string a beaded straw onto the beading wire. Grasp the beading wire where it exits the straw, remove the straw, and measure the wire. Double that amount, and add the length of the remaining beads, plus 6 in. (15cm). Cut a piece of beading wire to that length. This 22-in. (56cm) necklace required approximately 1 yd. (.9m) of beading wire.
[3] Center the pendant between two 4mm beads (photo c).
[4] Over both wire ends, string three to five accent beads (photo d).
[5] Separate the wire ends, and on each end, string a 4mm, a 6mm bead, a 4mm, and a peyote-covered straw (photo e).
[6] On each end, string 4½ in. (11.4cm) of assorted accent beads, a crimp bead, a 6º, and one half of the clasp. Go back through the last three or four beads strung (photo f), crimp the crimp bead (Basics), and trim the excess wire.

Assembly, over-the-head necklace (blue necklace)
[1] Follow steps 1 and 2 of assembling the orange necklace. This 32-in. (81cm) necklace required approximately 4½ ft. (1.4m) of beading wire.

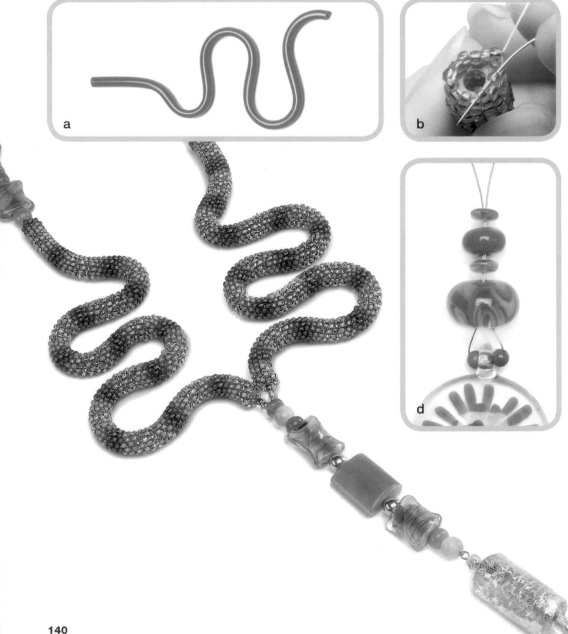

a

b

c

d

MATERIALS
necklace 22–32 in. (56–81cm)
- focal bead or pendant
- assorted 4–20mm accent beads and spacers
- 1–2g size 6º seed beads
- 5g size 11º seed or cylinder beads, in each of **5–7** colors
- clasp (optional)
- 3-in. (7.6cm) head pin (optional)
- 2 crimp beads
- nylon beading thread or Fireline 6 lb. test
- flexible beading wire, .018 with 7 internal strands
- beading needles, #12
- **1–2** curvy drinking straws
- metal file or coarse nail file
- T-pin (optional)
- chainnose pliers (optional)
- crimping pliers
- roundnose pliers (optional)
- wire cutters

[2] On a head pin, string a focal bead and accent beads as desired, and make a plain or wrapped loop (Basics) above the beads **(photo g)**.

[3] Center the loop on the beading wire. Over both wire ends, string beads as desired **(photo h)**.

[4] Separate the wires, and, on each end, string two to four accent beads or spacers and a peyote-covered straw **(photo i)**.

[5] On each end, string approximately 4 in. (10cm) of accent beads, a crimp bead, 1–2 in. (2.5–5cm) of accent beads, and 2–3 in. (5–7.6cm) of 6ºs **(photo j)**.

[6] With one wire end, go through the beads on the other end in reverse until you get one or two beads past the crimp bead **(photo k)**. Repeat with the other end, going in the opposite direction. Snug up the beads, crimp the crimp beads, and trim the excess wire. **o**

Margaret Zinser made the focal bead shown here. To see more of her beads, visit her Web site, mzglass.com.

e

f

EDITOR'S NOTE:
To make a necklace with a centered peyote stitch component, as in the teal necklace (above, right), work peyote stitch around a short section of straw. Use a T-pin to pierce the bottom edge at the center of the straw. Center your focal beads on the beading wire, pass both wire ends through the hole you made in the straw, and guide one wire end out through each side of the straw. String beads on each side of the necklace as desired.

g

h

i

j

k

Shape a 3-in. (7.6cm) piece of 20- or 22-gauge wire into a hook as shown above, or simply hang your ornament from a traditional ornament hook.

Dainty Russian
ornament

Embellish a holiday decoration with crystal fringe.

designed by **Paula Adams**

step*by*step

Bottom half

[1] On 4 yd. (3.7m) of Fireline or conditioned thread (Basics, p. 10), pick up seven color A and three color B cylinder beads five times for a total of 50 beads.

[2] Center the beads on the thread, sew through them again to form a ring, and exit the third A.

[3] Using As, work two rounds of tubular, even-count peyote stitch (Basics).

[4] Continue in peyote stitch, working a repeating pattern for each round and stepping up at the end of each round as follows:

MATERIALS
one ornament
- Swarovski crystals
  10 13mm faceted teardrops
  10 6mm or 4mm rounds or bicones
  10 6mm faceted rondelles
  10 5mm or 3mm bicones
  10–11 4mm bicones
- 4mm or 5mm round bead
- Japanese cylinder beads
  4g in each of **2** colors: A, C
  3g in each of **2** colors: B, D
- 3 in. (7.6cm) 20- to 22-gauge wire
- Fireline 6 lb. test or nylon beading thread conditioned with beeswax
- beading needles, #12
- chainnose pliers
- roundnose pliers
- wire cutters
- wire hook

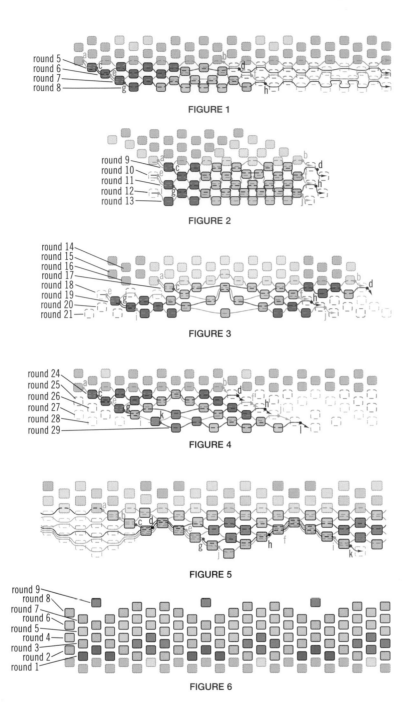

round 5
round 6
round 7
round 8

FIGURE 1

round 9
round 10
round 11
round 12
round 13

FIGURE 2

round 14
round 15
round 16
round 17
round 18
round 19
round 20
round 21

FIGURE 3

round 24
round 25
round 26
round 27
round 28
round 29

FIGURE 4

FIGURE 5

round 9
round 8
round 7
round 6
round 5
round 4
round 3
round 2
round 1

FIGURE 6

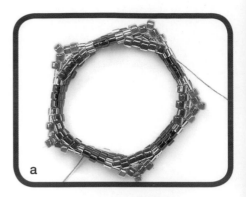

a

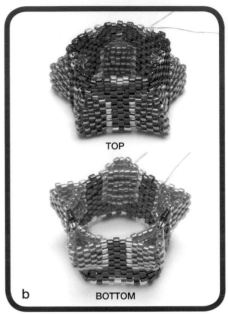

TOP

b

BOTTOM

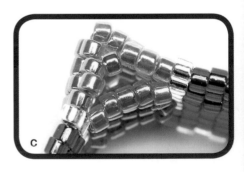

c

Round 5: Alternate 4 As and a B **(figure 1, a–b).**

Round 6: Alternate 3 As and 2 Bs **(c–d).**

Round 7: 2 As, B. Begin forming the points by working an increase, adding 2 Cs for the next stitch. Then add a B **(e–f).**

Round 8: A, B, 3 Cs, B **(g–h).**

[5] Sew through to exit the B prior to the first point, and work a support round inside the point: Pick up five Cs and sew through the next B. Sew through the beads on the round to exit the B prior to the next point. Repeat around the ring. End with your thread exiting the B after the last point. Red

beads are used in **photo a** to show the support round.

The round following a support round will always start with the thread exiting a B after a point.

Round 9: Alternate 2 As and 4 Cs **(figure 2, a–b).**

Round 10: A, B, C, increase by adding 2 Cs, C, B **(c–d).** Repeat around the ring. Work a support round after the step up.

Round 11: Alternate 2 As and 5 Cs **(e–f).**

Round 12: A, B, 4 Cs, B **(g–h).** Repeat around the ring, and work a support round after the step up.

Rounds 13–16: Repeat rounds 11 **(i–j)**

and 12 twice **(photo b).**

Round 17: 2 Cs, decrease by sewing through the next two Cs, 2 Cs, 2 As **(figure 3, a–b).**

Round 18: 3 Cs (stitching the second C in the decrease) B, A, B **(c–d** and **photo c).** Work a support round after the step up.

Round 19: 2 As, B, 2 Cs, B **(e–f).**

Round 20: 2 As, B, decrease by sewing through two Cs, B, A **(g–h).**

Round 21: 2 As, B (in the decrease), 2 As **(i–j).**

Rounds 22 and 23: As, totaling 24 beads per round **(photo d).**

Round 24: 3 As, B, A **(figure 4, a–b).**

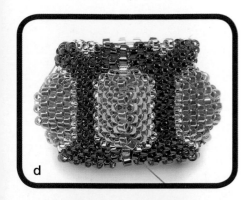

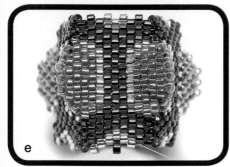

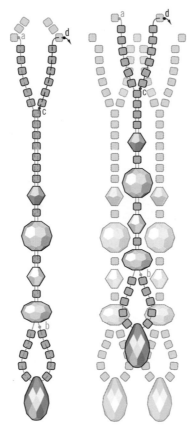

FIGURE 7   **FIGURE 8**

EDITOR'S NOTE:
Keep your tension tight as you work the decrease sections and the support rows. The beads fit snugly, so your matte beads may tend to break.

Round 25: 2 As, 2 Bs, A **(c–d)**.
Round 26: A, B, decrease by sewing through two Bs, B, A **(e–f)**.
Round 27: B, D (in the decrease), B, A **(g–h** and **photo e)**.
Round 28: Alternate 2 Ds and 2 Bs **(i–j)**.
Round 29: D, C, B, C **(k–l)**.
[6] Refer to the pattern in **figure 5** as you work rounds 30–35.
Round 30: Cs, totaling 20 beads **(a–b)**.
Round 31: C, B, C, D **(b–c)**.
Round 32: Alternate 2 Bs and 2 Ds **(c–d)**.
Round 33: Decrease by sewing through the next two Bs **(d–e)**, B, D, B **(e–f)**.
Round 34: 2 Bs **(g–h)**, decrease by

sewing through the next four Bs **(h–i)**.
Round 35: Sew through the Bs and stitch a B at each point **(j–k)**.
[7] Secure the working thread in the beadwork by tying a few half-hitch knots (Basics) between beads, and trim.

Top half
[1] Turn the beadwork over, thread a needle on the tail, and work the top half of the ornament in peyote stitch as follows (refer to the pattern in **figure 6** as you work rounds 1–9):
Round 1: B, 2 As, B, decrease by sewing through two Bs. After adding the last B, sew through three Bs to step up.
Round 2: B, A, B, D (in the decrease, as shown in **photo e**).
Round 3: Alternate 2 Bs and 2 Ds.
Round 4: B, C, D, C.
Round 5: Cs, totaling 20 beads.
Round 6: Alternate 3 Cs and a B.
Round 7: Alternate 2 Cs and 2 Bs.
Round 8: C, B, decrease by sewing through two Bs, B.
Round 9: B, D (in the decrease), B.
Round 10: Alternate 2 Ds and a B.
Round 11: Alternate a D and 2 As.
Round 12: A, B, A.
Round 13: Alternate 2 Bs and an A.

Round 14: Decrease to ten beads, sewing through the next two Bs, and then stitch 2 Bs.
Round 15: Alternate a B and a D (in the decrease).
Round 16: Cs, totaling ten beads.
Round 17: Alternate a C and a B.
Round 18: Bs, totaling ten beads.
Round 19: Decrease to five beads, sewing through the next two Bs, and then stitch a B.
Rounds 20 and 21: As, totaling five beads.
[2] Sew through the five As on the last round again, and snug them in a tight ring. Secure the thread, and trim.

Finishing
[1] Make a wrapped loop (Basics) at one end of a 3-in. (7.6cm) piece of wire. String a 4mm or 5mm round bead and the ornament, bottom end first. Position the wrapped loop and bead below the last round on the top of the ornament. String a 4mm bicone crystal if desired, and make a wrapped loop (**photo f**).
[2] To add fringe: Secure 1 yd. (.9m) of thread in the beadwork near the bottom edge of the ornament, and exit a B at one of the points (**figure 7, point a**). Pick up 13 Bs, a 4mm bicone, a B, a 5mm or 3mm bicone, a B, a 6mm or 4mm crystal, a B, a 6mm rondelle, five Bs, a teardrop-shaped crystal, and five Bs **(a–b)**. Skip the ten Bs and the teardrop, and sew back through the fringe beads, exiting the seventh B above the 4mm **(b–c)**. Pick up six Bs and sew through the B at the next point **(c–d)**. Repeat with the remaining points.
[3] Weave through to the edge B between two points (**figure 8, point a**). Pick up ten Bs and the fringe pattern from the 4mm bicone to the Bs after the teardrop **(a–b)**. Skip the ten Bs and the teardrop, and sew back through the fringe beads, exiting the fourth B above the 4mm bicone **(b–c)**. Pick up six Bs and sew through the corresponding B on the other side of the point **(c–d)**. Repeat with the remaining points.
[4] Secure the thread, and trim. Attach the wrapped loop to a wire hook. ○

Peyote stitch

Magnetic closures (opposite), hidden where the back peyote spiral section meets the sculptural peyote sections, are an ingenious solution for closing this intricate piece.

Four-in-one necklace

Enjoy adding one or more of these useful elements to your beading repertoire.

designed by **Kat West**

EDITOR'S NOTE:
Jeannette Cook developed a technique for rectangular curled wrap, which Kat West adapted for this necklace. The wraps are placed between the front and back spirals and on both sides of the cabochon and then embellished heavily to hide the joins. For instructions on how to stitch these curled wraps, refer to Cook's book *A Sculptural Peyote Projects Primer*, available at beadyeyedwomen.com.

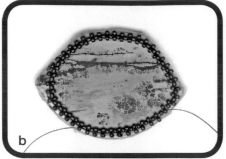

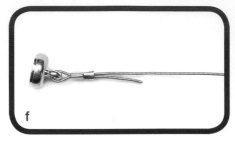

step*by*step

Cabochon centerpiece

[1] On a comfortable length of cond-itioned thread (Basics, p. 10), pick up enough 11º seed beads to go around the perimeter of your cabochon about ⅛ in. (3mm) inside the outer edge. Add or remove a bead, if necessary, so you have an even number of beads. Tie the tail and working thread with a surgeon's knot (Basics) to create a ring. Go through the first bead strung, and then work a round in tubular, even-count peyote stitch (Basics). Keep the tension fairly loose.

[2] Leaving the protective layer on, press double-sided tape along the outer edge of the back of the cabochon so that the tape extends ⅛ in. (3mm) beyond the edges. If your cab has sharp angles or an irregular shape, cut the tape into sections and work with small pieces **(photo a)**. On a curved edge, make several small cuts in the tape's outer edge to help it conform to the shape. Press the tape down all around the cab.

[3] Remove the protective layer from the tape, and position the peyote strip close to the cab's edge, adhering the strip to the cab **(photo b)**.

[4] Continue working in peyote stitch to fill the space between the peyote strip and the cab's edge, and then add a row or two past the edge to cover the sides of the cab **(photo c)**. Increase or decrease (Basics) as necessary to follow the lines of an angular or irregularly shaped cab.

[5] Change to working with cylinder beads, and cover the edge of the cab and the tape in peyote stitch. End by working one or two rows of peyote over the top surface of the cab using 14ºs or 15ºs **(photo d)**.

[6] Once you have encircled the cab, you can either cover the back with beads or leave it open. To cover the back, work rounds of peyote stitch, decreasing the number of stitches in each round, as necessary.

Necklace front

Virginia Blakelock developed this sculptural peyote tube, which she refers to as a Cellini spiral.

[1] On 2 yd. (1.8m) of thread, pick up two 11ºs, two 8ºs, two 6ºs, two 4mm bicone crystals, two 6ºs, two 8ºs, two 11ºs, and two cylinder beads. Leave a 1-yd. (.9m) tail. Go through all the beads again in the same direction, and tighten the thread so the beads form a ring.

[2] Work around the ring in tubular, even-count peyote stitch (Basics), picking up the same bead type as the bead you just exited for each stitch **(photo e)**. Step up (Basics) at the end of each round. Keep the tension tight.

[3] When you've completed one fewer than the desired number of spirals (in the necklace shown, that would be four of a total of five spirals), sew back through the line of crystals. Set the thread aside.

[4] Thread a needle on the tail. Work one round of peyote using 6ºs and one round using 8ºs. Using 11ºs, work as many rounds as needed to create a tube that will reach about halfway across the cab at the point where you plan to attach it to the necklace. Set this section aside.

[5] Repeat steps 1–3, making a shorter tube (two of a total of three spirals) or as desired. Then repeat step 4, making the tube of 11ºs about 1 in. (2.5cm) longer than the tube on the five-spiral section.

Necklace back

[1] On a comfortable length of thread, leaving an 18-in. (46cm) tail, pick up two 11ºs, two cylinders, two 11ºs and two 8ºs. Repeat this pattern once, then go through all the beads again in the same direction. Tighten the thread so the beads form a ring.

[2] Work in tubular peyote again, picking up the same bead as the bead you just exited for each stitch. Continue stitching until the tube is 9½ in. (24.1cm) or the desired length. Do not cut the thread.

[3] Cut 15 in. (38cm) of flexible beading wire. On one end, string two crimp beads and half of the magnetic clasp. Go back through the crimp beads. Crimp the crimp beads (Basics and **photo f**).

[4] Run the beading wire through the tube so the clasp is at the same end as your working thread. Using cylinder beads, continue to stitch around the tube, decreasing in each round until the tube fits snugly around the clasp **(photo g)**.

g

h

i

j

k

l

m

[5] Sew through the beading-wire loop several times to hold the tube in place against the clasp. Secure the tail in the tube, and trim.

[6] String two crimp beads and the other half of the clasp on the other end of the beading wire. Adjust the crimp beads and clasp so they extend about ½ in. (1.3cm) past the end of the tube, and crimp the crimp beads.

[7] Thread a needle on the 18-in. (46cm) tail. Decrease, and close the tube around the clasp as in steps 4 and 5.

Assembly

[1] Arrange the two necklace-front sections so their tubes of 11ºs touch. String 18 in. (46cm) of beading wire through the two sections.

[2] Zip up (Basics) the tubes **(photo h)**.

[3] Attach a clasp half to each end of the beading wire as in step 3 of the necklace back. Allow each clasp section to extend about ½ in. (1.3mm) past the edge of the spiral tube.

[4] Start a new thread at one end of the front spiral, and exit the last cylinder in the end spiral. Then, using

cylinders or 11ºs, decrease until the tube closes around the clasp, as in step 4 of the necklace back. Sew through the beading wire loop as in step 5 of the necklace back.

[5] Start a new thread in the end row of the Cellini spiral (not the tube stitched around the clasp), and exit the end bead. Pick up where you left off on the spiral, and resume stitching **(photos i and j)**. Connect the clasp on the necklace back to the clasp on the front to judge the length of the closure. Continue stitching until you've added enough spirals to hide the clasps.

[6] Repeat steps 4 and 5 on the other end of the necklace front.

[7] You can attach the pendant in one of two ways. The simpler method is to center the cabochon on the tube and sew it in place. Or, you can design a

peyote strip to use as a bail. Choose any mix of beads from the necklace, make it slightly narrower than the top of the cab and long enough to encircle the tube. Sew one edge to the cab **(photo k)**, place the bail over the tube, and sew the bail's other edge to the cab **(photo l)**.

[8] Connect the clasps on the necklace back to the clasps on the necklace front **(photo m)**.

[9] Embellish the bezel, the bail, and the spirals with crystals, drop beads, and 15ºs, as desired. ●

MATERIALS

cabochon centerpiece
- cabochon (blue druzy from Angela Fowler, 713-861-2315, angelafowler.com)
- seed beads
  5g size 11º
  5g size 14º or 15º
- 5g size 11º Japanese cylinder beads
- nylon beading thread conditioned with beeswax, or Silamide
- beading needles, #12
- ¼-in. (6mm)-wide Terrifically Tacky Tape

necklace 22 in. (56cm)
- **120** or more 4mm bicone crystals
- 10g small bead drops (optional)
- seed beads
  50g or more size 6º
  100g or more size 8º
  60g or more size 11º
- 20g size 11º Japanese cylinder beads
- **2** magnetic clasps
- **8** crimp beads
- flexible beading wire, .019
- beading needles, #10 or #11
- crimping pliers
- wire cutters

Oriental expression

Pagoda-like tops stitched in Ndebele herringbone cap a cascade of stone, ceramic, or glass beads suspended from small-link chain, making earrings that are lightweight and quick to stitch.

designed by **Karen Joelson**

step*by*step

Bead cap

[1] On 1 yd. (.9m) of Fireline, leaving a 6-in. (15cm) tail, sew a six-bead ladder (Basics, p. 10) using cylinder beads. Reinforce the ladder by zigzagging back through the beads. Join the first and last cylinders to form a ring.

[2] Work three Ndebele herringbone stitches (Basics) to finish the first round.

[3] Work the remaining rounds in herringbone: For each stitch, pick up two cylinders, sew down through two cylinders and up through two. Step up to the next round, sewing up through three cylinders. Repeat to sew a total of four rounds in herringbone.

[4] For the next round, continue in modified herringbone stitch, but add a 15º seed bead between each pair of bead stacks **(photo a)**. Step up to begin the next round. For rounds 7–10, increase the number of 15ºs between pairs of bead stacks by one bead until you have five 15ºs between the stacks **(photo b)**.

[5] Add a 4mm bicone crystal to the tip of a stack as follows: Exit a stack, pick up a 4mm and a 15º, skip the 15º, sew back through the 4mm and down through the three adjacent cylinders in the same stack. Sew across the segment of five 15ºs and up through three cylinders in the next stack. Repeat for each pagoda tip (photo c). Secure the thread with a few half-hitch knots (Basics), and trim.

Assembly

[1] Cut three pieces of chain measuring ⁷⁄₁₆ in. (1.1cm), ⁵⁄₈ in. (1.6cm), and ¹⁵⁄₁₆ in. (2.4cm).

[2] On a head pin, string a flat spacer, a 6–8mm bead, and a flat spacer. Make the first half of a wrapped loop (Basics). Slide the end link of a piece of chain onto the loop **(photo d)** and finish the wraps. Repeat to make a total of three dangles.

[3] Cut a 3-in. (7.6cm) piece of wire and make the first half of a wrapped loop on one end. Slide the three dangles onto the loop. Finish the wraps **(photo e)**.

[4] On the wire, string a 2mm bead, the herringbone bead cap, a flat spacer, and a 4mm **(photo f)**.

[5] Make the first half of a wrapped loop. Slide an earring finding into the loop and finish the wraps. Make a second earring to match the first. ●

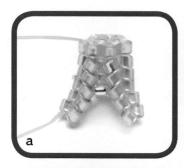
a

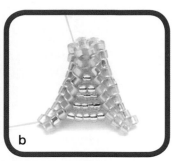
b

c

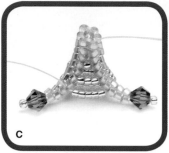
d

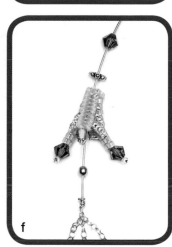
e

f

MATERIALS

earrings

- 6 6–8mm focal beads
- 8 4mm bicone crystals
- 2 2mm round silver or gold-filled beads
- 120 Japanese cylinder beads
- 96 size 15º Japanese seed beads
- 14 3–4mm flat silver or gold-filled spacers

- 6 in. (15cm) 24-gauge silver or gold-filled wire, half-hard
- 5 in. (13cm) silver or gold-filled chain
- 6 2-in. (5cm) head pins
- pair of earring findings
- Fireline 6 lb. test
- beading needles, #12
- chainnose pliers
- roundnose pliers
- wire cutters

Flower garden

Embellishments of simple fringe turn a quick Ndebele herringbone base into a bouquet for your wrist.

designed by **Barbara Woodall**

step*by*step

Base

[1] On 3 yd. (2.7m) of thread, leave a 12-in. (30cm) tail, and pick up two 6º seed beads. Make a bead ladder (Basics, p. 10) eight 6ºs long. Work a row of Ndebele herringbone stitch (Basics) off of the ladder using 6ºs. Continue working herringbone until the base fits around your wrist, with the ends overlapping ¼ in. (6mm) to accommodate the flower-and-loop clasp.

[2] Thread a needle on the tail, and sew to the middle of the fifth row of herringbone. Pick up an art-glass flower-shaped bead to use as the clasp. Secure it to the base by picking up an 11º, the flower, and a drop bead (the drop bead must be large enough to hold the flower in place). Sew back through the flower and the 11º and into the base. Retrace the thread path twice to reinforce. Tie a few half-hitch knots (Basics) between beads, and trim the tail.

[3] On the working thread, pick up enough 6ºs to make a loop large enough to fit over the clasp. Sew back through the last row of herringbone, and work a row of flat even-count peyote stitch (Basics) on the loop, using 6ºs **(photo a)**. Retrace the thread path twice to reinforce it. Secure the tail, and trim.

Embellishments

Use comfortable lengths of thread to embellish. As you run out of thread, secure the tails in the beadwork. Starting with the art-glass flowers, fill in the base, overlapping with the remaining embellishments as desired. I made a new base for each reference photo to show the embellishments more easily.

Art-glass flowers

Arrange the art-glass flowers on the base at even intervals. Sew them onto the base the same way you attached the flower for the clasp.

Drop-bead flowers

Exit between two beads on the base, and pick up a 6mm accent bead. Sew back into the base, then exit next to the 6mm. Pick up seven drop beads and sew them into a ring, positioning the ring snugly under the 6mm **(photo b)**. Retrace the thread path to reinforce the ring. Sew into the base every few drops to anchor the ring to the base.

Flower clusters

Exit between two beads on the base, and pick up a small glass flower-shaped bead and an 11º. Sew back through the flower and into the base **(photo c)**. Exit next to the small flower, and pick up another small flower and 11º. Sew back through the flower and into the base. Continue to add small flowers as desired, using up to five. You can also tuck leaf-shaped beads next to the cluster by exiting close to the outside of the cluster, picking up a leaf, and sewing back into the base **(photo d)**.

Vine

Start at one end of the base and exit between two beads that don't already have any embellishments. Pick up several 11ºs and sew into the base a few rows away, leaving a little slack so the beads curve **(photo e)**. Pick up a leaf and sew into the next row. Repeat down the length of the bracelet, varying the number of 11ºs and leaves, filling in the gaps along the base. Secure the tails, and trim. ●

MATERIALS
bracelet 7 in. (18cm)
- **4** art-glass flower-shaped beads (Marcia Kmack, Cave Creek Glassworks, 480-488-2634, cavecreekglassworks.com)
- **15** assorted small glass flower-shaped beads
- **30** assorted glass leaf-shaped beads
- **5** 6mm accent beads
- **10g** fringe drop beads
- **30g** size 6º seed beads
- **10g** size 11º seed beads
- nylon beading thread
- beading needles, #12

EDITOR'S NOTE:
To adjust the width of your bracelet, use more or fewer 6º seed beads in your base.

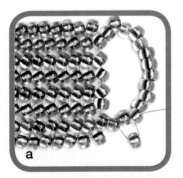

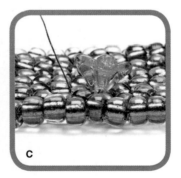

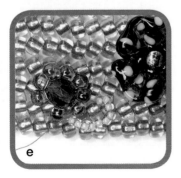

For an added burst of color, stitch a few straight fringes in a contrasting color in the middle of a cluster of glass flowers.

Herringbone stitch

Pillars
of strength

Twisted bugle beads line up like Ionic columns when they're inserted between Ndebele herringbone stitches. Graduated lengths of seed beads lend a graceful taper to each end.

designed by **Jill Wiseman**

MATERIALS
bracelet 7½ in. (19.1cm)
- 3g 12mm twisted bugle beads
- Japanese seed beads
  5g size 8º
  11g size 11º
- Fireline 6 lb. test
- beading needles, #10

FIGURE 1

FIGURE 2

---

step*by*step

Bracelet

[1] On a comfortable length of Fireline, leave a 6-in. (15cm) tail, and pick up four 8º seed beads. Sew back through all the beads and position them so you have two pairs side by side (**figure 1, a–b**). Work in ladder stitch (Basics, p. 10) until you have a strip that is four beads wide by two beads tall (**b–c**).

[2] Work two stitches in flat Ndebele herringbone (Basics and **figure 2, a–b**). Step up to complete the row (**b–c**). Work another row of herringbone.

[3] Work one herringbone stitch (**figure 3, a–b**). Pick up an 11º, sew through the next 8º, and work another stitch (**b–c**). Pick up four 11ºs, and sew up through the last 8º added (**c–d**).

[4] Repeat step 3, but pick up two 11ºs between stitches instead of one (**d–e**).

[5] Repeat step 3 seven times, increasing the number of 11ºs picked up between stitches by one on each row until you have completed a row with nine 11ºs between the two herringbone stitches.

[6] Work as in step 3, but replace the group of 11ºs with an 11º, a 12mm bugle bead, and an 11º (**figure 4, a–b**).

[7] Work one herringbone stitch (**b–c**). Pick up an 11º, sew through the bugle picked up in the previous stitch, and pick up an 11º (**c–d**). Work the next herringbone stitch, add four 11ºs, and step up (**d–e**).

[8] Repeat steps 6 and 7 until the bugle bead section is the desired length. To determine how long the bugle bead section should be, first add the length of the clasp to the length of the two 11º end sections of the bracelet, then subtract that sum from your wrist length.

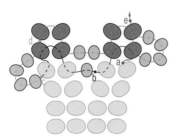

FIGURE 3

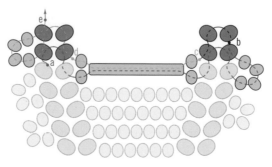

FIGURE 4

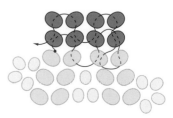

FIGURE 5

The bugle beads In the brown bracelet are 2.7mm in diameter, while the others are 2mm in diameter. Either size works fine in this design.

The clasp will require approximately 1 in. (2.5cm). The herringbone rows with 11ºs between them are approximately 1¼ in. (3.2cm) per side, or 2½ in. (6.4cm) total. For a 7½-in. (19.1cm) bracelet, the bugle bead section should be 4 in. (10cm) long. Add thread (Basics) as needed.

[9] Work a section using 11ºs between the stitches, as in step 3. Begin with nine

11ºs, and decrease the number of 11ºs used between stitches by one bead per row until you have completed a row with one 11º between stitches.

[10] Work two more rows of herringbone, as in step 2 **(figure 5)**. Sew through the last row in ladder stitch to straighten the beads. Secure both tails with a few half-hitch knots (Basics) between beads, and trim.

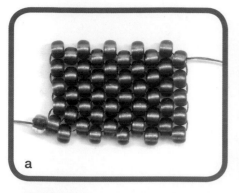

a

b

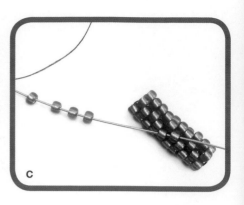

c

d

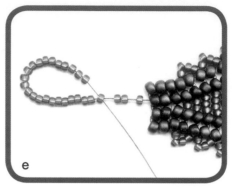

e

f

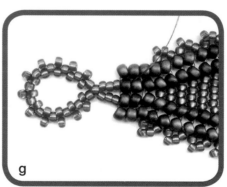

g

Clasp

[1] On 2 ft. (61cm) of Fireline, leave a 6-in. (15cm) tail, and pick up a stop bead (Basics) and ten 11ºs. Work in flat, even-count peyote stitch (Basics) to make a strip that is ten beads wide and ten rows tall **(photo a)**. The completed strip will have five beads on each flat edge.

[2] Remove the stop bead, and zip up (Basics) the jagged edges **(photo b)** to form a tube. Secure the tails with a few half-hitch knots, and trim.

[3] Secure 18 in. (46cm) of Fireline at one end of the bracelet, exiting the second 8º in the end row. Pick up four 11ºs, and sew diagonally through two 11ºs at the middle of the peyote toggle bar **(photo c)**. Pick up four 11ºs, and sew through the third 8º in the end row **(photo d)**. Retrace the thread path two or three times, secure the tails, and trim.

[4] Secure 18 in. (46cm) of Fireline at the other end of the bracelet, exiting the second 8º in the end row. Pick up approximately 27 11ºs, or enough 11ºs to form a ring around the toggle bar. Sew through the fourth 11º picked up **(photo e)**, pick up three 11ºs, and sew through the third 8º in the end row **(photo f)**.

[5] If desired, work a row of peyote stitch around the loop **(photo g)**. Retrace the thread path two or three times, secure the tails, and trim. ●

EDITOR'S NOTE:

While it's not necessary to finish the ends of the toggle bar, it adds a professional touch to the clasp. To do so, exit any 11º seed bead at one end of the bar, and sew an 8º over the open end. Retrace the thread path a few times, and repeat at the other end.

Blended
colors

Use beads of similar shades but different finishes for a band with texture and dimension.

designed by **Bonnie O'Donnell-Painter**

The band transitions seamlessly into a peyote closure.

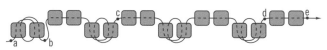

FIGURE 1

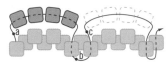

FIGURE 2

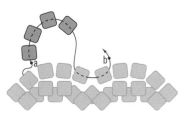

FIGURE 3

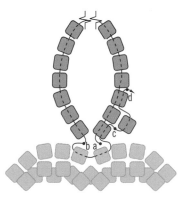

FIGURE 4

step*by*step

Choose your first color, and work the first five rounds as described below. Refer to the pattern on p. 159 as you work to graduate your band's colors. Subtract ¾ in. (1.9cm) from the desired length of the band to allow for the clasp.

[1] The initial round is a modified ladder stitch. On 3 yd. (2.7m) of Fireline or conditioned thread (Basics, p. 10), center two cylinder beads. Sew back through the cylinders again in the same direction **(figure 1, a–b)**. Pick up four cylinders, and sew back through the last two in the same direction **(b–c)**. Repeat twice **(c–d)**, and then pick up two cylinders **(d–e)**.
[2] To form a ring, sew down through the first bead picked up in step 1 and up through the next bead. (The ring won't lie right until the first few rounds are added.)
[3] Pick up four beads, skip two beads, and sew down through the next bead in the ring **(figure 2, a–b)**. Sew up through the next bead in the ring **(b–c)**. Repeat three times, sewing down through the first bead in the ring to finish the round. Then sew

up through the first bead in the new round to step up.
[4] Continue adding rounds as in step 3, sewing into the beads on the previous round **(figure 3, a–b)**. Remember to step up at the end of each round. After the first few rounds, pinch your work so it lies flat in two layers. Add thread as needed (Basics). When your band is the desired length, set the working thread aside, and thread a needle on the tail. Exit the first bead of the center herringbone stack.
[5] Working only off the center stack on both sides, stitch three rounds of tubular herringbone (Basics) to the center stack **(photo a)**. Set aside the band.
[6] Start 1 yd. (.9m) of thread. Stitch an even-count peyote (Basics) strip of cylinders, 16 beads long and 12 rows wide (six cylinders along the edges). Roll the strip into a tube and zip up (Basics) the ends.
[7] Sew through the center of the toggle bar. Pick up a 4mm crystal and a cylinder. Skip the cylinder, and sew back through the 4mm. Repeat on the other end **(photo b)**. Retrace the thread path, secure the tails with

half-hitch knots (Basics) in the beadwork, and trim.

[8] Pick up the tail from the band, and attach the toggle bar by sewing through two beads near the middle of the toggle bar and back into the band **(photo c)**. Retrace the thread path, secure the tail, and trim.

[9] Pick up the working thread, and exit the second bead of the center herringbone stack on one side of the band. Pick up an odd number of cylinders, enough to fit around the toggle. Sew through the two adjacent cylinders on the other side of the band **(photo d)**. Retrace the thread path **(figure 4, a–b)**. Exit the first cylinder in the loop **(b–c)**.

[10] Pick up a cylinder, skip a cylinder in the loop, and sew through the next cylinder **(c–d)**. Continue working in peyote stitch (Basics) until you reach the last cylinder in the loop. Step up through the first cylinder added in the new round.

[11] Pick up three 15º seed beads and sew through the next cylinder. Continue around the loop, and repeat for a second round of 15ºs.

[12] Secure the tail in the beadwork, and trim. ●

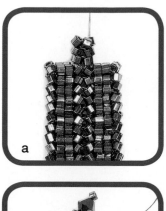

a

b

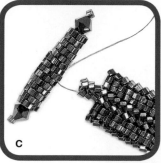

c

d

EDITOR'S NOTE:
You can use a button in place of the toggle bar. Just make the loop of cylinders large enough to accommodate the button.

Captured
gemstones

designed by **Debi Larson**

Twisted tubular herringbone spikes complement
the natural color of these gemstone nuggets.

step*by*step

Spiked components

[1] Center four 11º triangle beads on 1 yd. (.9m) of thread. Make a bead ladder (Basics, p. 10) two 11ºs tall and 10 11ºs long for the bracelet, or two 11ºs tall and 12 11ºs long for the necklace. Sew through the first two and the last two 11ºs to form a ring.

[2] Work one round of tubular Ndebele herringbone (Basics), sewing through only one 11º in the bead ladder instead of the stack of two.

[3] Pick up two 11ºs and start a round of modified twisted herringbone by sewing through the next 11º in the previous round and through the next two stacked 11ºs **(figure)**. Repeat to complete the row, stepping up through three stacked 11ºs for the last stitch.

[4] Repeat step 3 twice. Secure the working thread by tying a few half-hitch knots (Basics) between the 11ºs.

[5] Turn over your work and use the tail to repeat steps 2–4 on the other side of the ladder.

[6] Make a total of two spiked components for a bracelet or four spiked components for a necklace.

Twisted tubes

[1] To decide how long to make each tube, temporarily string three gemstones and two spiked components (or five gemstones and four spiked components for the necklace), bead caps, and accent beads on flexible beading wire **(photo a)**. Measure all of the parts you strung and add the length of your clasp. Subtract the combined length from the desired length of your bracelet or necklace. Divide the result in half to determine how long to make each twisted tube. Remove the beads and components.

[2] On 3 yd. (2.7m) of thread, leave a 12-in. (30cm) tail, and work steps 1–3 of the spiked components. Repeat step 3 until you reach the desired length. Secure the working thread as before.

[3] Using the tail that is exiting the ladder, pick up an 11º and sew into the next 11º in the ladder. Sew through the next 11º in the ladder. Pick up an 11º and sew through the next 11º in the ladder. Repeat around the ring, and step up through the first 11º added in this new round. Sew through all the 11ºs added in this round to pull them into a tight ring **(photo b)**. Secure the tail, and trim.

[4] Make a second tube to match the first.

Assembly

[1] On one end of the beading wire, string a crimp bead and half of the clasp. Go back through the crimp bead. Crimp the crimp bead (Basics) and trim the tail.

[2] String an accent bead, a bead cap, one twisted tube, the repeating pattern of gemstones and spiked components, a twisted tube, a bead cap, and an accent bead. String a crimp bead and the other half of the clasp, and crimp, making sure the components and twisted tubes are snug against the gemstones. ●

MATERIALS

both projects
- 2 4–6mm accent beads
- clasp
- 2 10mm bead caps
- 2 crimp beads
- nylon beading thread or Fireline 6 lb. test
- flexible beading wire, .014–.019
- beading needles, #12
- crimping pliers
- wire cutters

bracelet 8 in. (20cm)
- 3 12mm gemstone beads
- 25g size 11º Japanese triangle beads

necklace 18 in. (46cm)
- 5 15 x 30mm gemstone beads
- 60g size 11º Japanese triangle beads

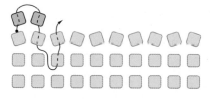

FIGURE

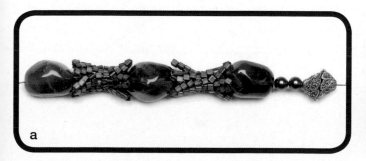

a

b

EDITOR'S NOTE:
Make sure that the gemstones are not so large that they put too much stress on the spikes of the components.

The blue neck piece, *Midnight in the Big City*, is 5 x 34½ in. (13 x 87.6cm). The purple lariat or belt is 2 x 35 in. (5 x 89cm).

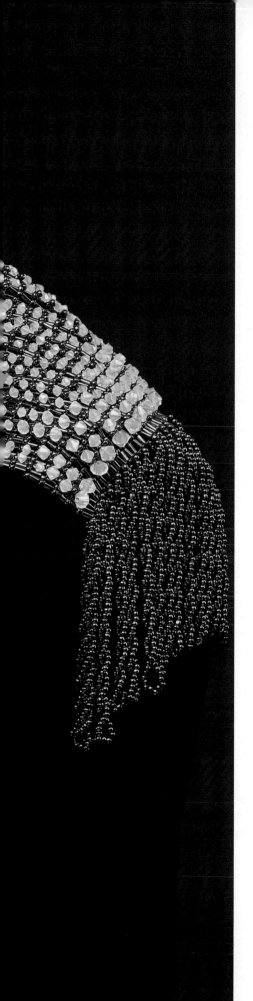

Defined
drape

Make an impressive adornment
for your neck, or a narrower
version for a lariat or belt.

designed by **Perie Brown**

MATERIALS
neck piece 5 x 34½ in.
(13 x 87.6cm)

- bicone crystals
  38 5mm
  118 4mm
  259 3mm

- 130g 3mm Japanese
  bugle beads
- 150g size 11º Japanese
  seed beads
- Fireline 6 lb. test
- nylon beading thread
- beading needles, #12

Herringbone stitch

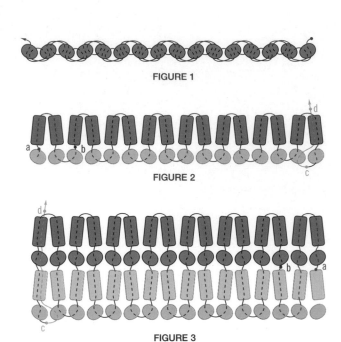

FIGURE 1

FIGURE 2

FIGURE 3

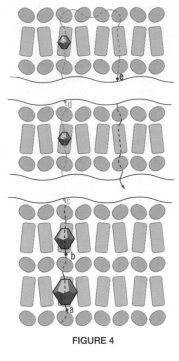

FIGURE 4

a

b

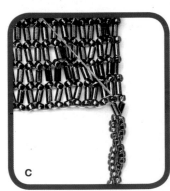

c

step*by*step

The illustrations show a portion of the width of the neck piece. The following instructions are for the blue neck piece, which is 58 beads wide and 150 rows long. Bead yours to the width or length desired by changing the number of 11º seed beads in the initial ladder, making sure the number is divisible by two. Work with 2–3-yd. (1.8–2.7m) lengths of Fireline, and end and add thread (Basics, p. 10) as needed.

Base

[1] Leaving an 8-in. (20cm) tail, make a ladder (Basics and **figure 1**) 58 11º seed beads long.
[2] With the thread exiting the last bead in the ladder, pick up two bugle beads and sew through the next two 11ºs **(figure 2, a–b)**. Complete the row by working in Ndebele herringbone **(b–c and Basics)**, and step up to the next row as shown **(c–d)**.
[3] Work a row of herringbone, picking up an 11º, two bugles, and an 11º

with each stitch. Sew through the bugle, two 11ºs, and bugle from the previous row **(figure 3, a–b)**. Repeat to complete the row **(b–c)**. Step up as shown **(c–d)**.
[4] Repeat step 3 until you have 150 rows of bugles. Work one row of 11ºs, then retrace the last row of 11ºs to mimic the thread path of the initial ladder. Secure the tails with a few half-hitch knots (Basics), and trim.

Twisted fringe

[1] Secure a comfortable length of thread at one end of the base and exit an end bead in the last row.
[2] Pick up a bugle, 100 11ºs, and a bugle. Slide the beads up to the base, and twist the thread between your thumb and index finger 20 times. Check how well it's twisting by folding the fringe in half **(photo a)**. When you let it go, it should begin to twist on its own **(photo b)**. Continue twisting as desired, keeping track of how many times, so each fringe looks the same.
[3] Sew through the next edge 11º **(photo c)**. Sew through the

next 11º and repeat step 2, adding fringe along the entire end of the base. Repeat along the other end. Secure the tails, and trim.

Crystal embellishment

[1] Secure a new length of thread at one end of the base and exit at **figure 4, point a**. Pick up a 5mm crystal, and sew through the next 11º in the column **(a–b)**.
[2] Pick up a 4mm crystal and sew through the next 11º in the column **(b–c)**. Repeat one to three times, varying the number of 4mms added in each column of crystals.
[3] Pick up a 3mm crystal and sew through the next 11º in the column **(c–d)**. Repeat six to 20 times, varying the number of 3mms added in each column of crystals.
[4] After completing one crystal row, sew through the next three 11ºs, a bugle, and an 11º to stagger the next crystal row **(d–e)**.
[5] Add crystals to every fourth column across the entire surface at one end of the base. Repeat at the other end. ●

Spiral
transcendence

Make a statement with cylinder beads, pearls, and fire-polished beads in a monochromatic palette.

designed by **Gwen Simmons**

step*by*step

Necklace

Side one, spiral tube

[1] On 2 yd. (1.8m) of conditioned thread (Basics, p. 10), leave a 6-in. (15cm) tail, and pick up two color A and two color B cylinder beads. Sew through all four beads again in the same direction. Alternating pairs of As and Bs, work in ladder stitch (Basics) until you have a two-bead ladder that is eight beads long **(figure 1)**. Join the ladder into a ring by sewing through the first two As, the last two Bs, and the first two As again.

[2] Work the next rounds as follows:

Round 3: Work one round of tubular Ndebele herringbone stitch (Basics), using an A and a B in each stitch.

Rounds 4–65: Working in spiral herringbone, pick up an A and a B, sew down through the next B, and continue up through two As in the next stack **(figure 2, a–b)**. Repeat around for four stitches **(b–c)**.

At the end of 65 rounds, the tube is approximately half the length it will be when finished. If you wish to adjust the length of the necklace, make this section longer or shorter as desired.

Fire-polished embellishment

Continue working in spiral herringbone as follows:

Round 66: Work the first stitch, but sew down through two Bs and come up through three As **(figure 3, a–b)**. This creates an opening where you'll insert a 4mm fire-polished bead on the next round. Complete the round **(b–c)**.

Round 67: Work the first half of the first stitch **(c–d)**. Pick up a 4mm, and sew up through two As in the next stack **(d–e)**. Complete the round **(e–f)**.

Round 68: Work the first stitch, but sew through two Bs, the 4mm, and three As on the next stack **(figure 4, a–b)**. Work the second stitch, and, following the method used in round 66, create an opening for a 4mm **(b–c)**. Complete the round **(c–d)**.

Round 69: Work the first stitch, retracing the thread path through the 4mm as in the previous round **(figure 5, a–b)**. Work the second stitch, adding a 4mm **(b–c)**. Complete the round **(c–d)**.

Round 70: Work the first stitch, sewing down through one B and up through two As on the next stack **(figure 6, a–b)**. Sew back down through the second B from the top on the previous stack, continue through the two As of the next stack **(b–c)**, and tighten to close up the gap above the 4mm. Work the second stitch, retracing the path through the 4mm **(c–d)**. Work the third stitch, leaving an opening for the next 4mm **(d–e)**. Work the fourth stitch **(e–f)**.

Round 71: Work the first stitch. Work the second stitch, retracing the path through the 4mm. Work the third stitch, adding a 4mm. Work the fourth stitch.

Round 72: Work the first stitch. Work the second stitch, closing the gap above the second 4mm. Work the third stitch, retracing the path through the 4mm. Work the fourth stitch, creating an opening for the fourth 4mm.

Round 73: Work two stitches. Work the third stitch, retracing the path through the 4mm. Work the fourth stitch, adding a 4mm.

Round 74: Work two stitches. Work the third stitch, closing the gap above the third 4mm. Work the fourth stitch, retracing the path through the 4mm.

Round 75: Work the first stitch, creating an opening for a 4mm. Work two stitches. Work the fourth stitch, retracing the path through the 4mm.

Round 76: Work the first stitch, adding a 4mm. Work two stitches. Work the fourth stitch, closing the gap above the 4mm.

Rounds 77–83: Repeat rounds 68–74.

Round 84: Work three stitches. Work the fourth stitch, retracing the path through the last 4mm.

Round 85: Work three stitches. Work the fourth stitch, closing the gap above the last 4mm as in round 76.

Rounds 86–93: Work in regular spiral herringbone.

Four-sided bead cage

Continue working in spiral herringbone as follows:

Round 94: Create an opening after the first stitch. Work three stitches.

Round 95: Add a 4mm after the first stitch. Work three stitches.

Round 96: Retrace the thread path through the 4mm. Work three stitches.

Round 97: Retrace the thread path through the 4mm, and create an opening for a 4mm after the second stitch. Work two stitches.

Round 98: Work the first two stitches, adding a 4mm after each. Work two stitches.

Round 99: Retrace the thread path through the 4mms. Work two stitches.

Round 100: Retrace the thread path through the 4mms, and create an opening for a 4mm after the third stitch. Work one stitch.

Round 101: Work the first three stitches, adding a 4mm after each. Work one stitch.

Round 102: Retrace the thread path through the 4mms. Work one stitch.

Round 103: Retrace the thread path through the 4mms, and create an opening for a 4mm after the fourth stitch.

Round 104: Work four stitches, adding a 4mm after each.

Rounds 105–106: Retrace the thread path through the 4mms.

Rounds 107–130: Repeat rounds 104–106 until you have 12 4mms in the first stack.

Rounds 131–142: Continue stitching as in rounds 104–106, closing the gap after the 12th 4mm of each stack. Work in regular spiral herringbone after each stack is closed.

Fringe

[1] After all four stacks are closed, resume spiral herringbone for approximately ten more rounds.

[2] Work three more rounds of spiral herringbone, retracing the thread paths between the stacks to separate them.

[3] Choose a stack, and extend it by several rows: Pick up an A and a B, and sew through the previous B and A. Continue through the last A added **(figure 7, a–b)**. Repeat until the stack is about ½ in. (1.3cm) long **(b–c)**.

[4] Pick up a 4mm and two As or Bs, and sew back through the 4mm and the other cylinder previous to the 4mm **(c–d)**.

[5] Sew back through the adjacent cylinder, the 4mm, and the first cylinder picked up in the previous step **(d–e)**.

[6] Pick up a 4mm, a stick pearl, a 4mm, a stick pearl, a 4mm, and two cylinders **(e–f)**. Sew back through the 4mms, stick pearls, and one cylinder

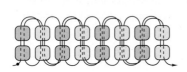

FIGURE 1

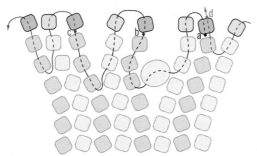

FIGURE 2

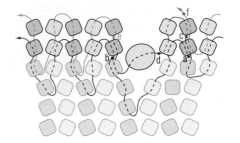

FIGURE 3

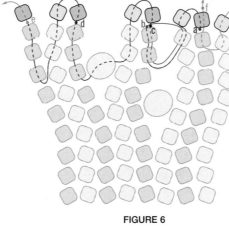

FIGURE 4

FIGURE 5

FIGURE 6

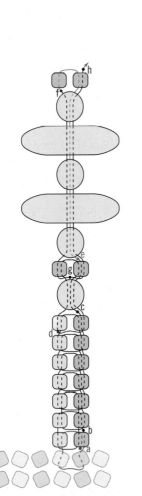

FIGURE 7

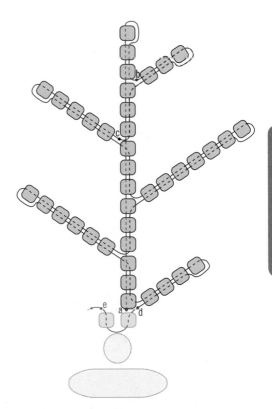

FIGURE 8

a

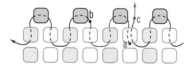

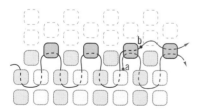

b

of the pair added in step 4 (f–g). Sew through the adjacent cylinder, sew back through the same five beads, and continue through the first cylinder picked up in the previous step (g–h).

[7] Pick up approximately 1 in. (2.5cm) of cylinders, skip the last one, and sew through the next two or three cylinders (figure 8, a–b).

[8] Pick up three to six cylinders, skip the last one, and sew back through the others and the next two or three stem cylinders (b–c).

[9] Repeat step 8 until you've made several branches on the stem (c–d). Sew into one of the cylinders below the last 4mm, and sew through the adjacent cylinder (d–e).

[10] Repeat steps 7–9 twice to make a total of three fringes. Sew back through the fringe beads and the separated stack, and exit the end cylinder of the adjacent separated stack.

[11] Repeat steps 3–10 on each separated stack, varying the length of each fringe. Secure the tails with a few half-hitch knots (Basics) between beads, and trim.

Side two, spiral tube

[1] Repeat the instructions for side one up through step 2 of the fringe.

[2] Choose a separated stack, and add 14 pairs of cylinders as in step 3 of the fringe.

[3] Pick up a 4mm, and wrap the stack around side one, between the fire-polished cage and the fringes (photo a). Sew into an end cylinder of the opposite separated stack of side two, and sew through the adjacent cylinder, the 4mm, and the adjacent cylinder of the extended stack (photo b). Retrace the thread path a few times to reinforce the connection.

[4] Sew back through the beadwork, and exit an end cylinder of one of the remaining stacks.

[5] Repeat steps 2 and 3 to join the two remaining stacks. Secure the tails, and trim.

Bead caps and clasp

[1] Secure 2 ft. (61cm) of conditioned thread at the ladder end of one side, and exit any cylinder. Pick up a cylinder, sew through the next cylinder, and exit the following cylinder (figure 9, a–b). Repeat around to add four cylinders (b–c).

[2] Working in the opposite direction, add a cylinder in each of the spaces between the beads added in step 1 (figure 10, a–b).

[3] Work two or three rounds of tubular, even-count peyote stitch (Basics). Sew through the final round of peyote to taper the end.

[4] Pick up a cylinder, a 4mm, a cylinder, a 4mm, a stick pearl, a 4mm, and three cylinders. Skip the last three cylinders, and sew back through the last six beads. Sew into the cylinder opposite the one your thread is exiting.

[5] Retrace the thread path several times, and then sew through the beadwork to exit a cylinder in the first row of peyote where the herring-bone tube and the peyote cap join. To camouflage the join with three-bead picots, pick up three cylinders, and sew through the next cylinder in the first peyote round. Repeat around, adding picots to the first two peyote rounds. Secure the tails, and trim.

[6] Repeat steps 1–3 on the other end. Pick up a cylinder, a 4mm, and enough cylinders to form a loop around the stick-pearl toggle. Sew back through the 4mm and into the bead cap. Repeat step 5.

FIGURE 9

FIGURE 10

Earrings

[1] Thread a needle on 2 ft. (61cm) of conditioned thread, leave a 6-in. (15cm) tail, and pick up four cylinder beads. Sew back through the first two cylinders (**figure 11, a–b**).

[2] Stitch two more pairs of cylinders, as shown (**b–c**).

[3] Pick up a stick pearl, a 4mm fire-polished bead, a stick pearl, and two cylinders. Sew back through the pearls, the 4mm, and a cylinder above the top pearl (**c–d**). Sew through the adjacent cylinder, the next three beads, and an end cylinder (**d–e**).

[4] Add fringe as in steps 7–10 of the necklace fringe.

[5] Sew back up through the pearls, the 4mm, and one stack of cylinders. Pick up five or six cylinders, and sew back through the adjacent cylinder. Retrace the thread path a few times. Secure the tails, and trim.

[6] Open the loop of an earring finding (Basics), attach the earring, and close the loop. Repeat to make a second earring. ⊙

MATERIALS

both projects
- nylon beading thread, conditioned with beeswax or Thread Heaven
- beading needles, #12

necklace 20 in. (51cm)
- **5–7** stick pearls
- **130–140** 4mm Czech fire-polished beads
- 10g Japanese cylinder beads, in each of **2** colors: A, B

earrings
- **4** stick pearls
- **2** 4mm Czech fire-polished beads
- 1g Japanese cylinder beads, in each of **2** colors: A, B
- pair of earring findings
- chainnose pliers

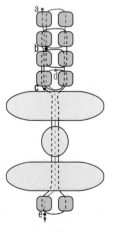

FIGURE 11

EDITOR'S NOTE:
If you want the spiral on the second side to go the opposite direction of the first side, work your spiral herringbone by going down two and up one bead on each stitch. You'll need to work the embellishment and cage beads in the opposite order also, adding a 4mm bead after the fourth stitch and working backward.

Spiraling
pearls

Combine freshwater pearls,
fire-polished beads, and
seed beads for a
fashionable necklace.

designed by **Paula-Ray Mandl**

step*by*step

[1] On 2 yd. (1.8m) of conditioned nylon thread or Fireline (Basics, p. 10), leave a 10-in. (25cm) tail, and pick up three color A 8º seed beads, a color B 8º, an 8mm pearl, a B, and a 4mm fire-polished bead **(figure 1, a–b)**. Tie the beads into a ring with a surgeon's knot (Basics). Sew back through the three As **(b–c)**.

[2] Pick up an A, a B, a pearl, a B, and a 4mm **(figure 2, a–b)**. Sew through the top A, snug up the beads, and sew through the A just added **(b–c)**. Move the new pearl loop to the left so it sits on top of the first pearl loop.

[3] Repeat step 2 until your necklace is the desired length, adding thread as needed (Basics).

[4] To attach the rivoli half of the clasp, sew through the end B. Pick up three cylinder beads, a 4mm, three cylinders, the 12mm rivoli, and three cylinders **(figure 3, a–b)**. Sew back through the 4mm **(b–c)**. Pick up three cylinders and a B, and sew back through the end A **(c–d)**. Make a half-hitch knot (Basics). Retrace the thread path a few times to reinforce the clasp connection. Secure the thread with a few half-hitch knots, and trim.

[5] To make a loop closure, thread a needle on the tail with the thread exiting an A. Pick up a B, three cylinders, a 4mm, and enough cylinders (approximately 24) to fit around the button **(figure 4, a–b)**. Sew back through the 4mm **(b–c)**, and pick up three cylinders and a B **(c–d)**. Sew through the last two As, and tie a half-hitch knot. Retrace the thread path a few times to reinforce the loop. Secure the thread with a few half-hitch knots, and trim. ●

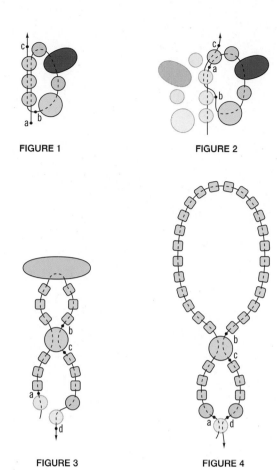

FIGURE 1

FIGURE 2

FIGURE 3

FIGURE 4

MATERIALS
necklace 19½ in. (49.5cm)

- **150** 8mm freshwater drop pearls
- **150** 4mm fire-polished beads
- size 8º Japanese seed beads
  3g color A
  7g color B
- **42** Japanese cylinder beads
- 12mm shank-enhanced Swarovski rivoli for clasp (Joyce Trimmings, ejoyce.com)
- Fireline 6 lb. test, or nylon beading thread conditioned with beeswax or Thread Heaven
- beading needles, #12

EDITOR'S NOTE:
For the clasp, you also can use a round Swarovski faceted button in place of the shank-enhanced 12mm Swarovski rivoli.

Spiral rope stitch

Follow the instructions to make the bracelet in the foreground. For the other bracelet, substitute 3mm crystals for the bugle beads, and replace the middle three 8°s of each loop with a 4mm bead.

Textural. variation

Show off core beads in this unusual twist on spiral rope.

designed by **Lisa Keith**

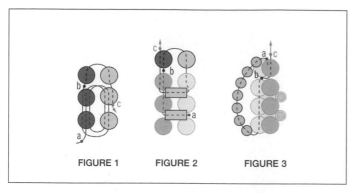

FIGURE 1   FIGURE 2   FIGURE 3

a

b

c

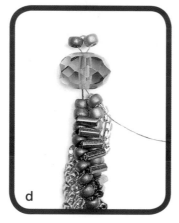

d

e

MATERIALS

bracelet 7 in. (18cm)
- 10g 3–4mm bugle beads
- seed beads
  10g size 6º, in each of
  2 colors: A, B
  15g size 8º, in each of
  2 colors: C, D
  1g size 15º
- clasp
- Fireline 6 lb. test, or nylon beading thread conditioned with beeswax or Thread Heaven
- beading needles, #10 or #12

necklace 20 in. (51cm)
- **5** 7 x 10mm rondelles or other large accent beads (optional)
- approximately **100** 3mm accent beads (optional)
- 20g 3–4mm bugle beads
- seed beads
  20g size 8º, in each of
  2 colors: A, B
  20g size 11º, in each of
  2 colors: C, D
  1g size 15º
- clasp
- Fireline 6 lb. test, or nylon beading thread conditioned with beeswax or Thread Heaven
- beading needles, #10 or #12

step*by*step

Bracelet

[1] Thread a needle on 2 yd. (1.8m) of Fireline or conditioned thread (Basics, p. 10), leave a 6-in. (15cm) tail, and pick up two color A 6º seed beads and two color B 6ºs. Sew through all four beads again, and continue on through the two As **(figure 1, a–b)**. The As and Bs are the core beads.

[2] Pick up an A and a B, and sew down through the B from the previous stitch **(b–c)**.

[3] Pick up a bugle bead, and sew up through the A of the previous stitch and continue through the last A added **(figure 2, a–b)**.

[4] Repeat steps 2 and 3 **(b–c)**.

[5] Pick up seven color C 8ºs, and cross them over the core. Sew into the fourth B below where your thread is exiting, sew up through three Bs **(figure 3, a–b)**, cross over, and continue through the next A **(b–c)**.

[6] Repeat steps 4 and 5 four times for a total of five color C loops **(photo a)**.

[7] Repeat steps 4 and 5 five times using color D 8ºs.

[8] Repeat steps 6 and 7, alternating five color C loops with five color D loops, until the bracelet is approximately ½ in. (1.3cm) short of the desired length. Add thread (Basics) as needed.

[9] Pick up approximately seven 15ºs and one half of the clasp, and sew through the last B **(photo b)**. Pick up a bugle, and sew up through the A **(photo c)**. Retrace the thread path of the loop a few times.

[10] If your thread is at least 15 in. (38cm) long, sew through the entire stack of As to snug up the core.

If your thread is shorter than 15 in. (38cm), secure it in the loops of 8ºs with a few half-hitch knots (Basics) between beads, and trim. Secure a new 15-in. (38cm) thread at the end that has a clasp, and sew through the stack of As.

[11] Repeat step 9 on the other end. Secure the tails, and trim.

Necklace

The necklace is made with 8º and 11º seed beads instead of 6ºs and 8ºs. If you choose to make it with 6ºs and 8ºs, the resulting necklace will be thicker than the one shown here. Make a continuous rope, or try interspersing large accent beads throughout.

[1] Follow steps 1–7 of the bracelet, substituting 8ºs for the 6ºs and 11ºs for the 8ºs. If desired, substitute a 3mm accent bead for the middle three 11ºs of each loop.

[2] Repeat steps 6 and 7 of the bracelet until the necklace is the desired length (if making a continuous rope) or until the first section is the desired length (if adding large accent beads).

To add a large accent bead between stitched sections, pick up a 7 x 10mm accent bead, an A, and a B. Sew back through the accent bead, and continue through the B from the previous stitch **(photo d)**. Pick up a bugle, and sew up through the adjacent A, the accent bead, and the A just added **(photo e)**. Pick up an A and a B, and sew through the B of the previous stitch, the accent bead, and the previous B. Sew back through the adjacent A, the accent bead, and the two As above.

[3] Continue stitching as in steps 6 and 7 of the bracelet until the next section is the desired length.
[4] Repeat steps 2 and 3 until the necklace is the desired length.
[5] Attach a clasp as in steps 9–11 of the bracelet. ●

EDITOR'S NOTE:
To vary the look, substitute crystals, pearls, gemstones, or drop-shaped beads for the bugle beads. Or, use a 3–4mm bead in the center of each loop.

Spicy stitched ensemble

Combine red and hessonite garnets in a double-spiral rope necklace with a coordinating centerpiece and earrings.

by **Julia Gerlach**

step*by*step

Necklace
Spiral rope

[1] On a comfortable length of Fireline or conditioned thread (Basics, p. 10), leave an 8-in. (20cm) tail, and pick up a stop bead (Basics). Pick up three cylinder beads, a Charlotte bead, a red garnet, and a Charlotte. Sew back through the cylinders in the same direction (figure 1, a–b).
[2] Pick up a Charlotte, a hessonite garnet, and a Charlotte, and sew back through the cylinders (b–c).
[3] Pick up a cylinder, a Charlotte, a red garnet, and a Charlotte. Sew through the last two cylinders of the previous stitch and the

cylinder just picked up (photo a). Position the new loop of beads on the right of the previous red-garnet loop.
[4] Pick up a Charlotte, a hessonite garnet, and a Charlotte, and sew through the last three cylinders (photo b). Flip your work so the loop with the hessonite garnet is on the left. Position the new loop of beads on the right of the previous hessonite-garnet loop.
[5] Repeat steps 3 and 4 until the rope is about 8½ in. (21.6cm) long, or half the desired length minus the length of the clasp.

To end a thread, sew back into the last loop added, secure it with a few half-hitch knots (Basics) between

beads, and trim. To begin a new thread, sew into a previous loop, make a few half-hitch knots between beads, and continue through the core cylinders to exit the same place you left off.
[6] To finish the first rope, pick up a cylinder, and sew back through the last cylinder added in the same direction (figure 2). Retrace the thread path twice. Secure the tail in a nearby loop with a few half-hitch knots between beads, and trim. Set the rope aside.
[7] Repeat steps 1–5 to make a second rope, but in steps 3 and 4, hold the new loops of beads to the left of the previous loops. This will make the beads spiral in the

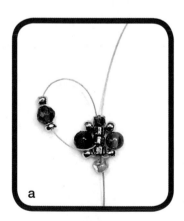

a

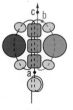

FIGURE 1

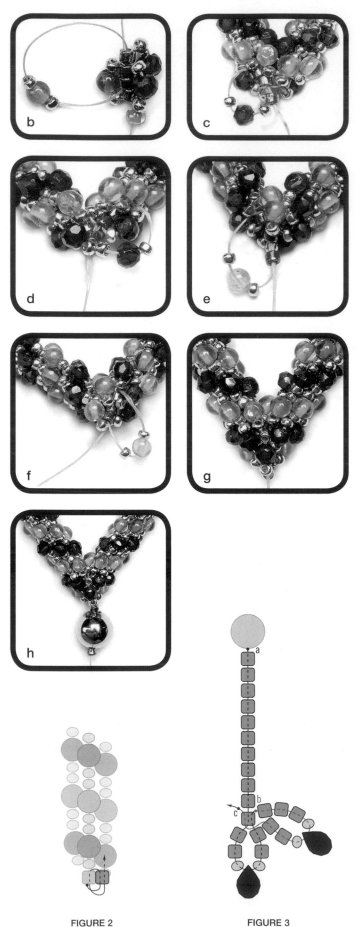

FIGURE 2

FIGURE 3

other direction. For the last stitch, instead of picking up a cylinder, sew through the cylinder stitched to the end of the first rope in step 6.

[8] To taper the combined ropes into a point, work three more double-spiral rounds as follows:

Taper, round 1: Pick up a cylinder, a Charlotte, a garnet (choose the appropriate color based on where you ended the design), and a Charlotte, and sew back through the last two cylinders on one of the ropes and the cylinder picked up in this step **(photo c)**. Do not flip the beadwork.

Pick up a Charlotte, a garnet in the same color, and a Charlotte, and sew back through the last two cylinders on the other rope and the last cylinder picked up **(photo d)**.

Taper, round 2: Flip the beadwork over so you're working on the other side of the ropes. Pick up a cylinder, a Charlotte, a garnet in the other color, and a Charlotte, and sew back through the last cylinder on one of the ropes, the cylinder added in the previous round, and the cylinder picked up in this step **(photo e)**. Do not flip the beadwork.

Pick up a Charlotte, a garnet in the same color, and a Charlotte, and sew back through the last cylinder on the other rope, the cylinder added in the previous round, and the last cylinder picked up **(photo f)**.

Taper, round 3: Work one normal round of double spiral (one stitch per side), choosing the appropriate garnet colors to match the design **(photo g)**.

Centerpiece

[1] Pick up the 7mm bead. If the bead's hole is large enough, pick up enough cylinders to equal the length of the 7mm, and string the 7mm over them **(photo h)**.

[2] Pick up 13 cylinders, a Charlotte, a teardrop-shaped garnet, a Charlotte, and two cylinders. Skip the last seven beads, and sew back up through the next cylinder **(figure 3, a–b)**.

[3] Pick up three cylinders, a Charlotte, a teardrop, a Charlotte, and two cylinders. Sew through the cylinder your thread is exiting from bottom to top **(b–c)**. Repeat four times to make a total of five loops, sewing through the same cylinder with each repetition.

[4] Sew through two cylinders **(photo i)**, and repeat step 3.

[5] Repeat step 4 twice.

[6] Sew through two cylinders, and make five more loops, each consisting of two cylinders, a Charlotte, a teardrop, a Charlotte, and a cylinder.

[7] Sew through two cylinders, and make five more loops, each consisting of a cylinder, a Charlotte, a teardrop, and a Charlotte.

[8] Sew through the 7mm, secure the thread in the spiral rope with a few half-hitch knots, and trim.

Clasp

[1] Remove the stop bead from one end of the necklace. Thread a needle on the tail, pick up seven cylinders and go through the loop of one clasp half. Sew back into the spiral rope **(photo j)**, and tie a half-hitch knot. Retrace the thread path two or three times, secure the thread, and trim.

[2] Repeat on the other end.

Earrings

[1] On 1 yd. (.9m) of Fireline or conditioned thread (Basics), leave a 6-in. (15cm) tail, and pick up seven cylinder beads. Tie the ends with a square knot (Basics), and sew through a few cylinders.

[2] Pick up a 4mm bead, ten cylinders, a Charlotte bead, a teardrop-shaped garnet, a Charlotte, and a cylinder. Skip the last five beads, and sew through the next cylinder in the opposite direction **(photo k)**.

[3] Work four rounds of five loops per round as in the centerpiece, but use two cylinders, a Charlotte, a teardrop, a Charlotte, and a cylinder for all the loops. Sew through two cylinders between each round.

[4] Sew through the 4mm bead, and reinforce the loop made in step 1. Secure the tails, and trim.

[5] Open the loop of an earring finding (Basics), and attach the loop of cylinders **(photo l)**. Close the loop.

[6] Make a second earring to match the first. ●

MATERIALS

both projects

- nylon beading thread conditioned with beeswax or Thread Heaven, or Fireline 6 lb. test
- beading needles, #13

necklace 18 in. (46cm)

- 7mm gold-filled round bead
- 16-in. (41cm) strand 3 x 2mm–6 x 4mm faceted teardrop-shaped garnets
- 2 16-in. strands 2.5–3mm garnets (round or rondelle)
- 2 16-in. strands 2.5–3mm hessonite garnets (round or rondelle)

- 3g size 11º Japanese cylinder beads
- hank size 13º gold-plated Charlotte beads
- clasp

earrings

- 2 4mm gold-filled round beads
- 40 teardrop-shaped garnets left over from necklace
- 2g size 11º Japanese cylinder beads
- size 13º Charlotte beads left over from necklace
- pair of earring findings
- chainnose pliers

i

EDITOR'S NOTE: Hessonite garnets are available in graduated colors from pale yellow to dark amber. Placing the darker beads near the clasp and the lighter beads near the front gives the illusion that the spiral rope gets thicker as it nears the centerpiece.

j

k

l

Crystal tiles

Four stitches are the foundation for this bracelet with custom netted toggle clasps.

designed by **Geneva Beck**

Use 3-yd. (2.7m) lengths of thread to work these bracelets, but don't trim the tails until after you add the crystal embellishment.

MATERIALS

bracelet 8½ in. (21.6cm)
- **170** 4mm bicone crystals
- Japanese seed beads
  30g size 11º
  5g size 15º
- Fireline 6 lb. test
- beading needles, #12

step*by*step

Base

[1] Using 11º seed beads, leave an 18-in. (46cm) tail and make a bead ladder (Basics, p. 10) two beads wide and three rows long **(figure 1, a–b)**.

[2] Pick up six 11ºs, sew back through the last two 11ºs your thread is exiting, and continue through four new 11ºs **(b–c)**. Working in right-angle weave (Basics), repeat for a total of four stitches **(c–d)**.

[3] Using two 11ºs per stitch, work two ladder stitches **(d–e)**.

[4] Work four right-angle weave stitches **(e–f)**. Alternate between ladder stitch and right-angle

weave sections, ending with two ladder stitches. My bracelet has nine ladder and eight right-angle weave sections.

[5] Continuing in the established pattern, work a second column, sharing the side beads of the right-angle weave sections **(figure 2, a–b)**. Work a total of four columns.

[6] At one end, sew through the beadwork to exit at **figure 3, point a**. Pick up an 11º, and sew through the two end 11ºs of the next ladder **(a–b)**. Repeat twice **(b–c)**.

[7] Using 11ºs, work a row of square stitch (Basics) off the last row of ladder stitch **(c–d)**.

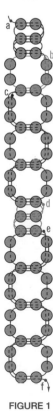

FIGURE 1

FIGURE 2

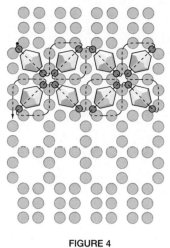

FIGURE 3

FIGURE 4

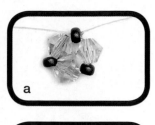

a

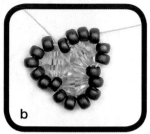

b

c

d

e

[8] Using one 11º per stitch, work five ladder stitches **(d–e)**. Using two 11ºs per stitch, work two rows of modified square stitch off the last two 11ºs in the ladder **(e–f)**.

[9] Sew through the next 11º **(f–g)**. Using one 11º per stitch, work three rows of ladder stitch, and attach the last ladder stitch to the first row of square stitch **(g–h)**. Secure the tail in the bead-work with a few half-hitch knots (Basics).

[10] Using the tail, repeat steps 6–9 on the opposite end of the bracelet.

Embellishment

Secure a new thread in the base, exiting at the corner of the first right-angle weave stitch at one end. Pick up a 15º, a 4mm bicone crystal, and a 15º. Stitch the thread path in **figure 4**, adding the bead sequence to the top of each right-angle weave stitch section.

Toggle

[1] On 2 yd. (1.8m) of thread, pick up an 11º and a 4mm. Repeat twice. Sew back through all the beads and tie the tail to the working thread with a square knot (Basics). Sew through the next 11º **(photo a)**.

[2] Pick up five 11ºs. Skip the next 4mm and sew through the next 11º. Repeat twice, continuing on through the first three 11ºs added in this step **(photo b)**.

[3] Pick up a 4mm and sew through the third 11º of the next set of five **(photo c)**. Repeat twice to complete the round.

[4] Repeat steps 2 and 3 until you have seven 4mm rounds. Sew through the beadwork to exit a center 11º **(photo d)**, and, using an 11º, work a ladder stitch. Using two 11ºs per stitch, work four ladder stitches, then work one more using one 11º.

[5] Attach the toggle bar to the base, sewing through the fifth 11º in the first square stitch row **(photo e)**. Retrace the thread path to reinforce the connection. Secure the tails in the beadwork, and trim.

[6] Repeat steps 1–5 to make a second toggle on the other end of the bracelet, but attach it to the fifth 11º from the other edge so the toggles are offset slightly when clasped. ●

EDITOR'S NOTE:
To make a pair of earrings, complete two right-angle weave sections. Sew a soldered jump ring to a corner, and attach the earrings to earring findings.

Colorful connections

Mix and match your favorite colors in this multihued peyote stitch beaded-bead bracelet.

designed by **Julie Glasser**

step*by*step

Peyote stitch tube beads

[1] On 2 ft. (61cm) of conditioned thread (Basics, p. 10), pick up a stop bead (Basics), leaving a 6-in. (15cm) tail. Pick up 12 cylinder beads of a single color, and work 12 rows of flat, even-count peyote stitch (Basics). The completed peyote strip should be 12 cylinders wide, with six cylinders on each flat edge.

[2] Zip up (Basics) the ends of the strip to form a tube. Remove the stop bead. Secure the tails with a few half-hitch knots (Basics) between beads, and trim.

[3] Repeat steps 1 and 2 to make 30 peyote tubes, three in each of ten colors. Set one aside to use as a toggle bar. To adjust the length of the bracelet, make more or fewer tubes as needed. When lined up side by side, the tubes

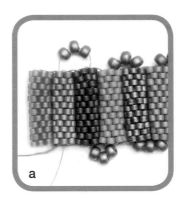

a

b

should be approximately ½ in. (1.3cm) short of the desired length.

Assembly

[1] Arrange the tubes side by side as desired.

[2] On 3 yd. (2.7m) of thread, leave a 12-in. (30cm) tail. Pick up two tube beads (**figure 1, a–b**). Working in ladder stitch (Basics), sew through both tubes again (**b–c**).

[3] Continue joining the remaining tubes (**c–d**), and exit one end of the last tube.

[4] To make the decorative edge, pick up three 8º seed

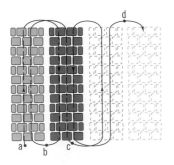

FIGURE 1

FIGURE 2

FIGURE 3

beads, and sew through the next tube. Repeat, adding 8°s on alternate edges **(photo a)** until you reach the other end of the bracelet. Tie the working thread to the tail at the beginning of the bracelet using a square knot (Basics).

[5] To make the toggle strap, use the working thread, and retrace the thread path back through the 8°s to the other end of the bracelet.

[6] Zigzag through the cylinders in the end tube to exit the seventh cylinder from one edge **(figure 2, point a)**. Pick up a cylinder and sew through the sixth cylinder in the tube **(a–b)**. Pick up a cylinder and sew through the first cylinder added in this

step **(b–c)**. Continue working in flat peyote stitch (Basics) until the toggle strap is at least five cylinders long **(c–d)**.

[7] Connect the toggle strap to two of the middle beads of the toggle bar **(d–e** and **photo b)**. Retrace the thread path several times. Secure the working thread, and trim.

[8] Thread a needle on the tail, and zigzag through the cylinders of the last tube to exit at **figure 3, point a**. Pick up 19 to 21 cylinders and sew through the middle two cylinders in the same direction to create a loop **(a–b)**. Pull to tighten, and retrace the thread path several times. Secure the tails, and trim. ●

Bonnie O'Donnell-Painter uses a different color scheme for each flower charm, providing bold contrast within the design.

Whimsical
herringbone
blooms

Delightful flower charms dangle from a right-angle weave base.

designed by **Bonnie O'Donnell-Painter**

MATERIALS
both projects
- nylon beading thread
- beading needles, #12

earrings
- 2 3mm Czech glass beads
- 1g size 11º seed beads, color A
- 1g size 15º seed beads, in each of **2** colors: B, C
- pair of earring findings

bracelet
- 6–7 5mm art-glass beads
- 26 3mm Czech glass beads
- 5g size 11º seed beads, color A
- 2g size 15º seed beads, in each of **2** colors: B, C
- 18mm-diameter button for clasp

step*by*step

Earrings
Base

[1] On 3 yd. (2.7m) of thread, pick up four color A 11º seed beads. Leaving a 6-in. (15cm) tail, sew back through the first A, and pull the beads into a ring **(figure 1, a–b)**.

[2] Pick up two color B 15ºs, one A, and two Bs. Sew back through the A the thread is exiting and the next A in the ring **(b–c)**.

[3] Pick up two Bs and one A. Sew back through the two adjacent Bs from the previous step and through two As in the ring **(c–d)**.

[4] Repeat step 3 **(d–e)**.

[5] Sew through two Bs from step 2, pick up an A, and sew through the two Bs from step 4. Sew through an A in the ring, two 15ºs, and the first A added in step 2 **(e–f)**.

[6] Sew through the four As, pulling them tight to form a new ring **(f–g)**.

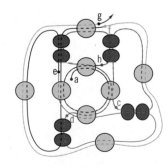

FIGURE 1

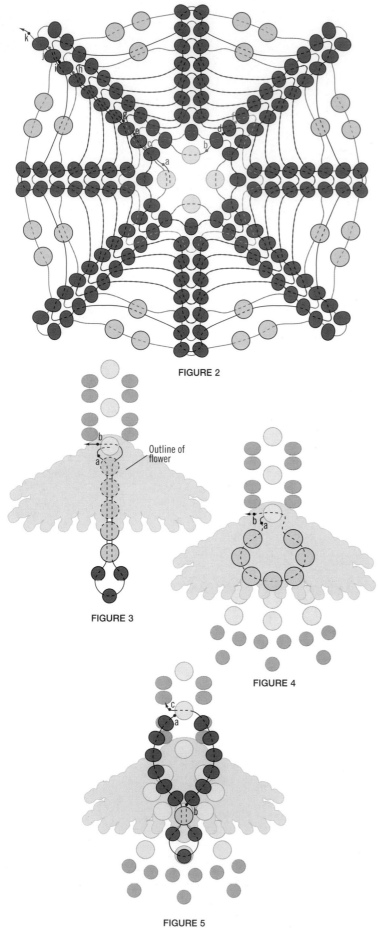

FIGURE 2

FIGURE 3

Outline of flower

FIGURE 4

FIGURE 5

[7] Repeat steps 2–6 three times. Finish by exiting any A on the last round.

Flower

[1] Pick up two color C 15°s. Sew through the next A in the ring (figure 2, a–b). Repeat around the ring, adding two Cs between each A. Step up through the first C added (b–c).

[2] Pick up two Cs, and sew down through the next C. For the next stitch, work an increase by picking up a B and sewing up through the next C (c–d).

[3] Repeat around the ring, working one regular stitch and one increase (d–e). Remember to step up after each round.

[4] To start the next increase round, work a stitch with two Cs and then a stitch with two Bs (e–f). Continue around the ring (f–g).

[5] Work four rounds of herringbone using Bs and Cs (g–h).

[6] On the next round, work herringbone with Bs and Cs, but increase using one A between each herringbone stack. Sew through the first bead in the new round (h–i).

[7] Work another herringbone round using Bs and Cs, sewing through the As added in the last round (i–j).

[8] Make one more round as follows: Work one herringbone stitch with Cs, increase to two As, sew through the two Bs of the next stack, and increase to two As. Repeat around (j–k). Sew back down a vertical stack of Cs, then exit at **point b**.

Embellishments

[1] Using the working thread, exit the center of the flower, and pick up five As and three Cs. Skip the Cs, sew back through the As, and sew back through the bead your thread is exiting (figure 3, a–b). Sew through the next A in the ring. Repeat to make three fringes.

[2] To make a loop, exit the same base ring, and exit an A on the outside of the flower. Pick up seven As, and sew back through the same A (figure 4, a–b and photo a). Sew through the next A on the ring. Repeat to make four loops.

[3] To make leaves, exit the ring of As right above the one you just added the loops to. Pick up six Bs, one A, and three Cs. Skip the three Cs, and sew back through the A (figure 5, a–b). Pick up six Bs, and sew back into the A on the ring (b–c and photo b). Sew through the next A on the ring. Repeat to make four leaves.

[4] Secure the thread with half-hitch knots (Basics, p. 10) between several beads. Trim the working thread, and thread a needle on the 6-in. (15cm) tail.

[5] On the tail, pick up one 3mm glass bead, three As, the loop of an earring finding, and three As. Sew back through the 3mm and the A opposite the bead your thread is exiting. Retrace the thread path. Secure the tail, and trim.

[6] Make a second earring to match the first.

Bracelet

The bracelet has many of the same components as the earring. Start by making the base for the earring, but in step 7, keep stitching until the base is the length of your wrist. Make six or seven flower charms the same as for the earrings. Set them aside to be stitched to the base later.

a

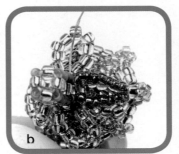
b

c

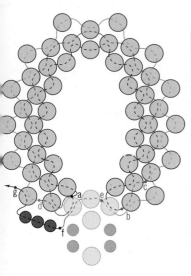

FIGURE 6

d

Clasp

[1] Use the tail to sew a button to one end of the base (photo c). Retrace the thread path, and secure it in the beadwork. Trim the tail.

[2] Secure 2 yd. (1.8m) of thread in the base, exiting one of the As on the last ring (figure 6, point a).

[3] Pick up enough As to fit around the button. Sew into the opposite A in the ring (a–b).

[4] Pick up an A, skip an A on the loop, and sew through the next A (b–c). Continue in peyote stitch (Basics) until you reach the beginning of the loop, sewing through the A in the ring and back through the last A added (c–d).

[5] Work one more row of peyote using As (d–e). Sew through the ring of As to get back to the other side (e–f).

[6] Pick up three Cs, and sew through the next A in the previous round (f–g). Continue to work in modified peyote, adding three Cs per stitch. Work three or four rows of modified peyote. Secure the threads, and trim.

[7] Arrange the art-glass beads and the flower charms as desired, and stitch them to the base in even intervals (photo d). ○

EDITOR'S NOTE:
If you need to add thread when making the base for the bracelet, try to keep all the knots in one line of beads so when you stitch the flowers and art-glass beads to the base, the knots don't get in the way.

Artful

centerpiece

Ndebele herringbone ropes set the stage for an art-glass pendant.

designed by **Michelle Bevington**

step*by*step

Ndebele herringbone ropes

[1] On 2 yd. (1.8m) of Silamide, leave a 12-in. (30cm) tail and make a ladder (Basics, p. 10) with four color A cylinder beads. Join the ladder into a ring by sewing through the first cylinder, back through the last ladder cylinder, and exiting the first cylinder.

[2] Working in tubular Ndebele herringbone stitch (Basics), stitch a rope approximately 17 in. (43cm) long. Do not secure the tails when you finish the rope because you may need to adjust the length later. Add thread (Basics) as needed.

[3] Repeat steps 1 and 2 to make three or four ropes, using a different color cylinder for each rope. Make all the ropes the same length.

Ndebele herringbone ropes and a peyote stitch bail complement art-glass beads by Brendan Blake (both beads at left) and Helen Stoughton (p. 190).

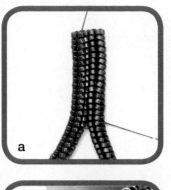

a

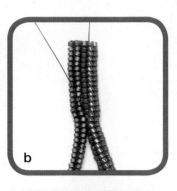

b

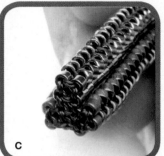

c

d

e

f

A

B

FIGURE 1

[4] Thread a needle on the 12-in. (30cm) tail of one rope, and, working in square stitch (Basics), connect the first 17 cylinders in one column to the first 17 cylinders of a second rope **(photo a)**. Sew through an adjacent cylinder. Continue in square stitch and work in the opposite direction to stitch the first 17 cylinders of a second column **(photo b)**. Secure the tail with a few half-hitch knots (Basics) between beads, and trim.

[5] If you made three ropes, connect the third rope by sewing one column to the first rope and another column to the second rope **(photo c)**. Secure the tail, and trim.

If you made four ropes, connect the third rope to the second, creating an L shape. Connect the fourth rope to the first and third ropes. Attach the inner rows on both sides first, then attach the outer rows. Secure the tail, and trim.

[6] Now that the ropes are connected at one end, check that the lengths are even. If they aren't, add or remove rows as needed.

[7] Repeat steps 4 and 5 to connect the other ends, being careful not to twist the ropes.

Pendant and bail

[1] On a 3-in. (7.6cm) head pin, string two or three spacers and/or bead caps and the focal bead. If the bead is shifting around on the head pin, string some small seed beads onto the head pin and into the hole of the focal bead. String spacers above the focal bead to mirror the ones below it, and make a wrapped loop (Basics and **photo d**).

[2] On 1 yd. (.9m) of nylon thread, working in flat, odd-count peyote stitch, make a bail **(figure 1)**, increasing and decreasing (Basics) as needed. Leave the ends unattached and do not secure the tails.

[3] To make the wire triangle that attaches the pendant to the bail, use one of the following methods:

• For a simple triangle, as in the pink and blue necklaces, p. 188, cut a 1½-in. (3.8cm) piece of 24-gauge wire, and bend it into an equilateral triangle wide enough to accommodate the tab of the bail. Cut the wire so the two ends overlap slightly **(photo e)**. Slide the pendant into the triangle. Slip a crimp bead onto one end of the wire. Slide the crimp bead over both wire ends **(photo f)**, and crimp it (Basics).

• For a triangle with a wrapped loop, as in the green necklace, p. 190, cut a 5-in. (13cm) piece of wire. Using the width of the tab of the bail as a guide, make two bends in the middle of the wire to form a triangle

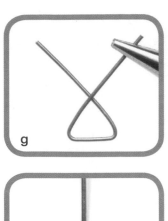

g

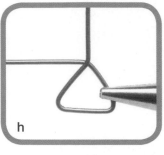

h

i

j

k

MATERIALS

necklace 18 in. (46cm)

- focal bead, approximately 27 x 22cm
- 10g Japanese cylinder beads, in each of **3** or **4** colors: A, B, C, (D)
- 1g size 15º Japanese seed beads
- **4–6** spacers or bead caps
- clasp
- 1½ in. or 5 in. (3.8cm or 13cm) 24-gauge wire, half-hard
- 3-in. (7.6cm) head pin
- **2** 4mm split rings
- 2 x 2mm crimp bead (optional)
- Silamide
- nylon beading thread
- beading needles, #12
- chainnose pliers
- crimping pliers (optional)
- roundnose pliers
- split-ring pliers (optional)
- wire cutters

SUPPLY NOTE:
See more beads by Brendan Blake on his Web site, bbglassart. com. Find Helen Stoughton's beads by searching for her seller ID, firefly*glass, on ebay.com.

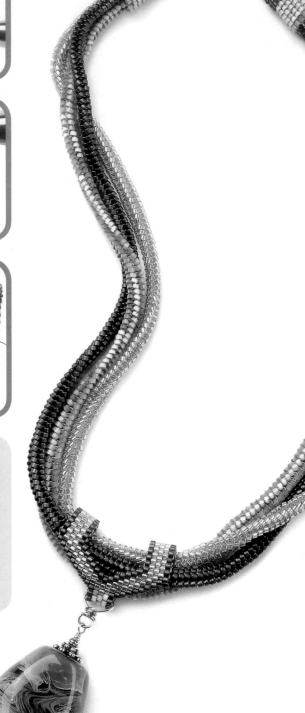

(photo g). At the point where the ends cross, make a small bend in each end to form a right angle (photo h). Wrap the horizontal wire around the vertical wire twice, and trim the wrapping wire (photo i).

With the vertical wire, make the first half of a wrapped loop. Attach it to the loop of the pendant (photo j), and finish the wraps.

[4] Slide the tab of the bail into the triangle, and zip up (Basics) the edges (photo k). Retrace the thread path, secure the tails, and trim.

Assembly

[1] Attach a split ring to each half of a clasp.

[2] On 2 yd. (1.8m) of thread, attach a stop bead (Basics). Working in square stitch, make a band that is nine beads wide and 16 to 18 rows tall (figure 2), starting at the lower left-hand corner of the pattern. To make the band into an end cap, wrap it around the end of the ropes, positioning the A cylinders at the end, and stitch the first and last rows together (photo l) using square stitch.

[3] Slide the end cap up so one row extends past the end of the ropes. Stitch it in place around the ropes with square stitch.

[4] Sew through the bead-work to exit an A at the edge of the end cap. Pick up an A, and sew down through the next A in the end cap and up through the following A (photo m). Repeat along the entire edge. Step up through

the first A added in this round.

[5] Pick up an A and sew through the next A on the previous round (photo n). Repeat, working two rounds of tubular peyote stitch (Basics).

[6] Work one round of pcyote using 15° seed beads. Work another round of peyote using 15°s, but work a decrease every third stitch. Work two more rounds of peyote using 15°s.

[7] Pick up five 15°s and one half of the clasp. Sew into the 15° opposite the one you just exited (photo o).

[8] Zigzag through the 15°s on one side of the tube, exit where you began the loop, and sew back through the loop. Zigzag through the 15°s on the other side of the tube, and sew through the loop again. Repeat this step twice. Sew into the beadwork, secure the tails, and trim.

[9] Slide the peyote bail onto the ropes, and then repeat steps 2–8 to finish the other end. ○

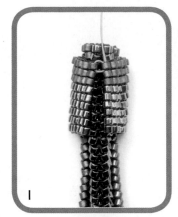

l

m

n

o

EDITOR'S NOTE:

If you're making the simple triangle for the bail and find both wire ends won't slide through the crimp bead, try flattening the crimp bead slightly with chainnose pliers. This will allow the two wire ends to nestle side by side.

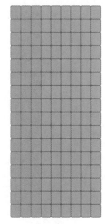

FIGURE 2

Sparkling crystal cabochons

Bezeled and embellished crystals make a stunning centerpiece with a secret.

designed by **Barbara Klann**

step*by*step

Embellished bezel – 14mm crystal

[1] On 1 yd. (.9m) of thread, and leaving a 10-in. (25cm) tail, pick up eight 15º seed beads. Tie the beads into a ring using a square knot (Basics, p. 10), and sew through the first 15º picked up. These beads make up rounds 1 and 2.

Round 3: Working in peyote stitch (Basics), pick up a 15º, skip a 15º on the ring, and sew through the next 15º **(figure 1, a–b)**. Repeat around the ring for a total of four stitches **(b–c)**. Step up through the first 15º picked up in this round **(c–d)**.

Round 4: Pick up two 15ºs, and sew through the next 15º on the previous round **(d–e)**.

Repeat around for a total of four stitches, stepping up through the first 15º of the first pair picked up in this round **(e–f)**.

Round 5: Pick up a 15º, and go through the second 15º of the pair **(f–g)**. Pick up two 15ºs, and go through the first 15º of the next pair on the previous round **(g–h)**. Repeat around, inserting one 15º in the middle of the pairs and two 15ºs between each pair on the previous round. Step up through the first 15º added in this round **(h–i)**.

Round 6: Work 12 peyote stitches, inserting one 15º between up-beads as well as in the middle of pairs on the previous round. Step up through the first 15º added in this round **(i–j)**.

Rounds 7 and 8: Switch to

cylinder beads, and work 12 peyote stitches per round **(j–k)**.

Round 9: Work 12 stitches, alternating between one and two cylinders per stitch **(k–l)**.

Round 10: Work 18 stitches, placing a cylinder between

up-beads and in the middle of each pair on the previous round **(l–m)**.

Rounds 11–13: Holding the 14mm crystal face-up on the beadwork, work 18 stitches per round, pulling tight so that the beadwork begins to

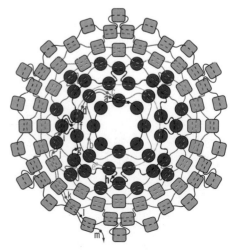

FIGURE 1

At first glance, this necklace seems to be an endless design with no clasp. Closer inspection reveals a clever tab that discreetly houses a snap or hook-and-eye closure.

MATERIALS

necklace 23 in. (58cm)

- Swarovski rivoli cabochons
  18mm
  14mm
- **40** 4mm bicone crystals
- 40g size 8º triangle beads
- 3g size 11º Japanese
  cylinder beads
- 3g size 15º Japanese
  seed beads
- snap or hook-and-eye
  closure
- nylon beading thread or
  Fireline 6 lb. test
- beading needles, #12

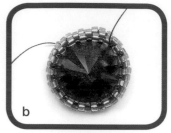

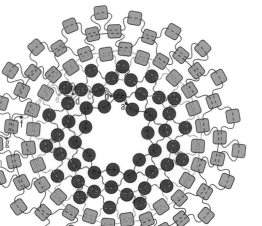

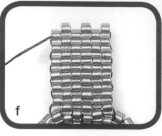

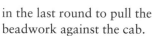

FIGURE 2

come up around the cab
(**photo a**).

Rounds 14 and 15: Switch to
15ºs, and work 18 stitches
per round (**photo b**).

[2] Sew diagonally through
the rows of 15ºs and three
rows of cylinders to exit a
cylinder along the edge of the
cab. Pick up a cylinder, a
4mm crystal, and a 15º, and
sew back through the 4mm
(**photo c**). Pick up a cylinder,
and sew into the next cylinder
along the edge of the cab
(**photo d**). Repeat around to
add a total of 18 4mms.
Secure the thread with a few
half-hitch knots (Basics)
between beads, and trim.

[3] With the tail, sew
diagonally through the
beadwork to exit a cylinder
two rows from the edge on
the underside of the cab. To
begin the extension for the
snap, work three peyote
stitches (**photo e**). Continue
working in flat, even-count
peyote until you have a tab
that is six beads wide and
has seven beads along each
flat edge (**photo f**).

[4] Sew one snap half to the
tab (**photo g**), secure the tail,
and trim.

Embellished bezel – 18mm crystal

[1] Bezel the 18mm crystal
in the same manner as the
14mm crystal, but use the
following bead counts:

Rounds 1 and 2: On 4 ft.
(1.2m) of thread, tie 14 15ºs
into a ring. Sew through the
first 15º (**figure 2, a–b**).

Round 3: Work seven peyote
stitches (**b–c**).

Round 4: Work seven peyote
stitches with two 15ºs per
stitch (**c–d**).

Round 5: Work 14 peyote
stitches with one 15º between
pairs and one 15º in the
middle of the pairs (**d–e**).

Rounds 6 and 7: Work 14

peyote stitches per round
with cylinder beads (**e–f**).

Round 8: Work 14 peyote
stitches, alternating between
adding one cylinder and two
cylinders (**f–g**).

Round 9: Work 21 peyote
stitches, inserting a cylinder
in the increase and between
pairs (**g–h**).

Rounds 10–12: Holding the
18mm cab face-up on the
beadwork, work 21 peyote
stitches per round with
cylinders. Pull the beadwork
tight so it comes up along
the edge of the cab.

Rounds 13–15: Work 21
peyote stitches per round
using 15ºs. Use thinner beads

in the last round to pull the
beadwork against the cab.

[2] Follow step 2 of the
14mm cab to add 21 4mm
crystals around the edge.

[3] Repeat steps 3 and 4
of the 14mm cab to add
an extension tab and the
other snap half.

Russian leaves

[1] On 1 yd. (.9m) of thread,
pick up a 15º, nine cylinders,
and a 15º (**figure 3, a–b**). Pick
up a cylinder, skip the last
two beads, and sew through
the next one in the opposite
direction (**b–c**). Work four
peyote stitches, sewing
through the first 15º picked
up for the last stitch (**c–d**).

[2] Pick up a cylinder, skip
the 15º, and sew through the
next cylinder (**d–e**).

[3] Work three regular
peyote stitches using
cylinders (**e–f**).

[4] Pick up a 15º and a
cylinder, and sew through the
last cylinder added in the

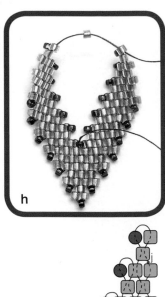

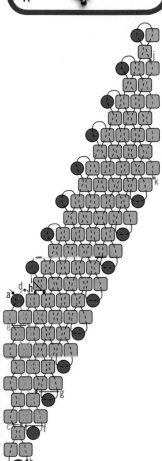

FIGURE 3

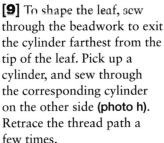

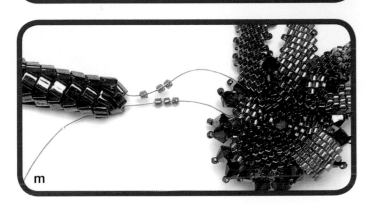

EDITOR'S NOTE:
Each of the two styles of size 8º triangle beads will look slightly different in the herringbone rope. The sharp Toho triangles used in the red necklace produce a more defined herringbone pattern. The rounded Miyuki triangles in the green necklace yield a more subtle result. Either choice is beautiful.

previous row **(f–g)**. Work three peyote stitches **(g–h)**.
[5] Pick up a cylinder, a 15º, and a cylinder, and sew back through the first cylinder picked up in this step **(h–i)**.
[6] Repeat steps 3–5 seven times, with a total of nine 15ºs on each edge **(i–j)**. Work four regular peyote stitches **(j–k)**.
[7] Sew through the bead-work to exit at **point a**.
[8] Repeat steps 2–6 to make the second half of the leaf in the mirror image of the first.

[9] To shape the leaf, sew through the beadwork to exit the cylinder farthest from the tip of the leaf. Pick up a cylinder, and sew through the corresponding cylinder on the other side **(photo h)**. Retrace the thread path a few times.
[10] Make two more leaves as follows: For the medium-sized leaf, start with seven cylinders instead of nine. Reduce the number of peyote stitches in each step by one. The completed leaf will have seven 15ºs on each edge. For the small leaf, begin with five cylinders, and reduce the number of peyote stitches by two. The completed leaf will have five 15ºs on each edge.
[11] Position the leaves as desired, and sew them to

the underside of the bezeled cabs. Secure the thread tails, and trim.

Herringbone rope
[1] On about 2 yd. (1.8m) of thread, and leaving an 8-in. (20cm) tail, make a six-bead ladder (Basics) with 8º triangles. Join the first and last bead to form a ring.
[2] Work in tubular herring-bone stitch (Basics) until your rope is the desired length.
[3] To close the end of the rope, pick up two 8ºs, skip over two beads on the previous row, and sew under the thread bridge on the next herringbone stitch. Sew back through the last bead picked up **(photo i)**. Pick up an 8º, and sew under the thread bridge on the next

herringbone stitch and back through the bead just added **(photo j)**. Sew down through the first 8º added in this step, go under the thread bridge on the previous row **(photo k)**, and go back up through the 8º. Pull to tighten.
[4] Using the tail at the other end of the rope, repeat step 3. Do not trim the tails.

Assembly
[1] Using a tail at one end of the rope, pick up three cylinders, and sew through a cylinder on the underside of one of the cabs **(photo l)**.
[2] Pick up three cylinders, and sew through an adjacent 8º on the rope **(photo m)**. Retrace the thread path a few times, secure the tail, and trim.
[3] Repeat steps 1 and 2 with the other tail, attaching it to the second cab. ●

Accent a beaded bezel

A peyote stitch pendant is front and center on a spiral rope neckstrap.

designed by **Laura McCabe**

a

b

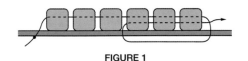

FIGURE 1

step*by*step

Pendant

[1] Glue the cabochon to a piece of Ultrasuede that is approximately ¼ in. (6mm) larger than the cab. If you are using E6000, allow time for the glue to dry.

[2] Tie an overhand knot (Basics, p. 10) at the end of 2 yd. (1.8m) of Fireline or conditioned thread (Basics).

Using a #12 sharps needle, sew through the fabric from back to front, next to the cab's edge.

[3] Pick up six color A cylinder beads, and position them along the cab's edge. Sew down through the fabric next to the last bead, and come up between the third and fourth beads. Sew through the last three As **(figure 1)**. Continue working

in beaded backstitch (Basics) around the edge of the cab, adding an even number of beads **(photo a)**.

[4] Sew through the ring of beads again so it's snug against the cab's edge.

[5] Using a regular beading needle and As, work in tubular, even-count peyote stitch (Basics) around the ring **(photo b)**. Changing cylinder colors for each

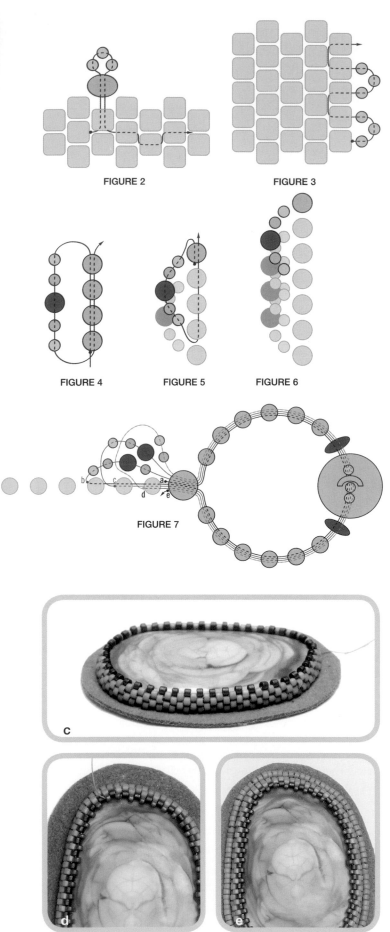

FIGURE 2

FIGURE 3

FIGURE 4

FIGURE 5

FIGURE 6

FIGURE 7

c

d

e

round, continue adding rounds of peyote until the top edge of the cab is covered **(photo c)**. If you have an irregularly shaped cab, you may need to work a few decreases (Basics) so the bezel stays tight around the cab.

[6] Work a round of peyote using 15º seed beads, to curve the beadwork inward so it's snug around the dome of the cab **(photo d)**.

[7] Weave through the bezel to the backstitched round, sew through the fabric between two beads, and tie a knot. Don't trim the thread.

[8] Using a sharps needle, sew back through the fabric next to the backstitched round. Using one of the cylinder colors, repeat steps 3 and 4, and backstitch an even number of beads around the bezel **(photo e)**. Sew through to the back of the suede, knot the thread, and trim.

[9] Embellish the bezel, if desired. Using a regular beading needle and 3 yd. (2.7m) of doubled Fireline or thread, knot the ends together, and sew through the fabric from back to front. Weave through the beadwork to the center round of peyote on the bezel. Begin embellishing every other or every third ditch as follows: Pick up a 2–3mm bead and three 15ºs, skip the 15ºs, and sew back through the 2–3mm bead and the next three or five beads on the bezel **(figure 2)**. Repeat around the cab. Secure the thread, and trim.

[10] Tie a knot at the end of a 2-yd. (1.8m) length of thread. Using a sharps needle, sew through the fabric, from back to front, next to the bezel's edge. Adhere the back of the Ultrasuede to a second piece of Ultrasuede.

[11] Trim the two layers of Ultrasuede no more than a cylinder's width larger than the bezel **(photo f)**. Sew through to the new back of the pendant near the edge, and whip stitch (Basics) the edges together **(photo g)**. Don't trim the thread.

[12] Bring the needle to the front of the pendant between two beads on the ring. Using a regular beading needle, work a round of tubular, even-count peyote using cylinders. Then work a round using 11ºs.

[13] Weave through the beadwork to the top edge of the pendant. Position the needle on the second-to-last round so it exits a cylinder up-bead one or two beads left of the pendant's center. Work in flat, even-count peyote (Basics), and stitch a strip of cylinder beads on the top edge of the pendant, six or eight beads wide and 32 to 38 rows long (16 to 19 beads on each side) **(photo h)**. Fold the strip, aligning the first and last rows, and zip it up (Basics and **photo i**) to form a tube for the bail.

[14] Add a three-bead picot along the edges of the bail as follows: Exit an edge bead on the bail, pick up three 15ºs, and sew through the next edge bead **(figure 3)**. Repeat. Secure the thread in the beadwork with a few half-hitch knots (Basics) between beads, and trim.

[15] Embellish the bezel with pearls: Secure a doubled length of Fireline or beading thread in the bezel with half-hitch knots, and exit an 11º on the outer edge. Pick up a pearl and a 15º. Skip the 15º, and sew back through the pearl and the next 11º on the bezel **(photo j)**. Repeat around the bezel. Add pearls to the bail, if desired. Secure the thread, and trim.

MATERIALS

both components
- Fireline 6 lb. test
- beading needles #12 and #12 sharps

pendant
- stone cabochon
- **20–30** 2–3mm glass or crystal rondelles (optional)
- 16-in. (41cm) strand keshi pearls
- Japanese cylinder beads 5g color A
  3g in **2–3** colors: B, C, D
- Japanese seed beads
  2g size 11º
  2g size15º

- nylon beading thread, conditioned with beeswax or Thread Heaven, color to match Ultrasuede
- E6000 adhesive or Peel 'n' Stick adhesive sheet (fabric and craft stores)
- Ultrasuede

spiral rope
- **2** 6mm beads or **20** 4mm round crystals and **18** 6–8mm pearls
- Japanese seed beads
  8g size 11º in **2** colors: A, B
  4g size 15º in **2** colors: C, D
- **2–8** 3mm beads
- clasp or shank button

Spiral rope

For the pattern that follows, color A 11ºs are the center (core) of the rope.

[1] Using a regular beading needle and 2 yd. (1.8m) of Fireline, pick up four color A 11ºs, a color C 15º, a color D 15º, a color B 11º, a D, and a C. Position the beads 14 in. (36cm) from the end, and sew through the four As again to form a ring **(figure 4)**.

[2] Pick up an A, C, D, B, D, and C. Sew through the top three As and the new A **(figure 5)**. Position the new loop of beads on the right of the previous loop, and hold both loops on the left side of the core beads.

[3] Repeat step 2 until the spiral rope is the desired length, making sure that the new loop is always on the right of the previous loop to maintain the direction of

the spiral **(figure 6)**. For a neckstrap with pearls and crystals (p. 196, left), make a spiral rope 6 in. (15cm) long.

Finishing

[1] Depending on the neckstrap you have chosen, pick up a 6mm bead or string a pattern of pearls, crystals, and seed beads on one end of the spiral rope. If you are stringing a pattern of beads, string the other side in the mirror image, and check the fit before going on to the next step.

[2] String six 11ºs, a 3mm bead, three 15ºs, a clasp half or a button, a 3mm, and six 11ºs. Sew back through the beads strung in the previous step and three core beads on the spiral rope **(figure 7, a–b)**. The 3mms will keep the clasp in place so it doesn't slide around on the loop.

[3] Pick up a C, D, B, and D. Sew through the 6mm or strung beads, the clasp loop, and back through to the second core bead from the end of the rope **(b–c)**.

[4] Pick up a C, D, and B. Sew through the 6mm and

clasp loop and back through to the end core bead **(c–d)**.

[5] Pick up a C and a D, and repeat the thread path as before **(d–e)**. Secure the tail in the core of the rope with a few half-hitch knots between beads, and trim.

[6] Repeat steps 1–5 on the other end, but string enough seed beads and 3mms in step 2 to make a loop around the button. ●

EDITOR'S NOTE:

Center-drilled pearl chips are an acceptable substitute for the keshi pearls, which can be difficult to find or may be available only in limited colors.

Monochromatic
palettes lend
sophistication
to these
bracelets. Or,
highlight your
accent beads
with contrasting
netting.

Captured cuff

A platform of two-drop peyote peeks through open netting sprinkled with lustrous pearls or glittering crystals.

designed by **Barbara Klann**

step*by*step

Base

[1] On 2 yd. (1.8m) of conditioned thread (Basics, p. 10), pick up a stop bead (Basics), and leave a 6-in. (15cm) tail. Pick up 24 color A 11º seed beads, and work in two-drop peyote stitch (Basics) until your bracelet is 24 beads wide and the desired length. Make sure that the number of rows is divisible by three.

[2] Remove the stop bead, secure the tails with a few half hitch knots (Basics) between beads, and trim.

MATERIALS
bracelet 7½–8½ in. (19.1–21.6cm)
- 49–55 4mm bicone crystals or pearls
- size 11º seed beads
  25–35g color A
  10g color B
- 5g size 15º seed beads
- 3 sew-on snaps, or alternate clasp
- nylon beading thread, conditioned with beeswax or Thread Heaven
- beading needles, #12

EDITOR'S NOTE:
If you've made your bracelet shorter (6½–7 in./16.5–18cm), instead of overlapping with snaps, attach a purchased clasp with reinforced loops of seed beads.

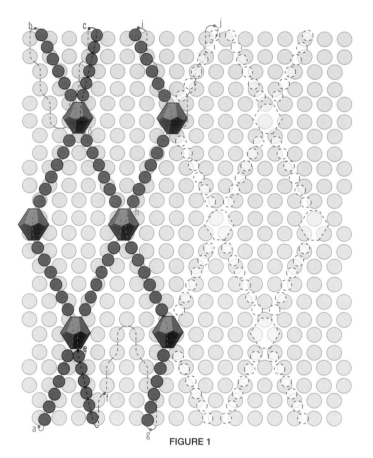

FIGURE 1

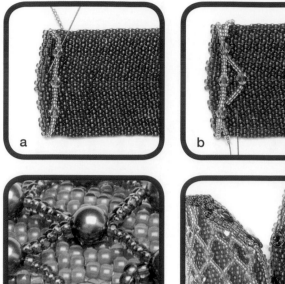

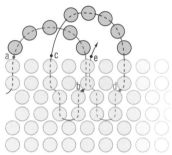

FIGURE 2

Netting

Maintain consistent tension while stitching the netting, but don't pull too tightly, or the base may curl.

[1] Secure 2 yd. (1.8m) of conditioned thread in the beadwork, exiting an end bead stack on one edge of the cuff **(figure 1, point a)**.
[2] Pick up six 15ºs, a 4mm crystal or pearl, six 15ºs, a 4mm, six 15ºs, a 4mm, and six 15ºs **(a–b)**. Sew through the end bead stack on the opposite edge of the bracelet, and sew through the base, skipping two bead stacks, to exit the fourth bead stack on the same edge **(b–c)**.
[3] Pick up six 15ºs and sew through the last 4mm added in the previous step **(c–d and photo a)**. Pick up six 15ºs, a 4mm, and six 15ºs, and sew through the first 4mm added in the previous step **(d–e)**. Pick up six 15ºs and sew through the fourth bead

stack on the opposite edge **(e–f and photo b)**. Sew through the base to exit the seventh bead stack along the same edge **(f–g)**.
[4] Pick up six 15ºs, a 4mm, and six 15ºs, and sew through the center 4mm added in the previous step **(g–h)**. Pick up six 15ºs, a 4mm, and six 15ºs, and sew through the seventh bead stack along the opposite edge **(h–i)**. Sew through the base and exit the tenth bead stack along the same edge **(i–j)**.
[5] Repeat steps 3 and 4, skipping two bead stacks with each horizontal movement, until you're ¼ in. (6mm) from the end, allowing room for the overlap of the snaps.
[6] Secure each end's center 4mm to the base with a few thread paths to maintain the netted spacing **(photo c)**. Secure your thread with a few half-hitch knots between beads, and trim.

Edging

[1] Secure 2 yd. (1.8m) of thread in the base and exit an end bead stack along one edge **(figure 2, point a)**.
[2] Pick up five color B 11ºs, skip three bead stacks, and sew through the base as shown **(a–b)**.
[3] Gently tighten the loop. Sew through the beadwork to exit at **point c**. Make sure to always exit in front of the loop you've just made.
[4] Pick up five Bs, skip three bead stacks, and sew through the base (entering the seventh bead stack), gently tightening the loop **(c–d)**.
[5] Sew back through the base to begin another loop

(d–e), and continue in this manner until you reach the end of the base. Secure your thread with a few half-hitch knots between the base beads, and trim the tails.
[6] Repeat steps 1–5 along the other edge.

Clasp

Secure 1 yd. (.9m) of thread in the beadwork, and attach the coordinating halves of three snaps at each end of the bracelet **(photo d)**. Secure the tails, and trim. ◗

Stacked cap bails

Take an artful approach to making a distinctive
beaded bail and cap for a special bead.

designed by **Michelle Bevington**

step*by*step

Components

Herringbone rope

[1] On a comfortable length of thread, leave an 8-in. (20cm) tail, and make a ladder (Basics, p. 10) with four color A cylinder beads. Join the beads into a ring by sewing through the first and last cylinders.

[2] Work in tubular Ndebele herringbone stitch (Basics) until your rope is approximately 26 in. (66cm). Straighten the last row by going through each bead in the opposite direction.

[3] Attach a split ring to each half of the clasp.

[4] Pick up five As and one split ring. Sew down through the top bead that is diagonal to the one your thread is exiting **(photo a)** and back up through an adjacent bead.

[5] Pick up six or seven As, and go through the split ring again. Sew down through the top bead of the remaining stack, crossing over the previous loop **(photo b)**. Retrace the thread path twice through both loops. Secure the tail in the beadwork with a few half-hitch knots (Basics) between beads, and trim.

[6] Repeat steps 4 and 5 on the other end of the rope.

End caps

On 2 ft. (61cm) of thread, pick up a color B cylinder, a color C cylinder, ten Bs, a C, and a B. Referring to **figure 1**, work ten rows in square stitch (Basics). Wrap the strip around the end of the herringbone rope to test the fit. It should fit snugly around the end of the rope

without any gaps or slack. Add or remove a row if needed, then set the strip aside. Repeat to make a second end cap.

Bail

[1] To make the bail tube, work with 2 ft. (61cm) of thread and pick up ten Bs. Work in square stitch to complete 14 rows **(figure 2)**.

[2] Stitch the ends of the strip together. Secure the tails, and trim.

[3] To make the bail loop, pick up two Cs on 2 ft. (61cm) of thread. Work in square stitch to complete 21 rows **(figure 3)**. Do not secure the tails.

MATERIALS

necklace 27 in. (69cm)

- art-glass bead, approximately 21 x 12mm
- mix of silver and accent beads for fringe
- **8** or more 5–12mm sterling silver dangles for fringe
- size 11º Japanese cylinder beads
  16g color A
  5g color B
  2g color C
- **1–3** 8–17mm sterling silver large-hole spacers or low-profile bead caps (optional)
- clasp
- **2** split rings
- 5 in. (13cm) 24-gauge sterling silver wire, half-hard
- nylon beading thread
- beading needles, #12
- chainnose pliers
- roundnose pliers
- split-ring pliers (optional)
- wire cutters

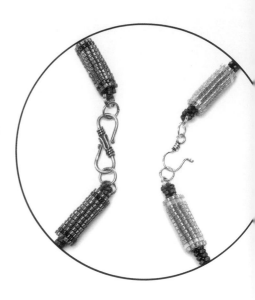

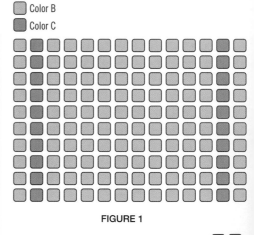

Color A
Color B
Color C

FIGURE 1

FIGURE 2

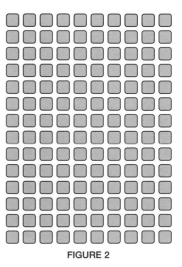

FIGURE 3

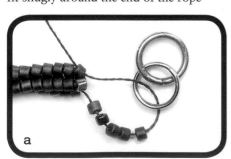

a

b

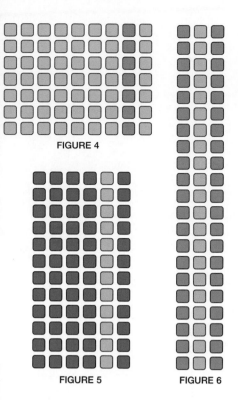

FIGURE 4

FIGURE 5   **FIGURE 6**

c

d

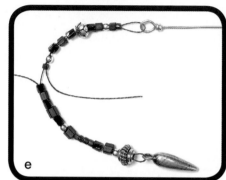
e

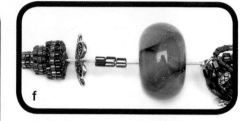
f

g

Bead cap

The bead cap is made of three square stitch strips sewn together in tiered layers.

[1] Working in square stitch, make the three strips that form the bead cap. Follow **figure 4** for the first (inner) layer, **figure 5** for the second layer, and **figure 6** for the third (outer) layer. Begin in the lower left corner of each pattern, and work the first row left to right. Do not trim the tails.
[2] Roll up the first strip, positioning the first row of beads in the center. Working in square stitch, join the last row to the second row **(photo c)**. Secure the tails, and trim.
[3] Wrap the second strip around the first so that the bottom edges are flush and the accent beads are visible on both pieces. Join the ends using square stitch **(photo d)**. Stitch the layers together between beads in several spots. Secure the tails, and trim.
[4] Repeat step 3 to attach the third strip to the second strip.

Pendant fringe

[1] Make a wrapped loop (Basics) on one end of the wire.
[2] On 2 ft. (61cm) of thread, pick up approximately 1½–2½ in. (3.8–6.4cm) of assorted beads. Pick up a silver

dangle, then sew back through the beads. Pick up ½–1 in. (1.3–2.5cm) of beads, sew through the wrapped loop, and then sew back through the beads just added **(photo e)**. Snug up the beads, and tie a square knot (Basics) with the tails.
[3] Sew each tail back through the beads in the opposite direction to secure it, and trim.
[4] Repeat steps 2 and 3 to add fringe as desired.

Assembly

[1] String the art-glass bead onto the wire so it covers the wrapped loop. Squeeze the loop slightly with pliers if necessary. If the bead hole is too small for the loop, string a large-hole spacer (or spacers) with an opening large enough to cover the loop. Add more fringe to cover the wrapped loop, if needed.

If the bead hole is large, string smaller beads to fit inside the hole to keep the art-glass bead from shifting. String a low-profile bead cap or a large-

hole spacer, if desired, and the beaded bead cap **(photo f)**.
[2] Above the bead cap, make a wrapped loop large enough to accommodate the two-bead-wide bail loop.
[3] Slide the pendant onto the bail loop, then stitch the ends together using square stitch.
[4] Center the bail loop on the bail tube, and stitch the top seven rows of the loop to the bail tube **(photo g)**. Secure the tails, and trim. Slide the bail onto the rope.
[5] Wrap an end cap around one end of the rope, leaving a row or two of the herringbone showing. Working in square stitch, join the first and last rows of the end cap to enclose the end of the rope.
[6] Stitch between beads to secure the end cap. Secure the tails, and trim.
[7] Repeat steps 5 and 6 on the other end of the necklace. ○

Choose a donut bead to build your palette around. Then get creative with your accent beads: crystals, pressed glass, stones, pearls – anything!

Netted donut pendant

Use netting and peyote as a textural backdrop to showcase accent beads in lush fringe.

designed by **Colleen McGraw**

step*by*step

Beaded donut

[1] With a #10 needle, on 2 yd. (1.8m) of Power Pro, pick up three color A cylinder beads and a color B cylinder, leaving a 6-in. (15cm) tail. Repeat until you have 36 beads. Tie the ends into a square knot (Basics, p. 10) to form a ring approximately the same size of the hole in your donut bead. Adjust accordingly, and make sure

EDITOR'S NOTE:

Donut beads vary in width, thickness, and hole size. Customize the rounds in your netting to accommodate your donut.

For example, I began with a ring of 28 beads instead of 36. Subsequently, I needed to add extra steps for the netting to fit around the wider edge of my donut. After rounds 1–5, I added two rounds of six As, a B, and six As before I began decreasing.

MATERIALS

pendant 3½–4 in. (8.9–10cm)
- 30–40mm donut bead
- **7** 8–10mm accent beads for fringe
- **3** 8–10mm accent beads for spiral ropes
- Japanese cylinder beads
  15g color A
  5g color B
  5g color C
- size 15º seed beads
  10g color D
  2g color E
  5g color F
- Power Pro
- nylon beading thread, conditioned with beeswax or Thread Heaven
- beading needles, #10 and #12

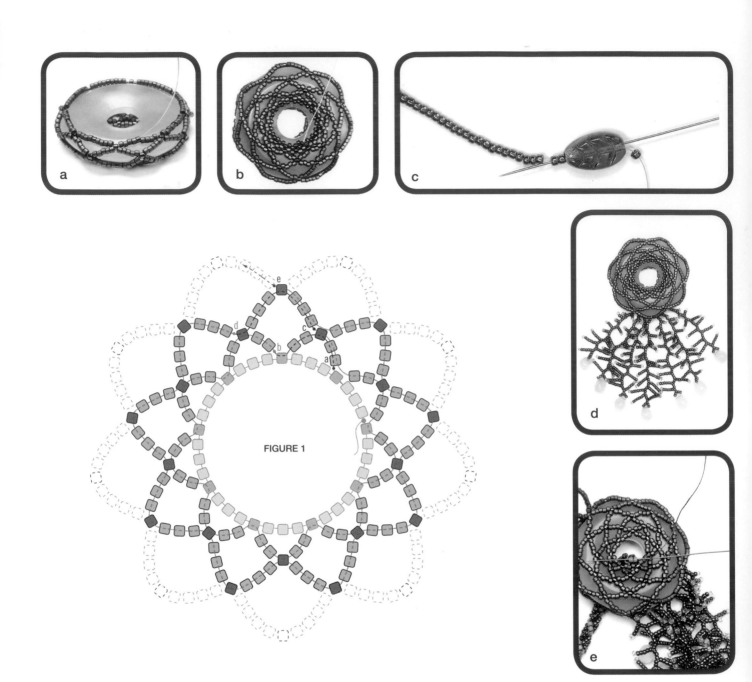

a

b

c

d

e

FIGURE 1

that the number of beads is
divisible by four.
[2] Sew through the ring until
you are exiting a B. Pick up
two As, a B, and two As, and
sew through the next B in the
base ring **(figure 1, a–b)**.
Continue around the ring,
working in flat circular netting.
Step up through the first two
As and B that you added **(b–c)**.
[3] Pick up three As, a B, and
three As, and sew through the

B of the next loop **(c–d)**.
Repeat around the ring,
stepping up through the first
three As and B that you
added **(d–e)**.
[4] Continue for two more
rounds, increasing one A on
each side of the B in each
round, or until your netting is
approximately the same
diameter as your donut's edge.
[5] Hold the donut on top of
your netting as you work the

decrease rounds. Pick up
four As, a B, and four As, (or
one fewer A on each side of
the B than in your last
round) and work a round of
netting, stepping up through
the first As and B that you
added in the round **(photo a)**.
Pick up three As, a B, and
three As for the next round.
Continue decreasing until
you've completed the round
and are exiting the B of a

loop that has two As, a B,
and two As.
[6] Pick up a color D 15°
seed bead, and work a round
of peyote stitch (Basics) off of
the last round of netting.
Repeat two or three rounds
until your inside diameter is
approximately the same size as
that of your donut **(photo b)**.
Secure the tails with half-hitch
knots between beads (Basics),
and trim.

FIGURE 2

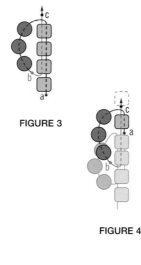

FIGURE 3

FIGURE 4

Mix matte and metallic cylinder beads for netting with subtle sparks of color.

Fringe

[1] With a #12 needle, secure 2 yd. (1.8m) of conditioned thread (Basics) in the bead-work, and exit a center cylinder at the bottom, on the outer rim of your netting.
[2] Pick up 42 Ds, an accent bead, and a color E 15º. Skipping the E, sew back through the accent bead and two Ds (figure 2, a–b and photo c), and pull tight.
[3] Pick up six Ds and an E. Skip the E, and sew back through the six Ds and two Ds in the stem (b–c). Continue, making shorter branches as you get closer to the donut.
[4] Exit the end of the stem, and sew into your netting. Exit at two- to four-bead intervals to complete three fringes on each side of this piece. Repeat steps 1–3 for each fringe, but decrease the

initial number of beads picked up so that the fringes are graduated in length (photo d). (My center fringe has 42 main Ds, the second has 36, the third has 32, and the fourth has 28.)
[5] Secure the tails in the beadwork, and trim.

Spiral ropes

[1] On 2 yd. (1.8m) of conditioned thread, leaving an 8-in. (20cm) tail for attaching the rope later, pick up four color C cylinders and three color F 15ºs (figure 3, a–b). Skip the three Fs and the first C, and sew through the last three Cs picked up (b–c).
[2] Push that loop over to the left. Pick up a C and three Fs (figure 4, a–b). Sew through the last two Cs and the C just added (b–c). Push the new loop to the left, on top of the previous loop.
[3] Repeat step 2 until your rope is the desired length.
[4] Pick up an accent bead and an F. Skip the F, and sew through the accent bead and into the beadwork. Secure the working thread, and trim.

[5] Repeat steps 1–4 to make two more ropes.
[6] Thread a #12 needle on the tail of your longest rope, and secure it to a few cylinders in the back of the beaded netting at the center of the inner circle (photo e).
[7] Repeat for the remaining ropes, attaching them one to three beads over, in the inner ring of netting, on either side of the central rope.

Bail

Secure 2 yd. (1.8m) of conditioned thread in the netting, and exit a B at the top of your netting. Pick up 16 to 24 As, and sew through the base B to form a loop. Retrace the thread path a few times, and trim the tails. Or, complete a spiral rope 1½ in. (3.8cm) long and attach both ends to the back, top of your netting as shown in the pendant above. ●

EDITOR'S NOTE:
If your fringe accent beads are top drilled, add one to four extra Ds on each side of the accent bead in step 2 of "Fringe." Skip those Ds and the accent bead, and sew back through the two Ds of the stem. When tightened, this forms a loop so they hang correctly.

Victorian spirit

Whether loomwoven or square stitched, these patterned panels connected by beaded strands make a great ensemble.

designed by **Jennifer Creasey**

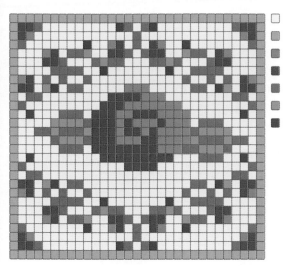

FIGURE 1

cream
gold
rose
dark rose
dark green
green
fuchsia

cream
gold
rose
dark rose
dark green
green

FIGURE 2

MATERIALS
necklace 36 in. (.9m)
- **16** 7 x 11mm teardrop-shaped crystals
- **43** 6mm bicone crystals
- **70** 4mm bicone crystals
- **242** 3mm round gold-colored beads
- Japanese cylinder beads (see the February 2007 Resource Guide at BeadAndButton.com for specific colors)
  20g cream, color A
  5g gold, color B
  5g rose, color C
  5g dark rose, color D
  3g dark green, color E
  2g green, color F
  1g fuchsia, color G
- nylon beading thread
- beading needles, #12
- beading loom (optional)

earrings
- **6** 7 x 11mm teardrop-shaped crystals
- **6** 6mm bicone crystals
- **6** 4mm bicone crystals
- **30** 3mm round gold-colored beads
- Japanese cylinder beads
  2g cream, color A
  2g gold, color B
  1g rose, color C
  1g dark rose, color D
  1g dark green, color E
  1g green, color F
- pair of earring findings
- nylon beading thread
- beading needles, #12
- beading loom (optional)
- chainnose pliers

step*by*step

Necklace
The rose-pattern panels can be made on a loom or in square stitch. Refer to either the Loomwork or Square stitch section of Basics, p. 10, before you begin.

Centerpiece panel
Thread a needle on 1 yd. (.9m) of thread. If using a loom, set it up with 32 warp threads, and tie the 1-yd. (.9m) working thread to the first warp, leaving a 6-in. (15cm) tail.

If using square stitch, pick up a stop bead (Basics), leaving a 6-in. (15cm) tail.

Follow the pattern in **figure 1** to make one panel using cylinder beads. Remove the stop bead (if working in square stitch), weave the tails or warp threads into the beadwork, and trim.

Strap panels
Make a total of eight strap panels as follows:

If using a loom, set it up with 11 warp threads. Following the pattern in **figure 2**, weave each panel from top to bottom, and leave a 16-in. (41cm) tail at the lower right-hand corner. Secure the beginning tail in the beadwork, and trim. Weave the warp threads into the beadwork to secure them, and trim.

If using square stitch, stitch each panel from top to bottom, and leave a 16-in. (41cm) tail at the lower right-hand corner. Remove the stop bead, secure the beginning tail in the beadwork, and trim.

EDITOR'S NOTE:
If you stitch the panels on a loom, you may be able to stitch more than one strap panel on a single set of warps, depending on the size of your loom. Stitch the first panel near the top of the loom, and end the working thread, leaving a 16-in. (41cm) tail. Drop down 8–12 in. (20–30cm), secure a new thread, and stitch another panel. Repeat, if you have space. When you cut the work off the loom, be sure to leave the tails on each end of the panel long enough that you can weave them in.

Strap

[1] Thread a needle on the 16-in. (41cm) tail at the bottom of one strap panel. Sew through the second-to-last row, then sew through the edge bead of the first row (figure 3, a–b).

[2] Pick up a 3mm gold bead, ten color A cylinder beads, a 3mm, a 4mm bicone crystal, a 3mm, a 6mm bicone crystal, a 3mm, a 4mm, a 3mm, ten As, and a 3mm (b–c). Sew into the centerpiece panel at the edge, sew through two beads in the second row, and sew through the adjacent bead in the first row (c–d).

[3] Sew through the 3mm, then pick up ten As (d–e). Sew through the next seven beads (e–f). Pick up ten As, and sew through the first 3mm picked up (f–g).

[4] Sew into the strap panel between the two beads you exited, and sew through the next four edge beads (g–h).

[5] Make two connecting strands more (h–i). Secure the thread in the beadwork with half-hitch knots, and trim.

[6] Repeat steps 1–5, joining the remaining seven strap panels to each other. Then attach the final strap panel to the other side of the centerpiece in the same way.

Fringe

[1] To make the fringe, secure 2 yd. (1.8m) of thread near the bottom of the centerpiece. Sew through the beadwork, and exit an edge bead on the bottom row.

[2] Pick up a 3mm, five As, a 3mm, a 4mm, a 3mm, a 6mm, a 3mm, a teardrop-shaped crystal, and a 3mm (figure 4, a–b). Skip the 3mm, and sew back through the next six beads. Pick up five As, sew through the 3mm, and sew through the second edge bead (b–c). Continue adding

fringe across the bottom row as shown in **figure 4**. Secure the tail, and trim.

Earrings

[1] Follow the pattern in **figure 2** to make two panels. Do not end the tails.

[2] Refer to **figure 5, a–b** to make the fringe, using the 16-in. (41cm) tail at the bottom of a panel. Secure the tail in the beadwork, and trim.

[3] To make a loop at the top, thread a needle on the remaining tail, and stitch through the beadwork to exit between the two middle

beads (c–d). Pick up four color B cylinders, sew back into the beadwork in the same place, and sew through two more beads (d–e). Retrace the thread path, then secure the thread, and trim.

[4] Open the loop of an earring finding (Basics), attach the earring, and close the loop.

[5] Repeat steps 2–4 to make a second earring to match the first. ◗

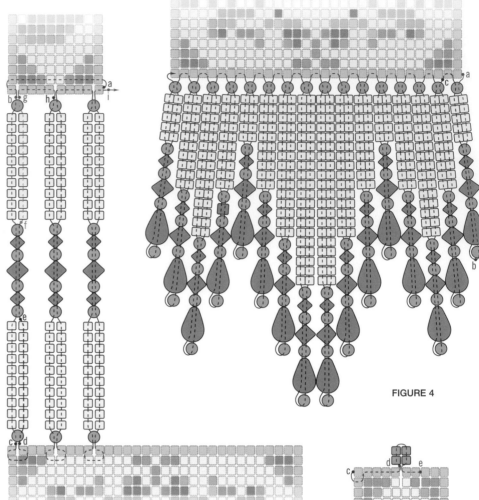

FIGURE 3

FIGURE 4

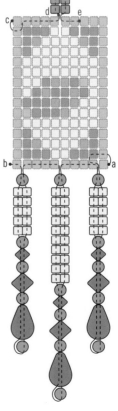

FIGURE 5

Accented
bracelets

Gemstones, pearls, or metal or glass beads fill in gaps made by alternating seed beads of different sizes.

designed by **Virginia Jensen**

step*by*step

Subtract the length of your clasp from the desired length of your bracelet. This is the length you will make your bead-woven band.

[1] Thread your beading loom (Basics, p. 10) with eight warp threads **(photo a)**. Leaving a 12-in. (30cm) tail, secure 3 yd. (2.7m) of thread to the first warp thread. Bring the working thread under the warp threads.
[2] Pick up one 8º seed bead and four 11ºs. Repeat twice, and then pick up an 8º. Push the beads between the warp threads **(photo b)**. Sew back through the beads, keeping your needle on top of the warp threads. Bring the working thread under the warp threads.

[3] Repeat step 2 twice.
[4] Pick up an 8º, four 11ºs, an 8º, an accent bead, an 8º, four 11ºs, and an 8º. Push the beads between the warp threads **(photo c)**. You may have to adjust the number of 11ºs to accommodate the accent bead. Sew back through the beads as before.
[5] To make a bracelet with accent beads running down the center only, as in the light-purple bracelet, p. 213, repeat steps 2–4. Or, to include two accent beads on every other or every third row, repeat step 2 once or twice, then pick up an 8º, an accent bead, an 8º, four 11ºs, an 8º, an accent bead, and an 8º **(photo d)**.
[6] Continue working in a pattern to the desired length. Cut the band off the loom.

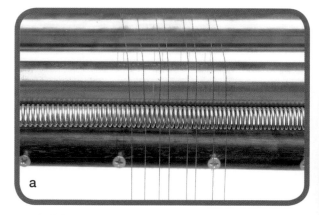

a

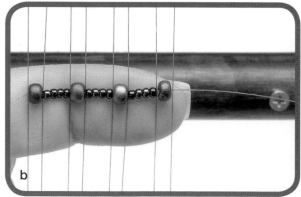

b

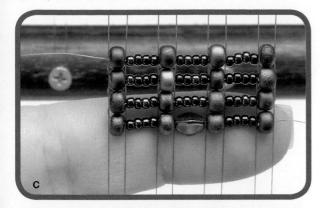

c

d

e

Secure only the warp tails by weaving them into the beads, away from the last few rows of beadwork and tying a few half-hitch knots (Basics) between beads.

[7] Use the working tails to attach the clasp by exiting the edge 8º in one end row of the band. Pick up two 11ºs, the first loop of one half of the clasp, and one 11º. Sew through the next 8º **(photo e)**.

Pick up two 11ºs, the second loop of the clasp, and two 11ºs. Sew through the next 8º. Pick up one 11º, the third loop of the clasp, and two 11ºs. Sew through the next 8º. Retrace the thread path a few times to reinforce the clasp. Secure the tail, and trim. Repeat on the other end to attach the other half of the clasp. **●**

MATERIALS
bracelet 7 in. (18cm)

- **9–19** 5–6mm accent beads
- 30g size 8º seed beads
- 20g size 11º seed beads
- 3-strand box clasp (Nina Designs, ninadesigns.com)
- nylon beading thread
- beading needles, #12
- beading loom

EDITOR'S NOTE:
Make a thinner bracelet by starting with six warp threads instead of eight. Adapt the pattern to accommodate two rows of alternating accent beads.

Silver
and
gemstones

Combining natural stone and sterling silver gives this bracelet substance and style.

designed by **Stephanie Riger**

The ends of this tube are sewn seamlessly to create a solid, slip-on bangle.

a

b

c

d

e

f

g

h

step*by*step

[1] Thread a Big Eye needle on the spool of Tuff cord, and pick up eight 4mm round sterling silver beads, a 4.5mm silver accent bead, a 5mm gemstone bead, and a 4.5mm accent bead. Repeat until all the beads are strung. Do not cut the cord.

[2] Leaving a 10-in. (25cm) tail, slide a bead down to the crochet hook, and work a bead chain stitch (Basics, p. 10). Repeat for the next four stitches **(photo a)**.

[3] To form a ring, connect the last stitch to the first by inserting the hook to the left of the first bead **(photo b)**. Push the bead over to the right, slide a new bead down, and work a bead slip stitch (Basics and **photo c**).

[4] Insert the scrap wire through the center of the ring to help identify where your

stitches will go **(photo d)**. (I curled the end of my wire to prevent it from slipping out of the work.) Remove the wire after a few rows.

[5] Continue to work in bead slip stitch, using medium tension, until all the beads are used. Work one slip stitch without a bead, pull through a 6-in. (15cm) tail, and cut the rope from the spool.

[6] Thread the tapestry needle on the 6-in. (15cm) tail, and sew into the center of the crochet rope 2 in. (5cm) from the end. Secure the tail by making half-hitch knots (Basics) between a few of the beads, and trim the tail close to the rope.

[7] Thread the tapestry needle on the 10-in. (25cm) tail. To position the tail, sew under the thread loop next to the first bead added **(photo e)**.

[8] Hold the two ends together to align the pattern

(photo f). Determine which bead on the last round matches the bead the thread is exiting on the first round. Sew through to the left of that bead, where you would insert the crochet hook if you were adding another bead slip stitch **(photo g)**. Push that bead over to the right, and pull the end rows together. Sew through the thread loop next to the next bead on the first round, and pull **(photo h)**. Repeat around until the ends are securely sewn together. Secure the tail as before, and trim. ●

EDITOR'S NOTE:
To make this bangle, substitute 37 4mm round crystals for the gemstones, 74 4mm bicone crystals for the 4.5mm silver accent beads, and 25g of size 11º metal beads for the 4mm round sterling silver beads.

MATERIALS
bangle 7 in. (18cm)
- **24** 5mm round gemstone beads
- **48** 4.5mm silver accent beads
- **192** 4mm round sterling silver beads
- 4 in. (10cm) scrap wire
- Tuff cord, size #2
- Big Eye needle
- tapestry needle
- steel crochet hook

Versatile rope
necklace

Swap out the decorative dangle to get five different looks.

designed by **Rona Loomis**

The rich gold seed beads of this necklace are beautifully accented by shimmering pearl fringes. Choose this, or one of the four other decorative dangles, to take a basic rope from simple to stunning.

Art glass

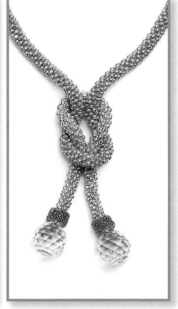

Crystal drops

Floral fringe

Grape clusters and leaves

MATERIALS

all projects
- silk thread, size FF
- steel crochet hook, size #10
- Fireline 6 lb. test
- beading needles, #12

base necklace 16–19 in. (41–48cm)
- 30g size 8º seed beads
- 2 3–4mm metal beads (to match clasp)
- 2 8–10mm end caps (bottom diameter)
- S-clasp with soldered jump rings
- glue (optional)

art-glass dangle
- 2 20mm art beads or other beads
- 4 6mm bicone crystals
- 2 2mm metal beads or size 11º seed beads
- 2 size 14º or 15º seed beads
- 2 6–8mm bead caps

crystal-drop dangle
- 2 20mm round top-drilled Swarovski crystals
- 2 8–10mm end caps (bottom diameter)

pearl-fringe dangle
- 2 6–8mm crystals
- 6 8mm pearls
- 6 6mm crystals
- 6 6mm pearls
- 42 4mm pearls
- 8 4mm spacers
- 14 2mm metal beads or 11º seed beads
- 2 8–10mm end caps (bottom diameter)

floral-fringe dangle
- 60 assorted pressed glass leaves and flower beads
- 5g size 11º seed beads
- 2 8–10mm end caps (bottom diameter)

grape-cluster-fringe dangle
- 12 pressed glass leaves
- 10g 4mm drop beads, in 1–3 colors
- 5g size 11º seed beads
- 5g size 14º or 15º seed beads

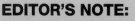

a

b

step*by*step

Crocheted rope

The necklace base is a 16–18 in. (41–46cm) crocheted rope. My base rope is worked using four 8ºs seed beads per round, or approximately 48 8ºs per inch. When determining your length, remember the fringed centerpiece rope will take up about 2 in. (5cm) of the base necklace's length when it is knotted to the base.

[1] String enough 8ºs on silk thread to make your base rope the desired length. Leaving an 8-in. (20cm) tail, work four bead chain stitches (Basics, p. 10). To form a ring, connect the first and last stitches with a slip stitch (Basics). Working in bead slip stitch (Basics), stitch the base until you've used all the beads. After you complete the last round, work one round of slip stitches with no beads, and pull the working thread through the last stitch, leaving an 8-in. (20cm) tail.
[2] Thread a needle on one tail. Sew into the center of the base rope, a few inches away from the end. Tie several half-hitch knots (Basics) between the beads, and trim. Repeat with the other tail.

[3] Secure 1 yd. (.9m) of Fireline in the base, and exit the center of the rope on one end. Pick up a bead cap, a 3–4mm metal bead, and the soldered jump ring of the S-clasp (photo a). Sew back through the bead and the bead cap. Sew into the center of the rope, and make a few knots. Retrace the thread path twice to reinforce the connection. Secure the tail, and trim. Repeat on the other end with a soldered jump ring.
[4] Repeat steps 1 and 2 to make a 7-in. (18cm) rope for the dangle centerpiece. Then choose one of the following fringe options to finish the ends.

Embellishments

For the art-glass and crystal-drop embellishments, secure 1 yd. (.9m) of Fireline, and exit the center of the center-piece rope at one end.

For the pearl, floral, and grape fringes, secure 3 yd. (2.7m) of Fireline, and exit one of the end 8ºs.

Art glass

Pick up a bead cap, a 2mm metal bead, a 6mm bicone crystal, an art bead, a 6mm, and a 15º seed bead. Skip the

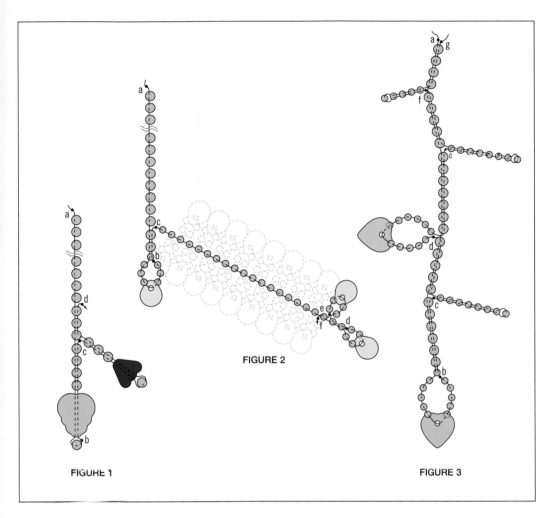

FIGURE 1

FIGURE 2

FIGURE 3

[2] Pick up 23 15ºs, a drop, and two 15ºs (c–d). Skip the last two 15ºs, the drop, and the next two 15ºs. Sew through the following two 15ºs, and pick up two 15ºs, a drop, and two 15ºs (d–e). Sew through the next 15º (e–f).

[3] Continue, adding 19 drops as in step 2. When one cluster is completed, make four more clusters at even intervals along the base of 11ºs. Sew into the rope and exit the next 8º.

[4] Pick up 27 11ºs, six 15ºs, a leaf bead, and five 15ºs (figure 3, a–b). Sew back through the first 15º added and the next six 11ºs (b–c).

[5] Pick up eight 15ºs, skip the last 15º, and sew through the remaining seven 15ºs and the next five 11ºs (c–d).

[6] Pick up five 15ºs, a leaf, and six 15ºs. Sew though the next seven 11ºs (d–e).

[7] Repeat step 5 (e–f). Pick up five 15ºs, skip the last 15º, and sew through the remaining five 15ºs and the next four 11ºs (f–g).

[8] Sew into the last row of the rope, and exit the next end 8º. Make two more fringes. Secure the tails, and trim. Repeat on the other end.

Finishing

When finished, the embellishments may hold the end caps or bead caps in place, but if they don't, dot glue on the inside of the end caps after all tails have been secured, slide the end caps into place, and let them dry. ●

15º, and sew back through the remaining beads and into the rope (photo b). Retrace the thread path two times, and secure the tails, and trim. Repeat on the other end.

Crystal drops

Pick up a end cap, and sew through the top of the crystal. Sew back through the end cap and into the rope. Reinforce the thread path two times, and secure the tails, and trim. Repeat on the other end.

Pearl fringe

[1] Pick up a end cap, eight 4mm pearls, a 2mm bead or an 11º seed bead, an 8mm pearl, an 11º, an 8mm, an 11º, an 8mm, and an 11º. Skip the 11º, and sew through the remaining beads and into the rope. Exit the next end 8º.

[2] Pick up three 4mm pearls, a 4mm spacer, a 6mm bicone crystal, a 4mm spacer, a 4mm pearl, a 4mm spacer, a 6mm crystal, three 4mm pearls, a 2mm or 11º, a 6mm crystal, and a 2mm. Skip the last bead strung, and sew through the remaining beads and into the base. Exit the next end 8º.

[3] Pick up three 4mm pearls, a 4mm spacer, a 4mm pearl, a 6mm pearl, a 4mm pearl, a 6mm pearl, a 4mm pearl, a 6mm pearl, and a 2mm. Skip the 2mm, and sew through the remaining beads and into the base. Secure the tail, and trim.

[4] Repeat on the other end.

Floral fringe

[1] Pick up a end cap, 40 11ºs, a leaf-shaped bead, and an 11º (figure 1, a–b). Skip the last 11º, and sew back through the leaf and the next four 11ºs (b–c).

[2] Pick up three 11ºs, a flower-shaped bead, and an 11º. Skip the 11º, and sew back through the flower and the next three to six 11ºs (c–d).

[3] Add leaves and flowers as desired in the same manner. When you finish the first fringe, sew back into the end round of the rope, and then exit the next 8º. Make a total of four fringes.

[4] Secure the tail, and trim.

[5] Repeat on the other end.

Grape clusters and leaves

[1] Pick up 28 11ºs, four 15ºs, a 4mm drop bead, and three 15ºs (figure 2, a–b). Sew back through the first 15º strung and the next two 11ºs (b–c).

Unexpected
element

Accent rows of single crochet with assorted shapes and sizes of seed beads and art-glass drops to make a casual, loopy bracelet.

designed by **Teresa Kodatt**

step*by*step

Loops

[1] String 5 in. (13cm) of assorted cube and 10º or 11º seed beads on the spool of thread. Then string an art-glass drop bead. Repeat until you have a total length of 3 yd. (2.7m). Do not cut the thread. Slide the beads approximately 12 in. (30cm) from the end of the spool.

[2] Leaving a 4-in. (10cm) tail, loosely crochet a row of chain stitches (Basics, p. 10) that is 1 in. (2.5cm) longer

than the desired length of your bracelet.

[3] To make the first bead loop, insert the crochet hook into the second chain stitch from the hook **(photo a)**. Slide about 1 in. (2.5cm) of beads next to the crochet hook, and work a bead single crochet stitch (Basics) to hold the loop in place **(photo b)**.

[4] Continue to add one loop in each chain stitch across the row. When you come to a drop, you can either use it in place of the loop or incorporate it into the loop. If you need to add

The red bracelet uses triangle beads in the mix, while the blue bracelet incorporates fringe drops.

MATERIALS
bracelet 7 in. (18cm) without clasp
- **40** art-glass drop beads
  (Pumpkin Glass, 309-266-7884, pumpkinglass.com)
- 20g 4mm Japanese cube, triangle, or fringe beads
- 20g size 10º or 11º Japanese seed beads
- toggle clasp or 20mm button
- **2** crimp beads
- spool of nylon or polyester thread, size 2
- flexible beading wire, .019
- Big Eye needle
- steel crochet hook, size 8 or 9
- G-S Hypo Cement
- crimping pliers
- wire cutters

more beads while working, complete a stitch, pull the thread through, and trim, leaving a short tail. String more beads on the spool. Tie the end of the spool and the short tail together right next to the last stitch, and dot with glue. Continue crocheting as before.

[5] When you reach the first chain stitch, turn, and work in single crochet to make another row of loops (**photo c**).

[6] Work one more row of loops, but use slip stitch (Basics) instead of single crochet. For the last stitch, work one chain stitch. Pull the thread through the chain stitch, leaving a 4-in. (10cm) tail.

Toggle clasp

[1] Center an 8-in. (20cm) length of flexible beading wire through the end crochet stitches on one end of the bracelet (**photo d**).

[2] Over both ends, string a crimp bead. On one end,

string half the clasp (**photo e**). Put the end the clasp is on back through the crimp bead (**photo f**), and crimp the crimp bead (Basics). Trim both wire ends.

[3] Repeat steps 1 and 2 on the other end of the bracelet.

Button clasp

[1] Center 8-in. (20cm) of flexible beading wire through the end crochet stitches on one end of the bracelet.

[2] On one wire end, string 12 11ºs, the button, and 12 11ºs. On the other wire end, string a crimp bead. Cross the first end through the crimp bead (**photo g**), and crimp the crimp bead (Basics). Trim the extra wire.

[3] Repeat on the other end of the bracelet, omitting the button. Make sure to string enough 11ºs to fit over the button. ⊙

EDITOR'S NOTE:
To create a loose first row of chain stitches, start with a slightly larger crochet hook. Then, you can switch to a smaller hook to crochet the rows with seed bead loops.

Tapestry
crochet purse

Take the challenge and
advance your crochet skills.

designed by **Carol Ventura**

stepbystep

The purse is stitched as a spiral, so it can be difficult to tell where one round ends and another begins. To keep track, slip a safety pin or stitch marker into the top of the last stitch of each round, or place a short piece of contrasting thread across the last stitch. Remove the marker as you come to it, and replace it at the end of the new round.

Read the Editor's Notes on p. 229 for more helpful hints before you begin.

Bottom

[1] String 5 ft. (1.5m) of color A 8º seed beads onto color A thread. String an equal amount of color B 8ºs onto color B thread. Slide the beads toward the balls of thread, leaving 1 yd. (.9m) of thread without beads.

[2] Using color A thread, chain four stitches (Basics, p. 10). Join the ends into a ring with a slip stitch (Basics) in the first chain stitch.

[3] Round 1: Place the A thread's tail on the chain stitches. Work six bead single crochet stitches (Basics) into the ring while carrying the tail. (See "Tapestry crochet basics," opposite, for instructions on carrying thread and changing colors.) Trim the tail. Mark the end of this and all subsequent rounds.

[4] Work the following rounds in bead single crochet using A beads and thread. Begin to carry the B thread.

Round 2: Increase in every stitch (12 stitches).
Round 3: Increase in every stitch (24 stitches).
Round 4: Increase in every second stitch (36 stitches).
Round 5: No increases.
Round 6: Increase in every third stitch (48 stitches).
Round 7: Increase in every fourth stitch (60 stitches).
Round 8: Increase in every fifth stitch (72 stitches).
Round 9: Increase in every sixth stitch (84 stitches).
Round 10: No increases.
Round 11: Increase in every seventh stitch (96 stitches).
Round 12: Increase in every eighth stitch (108 stitches).
Round 13: Increase in every ninth stitch (120 stitches).
Round 14: Increase in every 10th stitch (132 stitches).
Round 15: No increases.
Round 16: Increase in every 11th stitch (144 stitches).
Round 17: Increase in every 12th stitch (156 stitches).
Round 18: Increase in every 13th stitch (168 stitches).
Round 19: Increase in every 14th stitch (180 stitches).
Round 20: No increases.

Sides

Work the design motif following the instructions below, or refer to the chart in **figure 1**. The design on the chart will match what you see on the fiber side of the bag. The images are reversed on the beaded side.

Round 21: 1 B, 14 As. Repeat until you're back at the start of the round.
Round 22: 2 Bs, 13 As. Repeat.
Round 23: 3 Bs, 12 As. Repeat.
Round 24: 4 Bs, 11 As. Repeat.
Round 25: 5 Bs, 10 As. Repeat.

MATERIALS

purse 7½ x 7½ in. (19.1 x 19.1cm) not including handles

- size 8º Japanese seed beads (Matsuno brand, Fire Mountain Gems, 800-355-2137, firemountaingems.com; see Editor's Notes)
  290g color A
  240g color B
- crochet cotton thread, size 3
  3 150-yd. (137m) balls, color A
  2 150-yd. (137m) balls, color B
- sewing thread, transparent
- sewing needles
- small safety pin, stitch marker, or contrasting thread
- steel crochet hook, size 1 (2.75mm)
- twisted-wire needles or bead spinner (optional)
- ¾ x 3-in. (1.9 x 7.6cm) piece of Velcro

Gauge

8 stitches = 1 in. (2.5cm)   8 rows = 1 in.

Round 26: 6 Bs, 9 As. Repeat.
Round 27: 3 Bs, 1 A, 3 Bs, 8 As. Repeat.
Round 28: 3 Bs, 2 As, 3 Bs, 7 As. Repeat.
Round 29: 3 Bs, 3 As, 3 Bs, 6 As. Repeat.
Round 30: 3 Bs, 4 As, 3 Bs, 5 As. Repeat.
Round 31: 3 Bs, 5 As, 3 Bs, 4 As. Repeat.
Round 32: 3 Bs, 6 As, 3 Bs, 3 As. Repeat.
Round 33: 3 Bs, 7 As, 3 Bs, 2 As. Repeat.
Round 34: 14 Bs, 1 A. Repeat.
Rounds 35 and 36: All As while carrying the B thread.
Rounds 37–41: 2 As, 1 B, 2 As, 3 Bs, 2 As, 1 B, 2 As, 2 Bs. Repeat.
Rounds 42–46: 13 As, 2 Bs. Repeat.
Rounds 47 and 48: 1 A, 9 Bs, 3 As, 2 Bs. Repeat.
Round 49: 1 B, 1 A, 7 Bs, 2 As, 1 B, 2 As, 1 B. Repeat.
Round 50: 2 Bs, 1 A, 6 Bs, 6 As. Repeat.
Round 51: 3 Bs, 1 A, 5 Bs, 1 A, 1 B, 2 As, 1 B, 1 A. Repeat.
Round 52: 3 Bs, 1 A, 5 Bs, 6 As. Repeat.
Round 53: 2 Bs, 2 As, 5 Bs, 2 As, 2 Bs, 2 As. Repeat.
Round 54: 10 Bs, 1 A, 3 Bs, 1 A. Repeat.
Rounds 55–74: Repeat rounds 35–54. Don't cut the threads.

Tapestry crochet basics

Tapestry crochet employs conventional crochet stitches, but the technique allows you to work with multiple colors of thread (and beads) without ending one thread strand to add another.

To start, string beads on two or more threads. As you work the first row of crochet or bead crochet stitches in one thread color, lay the tail of the second thread along the previous row of stitches.

Work your crochet stitches over the tail (figure 1). When you're ready to change colors, go through the top two loops of the next stitch in the row below and, using the working thread, pull up the first loop

(figure 2). Thread over with the carried thread (figure 3) and pull it through both loops on the hook (figure 4). Continue working with the new thread, carrying the previous one until you switch colors.

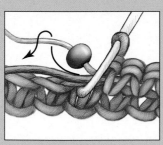

FIGURE 1

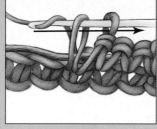

FIGURE 2

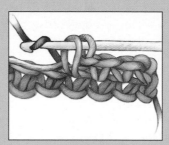

FIGURE 3

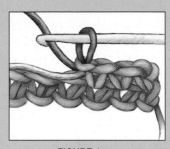

FIGURE 4

The stitch increases on the base of the purse create a petal effect. When you begin to make the sides, the tips of the petals form triangles along the base of the bag.

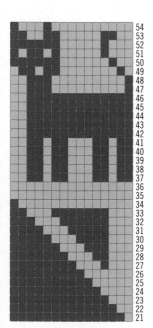

FIGURE 1

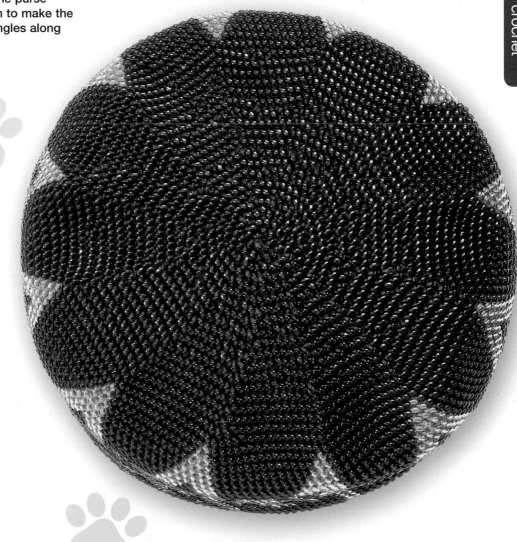

Crossed handles

The edge rows around the rim and the handles are always stitched in the same direction; a change in direction will alter the uniform slant of the beads.

[1] Cut the A thread, leaving a 3-in. (7.6cm) tail. Using the B thread, chain 100 stitches without beads. Connect the chain to a stitch 90 stitches away from the base of the chain with a bead single crochet **(figure 2, a–b)**.

[2] Pick up the A thread and carry it while working 44 Bs across the rim **(b–c)**. Cut the A thread flush with the stitches.

[3] Using the B thread, chain 100 stitches without beads. Connect the chain to a stitch 45 stitches from the base of the first chain with a bead single crochet **(c–d)**.

[4] Pick up the A thread and carry it while working in Bs across the rim to the stitch where the first chain is attached **(d–e)**, then continue across the chain **(e–f)**.

[5] Continue carrying the A thread and carry the 3-in. (7.6cm) tail as well. Stitch across the rim to the chain **(f–g)**, then across the chain **(g–h)**. Repeat **(h–i, i–j, j–k, k–l)**. Each handle now has one row of Bs on each edge of the chain; the rim has one row of Bs with two rows between **points j** and **k**.

[6] Continue across the rim with Bs **(l–m)**, but skip one stitch (decrease) at the inside corner between the rim and the handle. Stitch across the handle **(m–n)**, then decrease at the corner before continuing around the rim **(n–o)**. Work across the rims and handles as before **(o–p, p–q, q–r)** with a decrease at each corner.

[7] Change to As, and continue across the rim **(r–s)**. (This section of the rim already has two rows of Bs.) Decrease at the corner, change back to Bs, then stitch across the handle **(s–t)**.

[8] Change to As, and stitch across the rim and handles, decreasing by one stitch at each corner, as before. Continue until you have two rows of As along all but one handle edge.

[9] Cut the B thread flush with the stitches. With the A thread, make a slip stitch, cut the thread, leaving a 3-in. (7.6cm) tail, and pull the tail through the loop on the hook. Weave the tail into the beadwork for 2 in. (5cm) to secure it, then cut it.

[10] Insert the hook into the corner between the rim and handle where you have only one row of As on the handle **(point u)**. Pull up a loop of A thread, leaving a 2-in. (5cm) tail. Make one bead single crochet. Carry the B thread and the 2-in. (5cm) tail, and stitch along the handle. Cut the B thread and end the A thread with a slip stitch, as in step 9. Secure and cut the tail.

Finishing

[1] Center one piece of Velcro between two handles on the fiber side of the purse. Using transparent thread, sew it about ⅜ in. (1cm) below the top edge. Sew the other piece of Velcro between the handles on the opposite edge.

[2] Block the purse with a steam iron on the fiber side. Work slowly; too much heat can break the beads. ◦

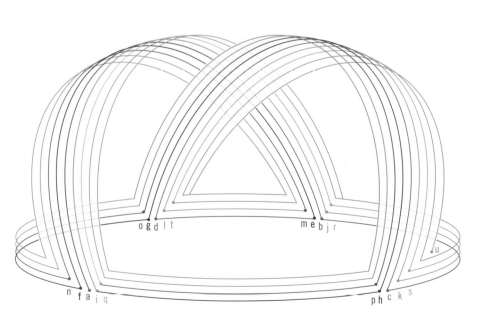

FIGURE 2

EDITOR'S NOTES:

• Matsuno 8° seed beads are slightly longer than other brands of Japanese seed beads. The extra length provides the coverage required for this crochet project.

• Use a bead spinner to simplify the seed bead stringing process.

• Before you start each round in the base, count the number of beads for that round. This will help you keep the correct number of beads and stitches in each round of the base.

• Keep the stitch tension very tight and even. Check the stitch gauge as you work.

• Before running out of beaded thread, cut a 2 ft. (61cm) tail with ten beads on the thread. Thread another 4 ft. (1.2m) of beads, then start to carry the new thread while crocheting the ten beads from the old thread. Switch threads and carry the old thread for ten stitches.

• As the base gets larger, let your stitch tension ease slightly. This will allow the edge of the base to expand more easily.

• Break small or misshapen beads off the thread with pliers.

• Snug each bead against the stitches as you work to help it lie in the correct position.

• Tighten the thread you are carrying every few stitches so it doesn't show on the front.

• Be careful not to place two beads in one stitch.

• The base will not lie flat as you stitch. You'll correct that when you block the finished purse.

The beaded handles cross from side to side, helping to contain the purse opening when it is set down.

Gather up your leftover beads and string them on head pins to turn them into dangles for fabulous fringe.

Fabulous
fibers

Kumihimo braiding is usually done on a *marudai*, a wooden loom, but it can be done on a simple braiding board as well.

designed by **Gloria Farver**

MATERIALS

lariat 1 yd. (.9m)

- **34–60** 3–6mm assorted accent beads
- **2** 4mm beads
- 2g size 11º metal or glass seed beads
- **10** assorted silver beads or spacers
- **2** 8mm cones
- 12 in. (30cm) 22-gauge wire, half-hard
- 13 in. (33cm) cable chain, 3.6mm links
- **34** 2-in. (5cm) head pins
- 3 yd. (2.7m) each of **4** fibers
- **8** bobbins or pieces of cardboard
- braiding board or marudai
- glue
- weight
- chainnose pliers
- roundnose pliers
- wire cutters

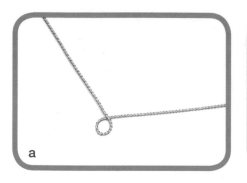

a

b

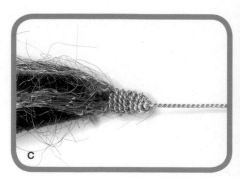

c

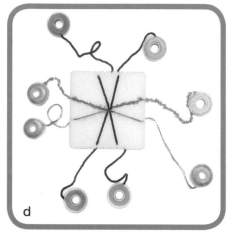

d

e

f

g

h

EDITOR'S NOTE:
Thinner fibers create narrower and more closely braided ropes. To make a thinner-fiber lariat as long as its thicker-fiber counterpart, you will need to compensate by using longer strands.

step*by*step

[1] Cut a 12-in. (30cm) piece of wire in half. Use roundnose pliers to grasp one wire at its center, and make the first half of a wrapped loop (Basics, p. 10 and **photo a**).

[2] Center four 3-yd. (2.7m) fiber strands in the wire loop. Make a wrap at the base of the loop **(photo b)**, and continue wrapping over the loop and the fibers to secure them **(photo c)** instead of wrapping over the wire stem.

[3] Position the wrapped loop in the center hole of the marudai or braiding board, and place a pair of fibers at the top, bottom, left, and right. Wrap the ends of the strands around bobbins or cardboard to keep them from tangling as you work **(photo d)**. Hanging a weight from the wire will keep the braid consistent by controlling the tension as you work.

[4] Place the bottom two fibers between the top two fibers **(photo e)**.

[5] Place the original top two fibers at the bottom **(photo f)**.

[6] Place the right two fibers between the left two fibers **(photo g)**.

[7] Place the original left two fibers at the right **(photo h)**.

[8] Repeat steps 4–7 until your lariat is the desired length. Remove the braided rope from the loom or braiding board and tie the loose ends in a square knot (Basics). Dot the knot with glue and allow it to dry.

[9] Remove the weight, and slide a cone over the wire at the beginning of the lariat. Pick up a 4mm bead and make the first half of a wrapped loop.

[10] Cut the chain into two 2½-in. (6.4cm) pieces, two 2-in. (5cm) pieces, and two 1½-in. (3.8cm) pieces. Slide one of each length of chain into the wire loop. Finish the wraps **(photo i)**.

[11] String an assortment of accent beads on head pins, starting and ending with an 11º seed bead, and then

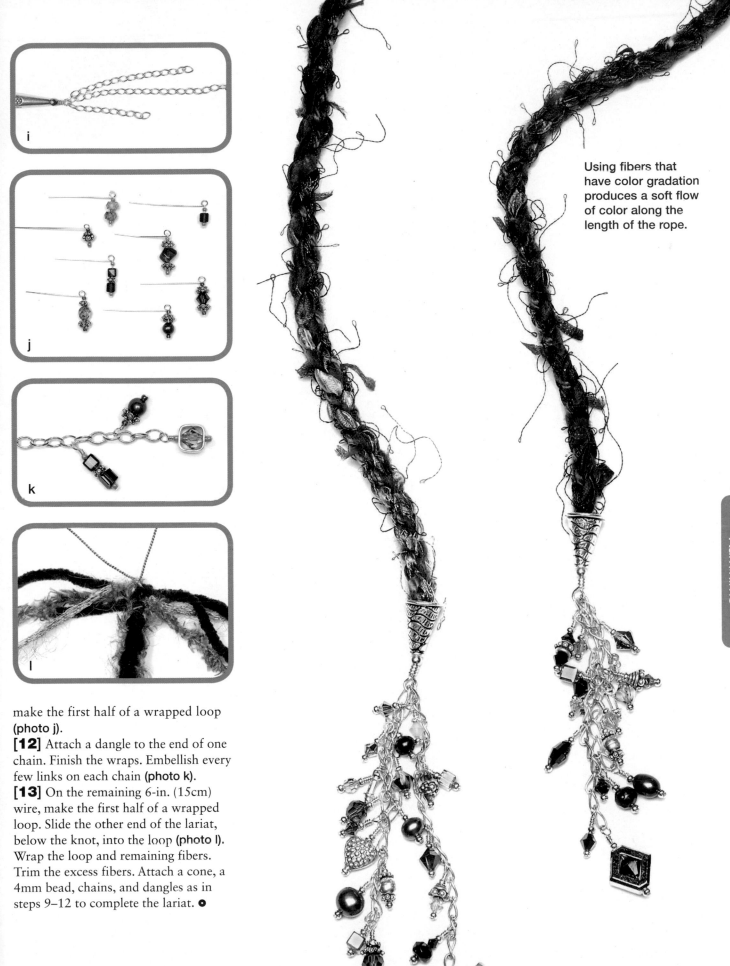

i

j

k

l

Using fibers that have color gradation produces a soft flow of color along the length of the rope.

make the first half of a wrapped loop (photo j).

[12] Attach a dangle to the end of one chain. Finish the wraps. Embellish every few links on each chain (photo k).

[13] On the remaining 6-in. (15cm) wire, make the first half of a wrapped loop. Slide the other end of the lariat, below the knot, into the loop (photo l). Wrap the loop and remaining fibers. Trim the excess fibers. Attach a cone, a 4mm bead, chains, and dangles as in steps 9–12 to complete the lariat. ●

Treasured beads

Tie a one-of-a-kind piece together using square knots.

designed by **Irina Serbina**

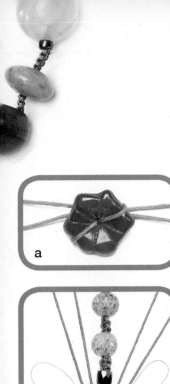

a

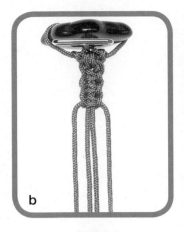

b

c

d

e

f

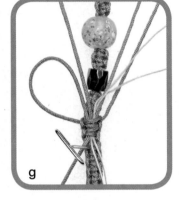

g

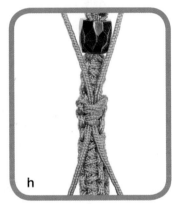

h

step*by*step

[1] Cut two 2-yd. (1.8m) pieces of cord.

[2] Center the clasp bead on the two cords, tying a square knot (Basics, p. 10 and **photo a**) that will secure the bead. Note the various beads used in the featured bracelets.

[3] Pin the clasp bead to a macramé board. Make three square knots (Basics) using the four cords (**Macramé square knot** box, and **photo b**).

[4] Slide a bead over all four cords and snug it up to the knots. Make two or three square knots (**photo c**).

[5] Repeat step 4, adding beads and tying knots, until your bracelet is ½ in. (1.3cm) short of the desired length.

[6] Add the last bead, and make three square knots. Leaving a ¼-in. (6mm) gap, tie a length of square knots (a sennit) long enough to fit around the clasp bead (**photo d**).

[7] Fold the sennit in half, and pin it in place. Position the center and working cords on either side of the ¼-in. (6mm) gap at the base of the sennit.

[8] Cut two 12-in. (30cm) pieces of silk beading thread and fold them in half. These will be lassos. Place the lassos on top of the folded sennit with the loops positioned toward the bracelet (**photo e**).

[9] Using the two outer working cords, tie three or four square knots to cover the gap. The knots should encircle the four cords in the gap, the two center cords, and the lassos (**photo f**).

[10] Place one end of a working cord through one of the lassos. Pulling on the lasso's ends, pull all but 1 in. (2.5cm) of the working cord back through the square knots and remove the lasso (**photo g**).

[11] Repeat step 10 with the other working cord. Place a

dot of glue on the cord ¼ in. (6mm) from the knot, and pull the remaining cord into the square knots (**photo h**). Let the glue dry, and trim the cords close to the knots. ●

Macramé square knot

Cross the right-hand cord over the core and the left-hand cord under the core. This creates a loop between each cord and the core. Pass the right-hand cord through the loop on the left from front to back and the left-hand cord through the other loop from back to front.

Cross the new left-hand cord over and the new right-hand cord under the core. Pass the cords through the loops, and tighten.

Macramé belt

Macramé knots make fashion
accessories that get noticed.

designed by **Irina Serbina**

step*by*step

[1] Cut five 7-yd. (6.4m)
pieces of leather cord. Cut
one 26-ft. (8m) piece of cord.
[2] Fold the 7-yd. (6.4m)
cord pieces in half. Attach
each to the belt ring with a
lark's head knot (Basics,
p. 10). Attach the sixth cord
to the ring **(photo a)**, folding
it so one side is 5 ft. (1.5m)

longer than the other and
positioning the longer end on
the outside.
[3] Using the longer end of
the sixth cord, cover the ring
with continuous lark's head
knots (Basics and **figure**). Pull
the cord snug around the
ring as you tie each knot.
[4] Number the cords 1–12
from left to right. Tie cords 5
and 8 in a square knot

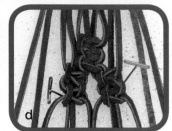

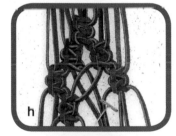

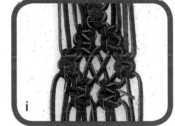

(Basics and **Macramé square knot** box, p. 235) around cords 6 and 7. Tie a second square knot with the same cords **(photo b)**.

[5] Tie two square knots with cords 3 and 6 around cords 4 and 5 **(photo c)**.

[6] Tie two square knots with cords 7 and 10 around cords 8 and 9 **(photo d)**.

[7] Tie two square knots with cords 1 and 4 around cords 2 and 3 **(photo e)**.

[8] Tie two square knots with cords 9 and 12 around cords 10 and 11 **(photo f)**.

[9] To form the decorative center detail, cross cords 7 and 8 over cords 5 and 6 **(photo g)**. Pin the crossed cords in position.

[10] Tie two square knots with the new cords 3 and 6 around the new cords 4 and 5 **(photo h)**.

[11] Tie two square knots with cords 7 and 10 around cords 8 and 9 **(photo i)**.

[12] Tie two square knots with cords 5 and 8 around cords 6 and 7. This completes the diamond **(photo j)**.

[13] Repeat steps 5–12, tying two more diamond patterns to form a cluster of three diamonds.

[14] Leave a 1½-in. (3.8cm) space, and start the next diamond cluster. Repeat the diamond cluster three times.

[15] Trim any cords that are significantly longer than the others. Embellish the cord ends with beads, tying an overhand knot (Basics and **photo k**) next to each bead. ○

FIGURE

Buttons sprout beaded blossoms

Enhance buttons with clusters of freshwater pearls and seed beads.

designed by **Anne Nikolai Kloss**

step*by*step

[1] Thread a needle on 1 yd. (.9m) of Fireline, and tie an overhand knot (Basics, p. 10) 4 in. (10cm) from the end. Sew through the center of a 1-in. (2.5cm) square of interfacing.

[2] Center a button on the interfacing and sew it in place with three or four stitches **(photo a)**.

[3] Exit upward through a button hole and pick up a 4–5mm freshwater pearl and a 15º seed bead. Snug up the pearl and seed bead to the button, and sew back through the pearl, the same button hole, and the interfacing **(photo b)**.

[4] Repeat step 3, adding six pearls in a circular pattern and filling in both button holes.

[5] Exit upward through a button hole and pick up seven to nine 15ºs. Sew down through the other hole and the interfacing **(photo c)**. Add three or four more seed bead loops to fill the center of the pearl cluster.

[6] Sew up through the interfacing half a bead away from the edge of the button. Pick up six 11ºs and lay them next to the button on top of the interfacing.

[7] Thread a second needle on 18 in. (46cm) of Fireline, tie an overhand knot at the end, and sew up through the interfacing between the

button and the row of 11ºs **(photo d)**. Go over the top of the base thread between the third and fourth 11º in the row, and sew down through the interfacing. This technique is referred to as "couching." Place the stitch close to the beads so you don't cut it when you trim the excess interfacing.

[8] Continue adding 11ºs around the button, working a couching stitch after every three beads.

[9] When you complete the ring, sew through all the 11ºs to reinforce the ring. Secure the threads and tails in the interfacing, and trim the tails **(photo e)**.

[10] Trim the interfacing around the button, being careful not to cut any of the couching stitches.

[11] Repeat steps 1–10 to make a total of five embellished buttons.

[12] Apply a thin layer of glue to one link of the bracelet blank and to the interfacing of one button. Let the glue set for a few minutes and then place the button on the link **(photo f)**. Press together firmly. Repeat to attach the remaining buttons. Allow the glue to set for 24 hours. ●

MATERIALS
bracelet 7½ in. (19.1cm)
- 5 ⅝-in. (1.6cm) two-hole buttons
- 35 4–5mm freshwater pearls
- Japanese seed beads
  3g size 11º
  1g size 15º
- Fireline 6 lb. test
- beading needles, #12
- link bracelet form with five ⅞-in. (2.2cm)-diameter links (Designer's Findings, 262-574-1324)
- E6000 adhesive
- 5 1-in. (2.5cm) square pieces Lacy's Stiff Stuff interfacing

a

b

c

d

e

f

EDITOR'S NOTE:
If you prefer to work with only one needle, add the 11º seed beads around the button using beaded backstitch (Basics, p. 10).

Leaves
and vines

Seed beads and dichroic glass pair up in a comfortable cuff.

designed by **Laurie Long Marcum**

MATERIALS

bracelet 7 in. (18cm)

- 1³⁄₁₆-in./30mm (maximum size) cabochon
- seed beads
  3g size 8º, in each of **2** colors: A, B
  4g size 11º, in each of **4** colors: B, C, D, E
  10g size 14º or 15º, color A
- nylon beading thread
- beading needles, #12
- all-purpose glue
- E6000 adhesive
- fine-tip permanent marker
- 3 x 10 in. (7.6 x 25cm) nonfusible Pellon
- **2** pairs of snaps, size 2/0
- 6 x 10 in. (15 x 25cm) Ultrasuede
- vellum or tracing paper
- T-pin (optional)

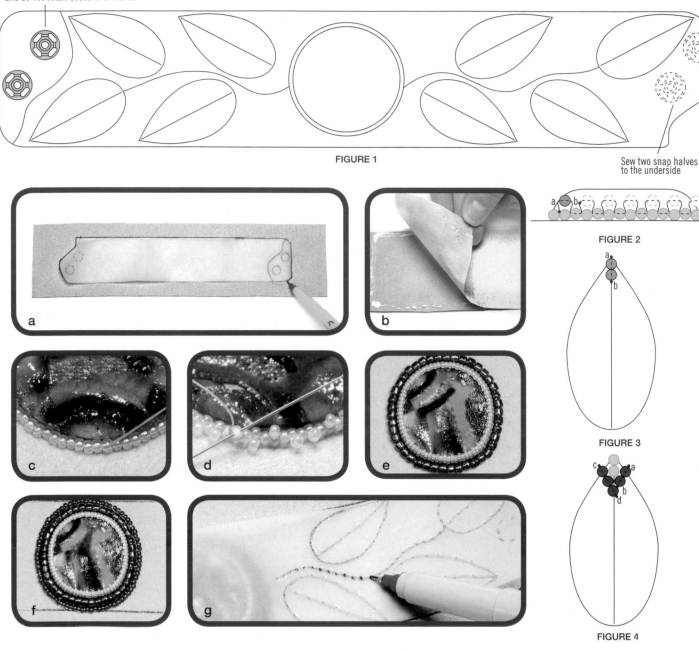

Sew two snap halves on the top, and do not stitch beads in this area

FIGURE 1

Sew two snap halves to the underside

a

b

c

d

e

f

g

FIGURE 2

FIGURE 3

FIGURE 4

step*by*step

Getting started

[1] Trace the template **(figure 1)** onto vellum or tracing paper. Cut it out, and test the fit. Adjust the template as needed by either folding the paper smaller or splicing in a section so that the template fits comfortably around your wrist when the snaps are lined up.

[2] Cut the Ultrasuede into two 3 x 10-in. (7.6 x 25cm) strips. On one piece, outline the template using a fine-tip permanent marker **(photo a)**.

[3] Squeeze a line of all-purpose glue around the edge of the back of the Ultrasuede, and adhere the strip of Pellon to it **(photo b)**. Keep the glue outside the template border since it is hard to get a needle through dried glue. Allow to dry.

[4] Coat the bottom surface of the cabochon with E6000 adhesive, and place it in the center of the Ultrasuede with the template outline. Wipe away any excess glue, and allow to dry.

Bezeling the cabochon

[1] Make an overhand knot (Basics, p. 10) at the end of a comfortable length

of thread. Come up through the Pellon and Ultrasuede right next to the cab, and work in beaded backstitch (Basics) with color A 15º seed beads around the cab. Finish with an even number of beads. Continue through the first 15º **(photo c)**.

[2] Pick up a 15º, skip a 15º on the round below, and sew through the next 15º **(figure 2, a–b)**. Repeat around, working in even-count peyote stitch (Basics). Step up through the first 15º added in this round **(photo d)**.

[3] Continue as in step 2, stitching two or three more rounds of peyote so that

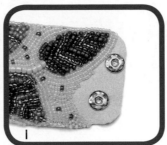

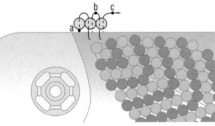

FIGURE 5

FIGURE 6

the beadwork frames the cab. Use thinner beads if necessary to allow the beadwork to decrease along the contour of the cab.
[4] Zigzag through the beadwork, and sew through the base to the underside.

Bead embroidery
[1] Come up through the fabric right next to the first round of 15°s, and work a round of beaded backstitch using color B 8°s (photo e).
[2] Work a round of beaded backstitch using color B 11°s (photo f).
[3] Use a fine-tip marker to draw the leaves and stems on the Ultrasuede.

If you wish to use the stems and leaves shown here, copy the lines from the template onto your vellum, and use a T-pin to puncture holes in the lines. Trace over the punctured lines to transfer them to your Ultrasuede (photo g).
[4] Secure a new thread, and come up through the fabric at the tip of a leaf. Pick up two color C 11°s, and sew back through the fabric close to the second bead (figure 3, a–b).
[5] Come back up through the fabric about half of a bead's width to the right of the leaf's tip. Pick up enough color D 11°s to reach the centerline, and sew through the fabric close to the last bead (figure 4, a–b).
[6] Come back up through the fabric to the left of the tip. Pick up enough Ds to reach the centerline, and sew through the fabric close to the last bead (c–d).
[7] Repeat steps 5 and 6 until you have filled the entire leaf (figure 5). Alternate between colors for the rows. Secure the thread, and trim.
[8] Repeat steps 4–7 for the remaining leaves using varying combinations of color B, C, D, and E 11°s. Keep the rows close to each other.
[9] Using color A 8°s, work beaded backstitch along the stem lines (photo h).
[10] Using 15°s and 11°s, work beaded backstitch randomly to fill in the background. Try to keep your stitching within the template lines.

Finishing
[1] Being very careful to avoid cutting any stitching, trim away the excess fabric along the edge of the template.
[2] Sew the female half of the snaps to the unbeaded section of the bracelet's top side (photo i), and sew the male

half of the snaps to the underside.
[3] Trace the bracelet on the other piece of Ultrasuede, and cut it out.
[4] Working with 1 yd. (.9m) of thread, make an overhand knot at the end. At one end of the bracelet, sew through the front of the bracelet from the inside out at the very edge (photo j). To whip stitch (Basics) the layers together, sew through both layers from back to front (photo k). Continue to whip stitch the unbeaded ends together.
[5] To finish the long edge, exit between the two layers, pick up two B 11°s, sew through both layers from front to back close to the second bead, and sew back through the second bead in the opposite direction (figure 6, a–b).
[6] Pick up an 11°, sew through the fabric close to the last bead, and sew back through the new bead in the opposite direction (b–c). Repeat along the entire long edge.
[7] Whip stitch the other end closed, and finish the second edge. Secure the threads, and trim. ●

EDITOR'S NOTE:
Instead of gluing the cabochon in place, try one of the double-sided tapes sold in the scrap-booking aisle of craft stores; they're thin and very strong. Look for the brand names Terrifically Tacky Tape, Curiously Sticky Tape, and Wonder Tape. Simply cut pieces of tape, and attach them to the back of the cab. Trim the tape around the cab, peel off the backing, and stick the cab in place.

Contributors

Penney Acosta received a degree in fine arts 35 years ago, but now works full time in an unrelated field. Contact her via e-mail at penneya2@aol.com.

Paula Adams, of Albuquerque, N.M., has designed and taught beadwork for over 20 years. Contact her via e-mail at paula@beadpatterns-paulaadams.com, or visit her Web site, beadpatterns-paulaadams.com.

Contact **Carol Alo** at (253) 468-0747, or via e-mail at carolalo71@hotmail.com.

Sandy Amazeen, from Williams, Ariz., divides her time between work, hiking, and dreaming up different ways of playing with beads and wire. Contact Sandy via e-mail at amamess@earthlink.net.

Geneva Beck started beading on doll costumes and now loves designing jewelry. Contact her at (334) 366-4085, or via e-mail at gbtimsbelle@aol.com.

Reach **Michelle Bevington** via e-mail at beadart@rain.org.

When not managing an audit department, **Connie Blachut** enjoys the creative expression of designing and making jewelry at her home in Plymouth, Mich. Contact her via e-mail at cblachut07@comcast.net.

Contact **May Brisebois** via e-mail at beadiful@bellsouth.net, or visit her Web site, maybdesigns.com, to view more of her work.

Reach full-time jewelry designer and teacher **Perie Brown** at (330) 455-1294, via e-mail at rkb9@aol.com, or visit her Web site, thebrownpear.com.

Contact **Jennifer Creasey** via e-mail at creasey@starband.net or visit her Web site, polarbeads.com.

Technical writer and jewelry designer **Miachelle DePiano**, from Gilbert, Ariz., can be reached at (480) 242-9094, via e-mail at cosmoaccessories@cox.net, or her Web site, cosmopolitanaccessories.net.

Phyllis Dintenfass loves creating with a variety of off-loom beading techniques and travels around the country teaching beadwork. Contact her via e-mail at phylart@new.rr.com, or visit her Web site, phylart.com.

Anna Elizabeth Draeger is an Associate Editor of *Bead&Button* magazine. Contact her via e-mail at adraeger@kalmbach.com.

Margaret Duffy says her inspiraton often comes from art, especially from the Renaissance and medieval periods. Reach her at mmduffy@mindspring.com, or visit her Web site, margaretduffy.com.

Contact frequent *Bead&Button* contributor **Gloria Farver** via e-mail at rfarver@wi.rr.com.

Though retired from her career as an art teacher, **Linda Frechen** hasn't stopped teaching; she's a beading instructor at Pam's Bead Garden in Plymouth, Mich. Contact her via e-mail at lfrechen@earthlink.net.

Contact **Julia Gerlach**, Managing Editor of *Bead&Button*, via e-mail at jgerlach@kalmbach.com.

A full-time jewelry designer, teacher, and writer, **Linda Gettings** teaches at Innovative Bead Expo shows. Her book, *Great Beaded Gifts*, was re-released in softcover in March 2007. Contact her at ladybeading@aol.com.

A self-taught jewelry artist who focuses on off-loom bead weaving, **Julie Glasser** is also a silversmith and creates designs combining both mediums. Contact her via e-mail at julri.designs@juno.com, or visit her Web site, julieglasser.com.

Contact **Mia Gofar** via e-mail at mia@miagofar.com or visit her Web site, miagofar.com.

Visit **Sandra D. Halpenny**'s Web site, sandradhalpenny.com.

Contact **Yvanne Ham** via e-mail at yvanne1@comcast.net.

Contact **Jane Hardenbergh** at service@twopurplepandas.com or her Web site, twopurplepandas.com.

Though **Dottie Hoeschen** has been beading for only the last seven years, she has been an artist in a variety of other media for 30 years. Contact her via e-mail at stonebrash@juno.com or her Web site, stonebrashcreative.com.

Jordana Hollander designs, weaves, sews, knits, crochets, and embroiders with beads. Contact her at jordana321@aol.com or view her creations at etsy.com under seller name "Jordana Dreams."

Virginia Jensen is a full-time beadweaver and beading teacher in Grand Junction, Colo. Visit her Web site, virjenmettle.com.

Karen Joelson enjoys all forms of off-loom beading techniques and wirework. Her passion for beading derives from a background in jewelry making and button collecting. Contact her via e-mail at auntteek1@aol.com.

When not creating kits, **Lisa Keith** teaches at the Baton Rouge Bead Company. Contact her via e-mail at lkeith@lj-studio.com, or visit her Web site, lj-studio.com.

Deanna Kittrell teaches chain mail classes in Sacramento, Calif. She also makes all of her own jump rings. Visit Deanna's Web site, dsdesignsjewelry.com.

Reach **Barbara Klann** in care of *Bead&Button*.

Bead artist and instructor **Anne Nikolai Kloss** is from Waukesha, Wis. Contact her at annekloss@mac.com.

Teresa Kodatt makes beads and jewelry, and teaches at her own bead store, Pumpkin Glass, in Morton, Ill. She can be contacted at teresa@pumpkinglass.com or via her Web site, pumpkinglass.com.

Debi Larson, of Bettendorf, Iowa, has been beading for nearly 19 years and teaching for five. Contact her via e-mail at debilarson@mchsi.com.

Jewelry artisan **Rona Loomis** specializes in bead crochet. Contact her via e-mail at beadedswan@aol.com, or visit her Web site, beadedswan.com.

A fiber, wire, and bead artist, **Melody MacDuffee** lives and works in Mobile, Ala. Contact her via e-mail at writersink@msn.com.

New York City jewelry designer and artist **Paula-Ray Mandl** can be contacted at prmandl@yahoo.com.

Laurie Long Marcum is a full-time manager of "Domestic Operations" in her home in Louisville, Colo. She hopes to make beading her full-time career someday. Contact her via e-mail at lauriemarcum@yahoo.com.

Contact **Laura McCabe** via e-mail at justletmebead@aol.com, or visit her Web site, justletmebead.com.

Reach **Marissa McConnell** via e-mail at kikathumper@yahoo.com or marissa@insomniacbeads.com, or visit evesadornments.com.

Colleen McGraw is the owner of Bead Metaler Teaching Studio in Las Vegas, Nev., where she is a full-time instructor for all levels of beadwork, wirework, and silver clay, as well as chain mail. Contact Colleen via e-mail at cfmcgraw@cox.net.

Contact **Vicky Nguyen** at (650) 328-5291, via e-mail at product@beadshop.com, or through the Web site, beadshop.com.

Shelley Nybakke is the owner of The Bead Parlor in historic downtown Bloomington, Ill. Contact Shelley at The Bead Parlor (309) 825-1877, via e-mail at shelley@thebeadparlor.com, or visit her Web site, thebeadparlor.com.

Bonnie O'Donnell-Painter studied jewelry and enameling at The Glassell School, part of the Museum of Fine Arts, Houston, Texas. She is now a studio jeweler who lives and works in Houston and can be contacted via e-mail at cubuffnut@aol.com.

Stephen Parfitt works in a number of mediums, including carving, metals, lampworking and beadwork, and enjoys making components for others to use in their designs. Contact him at (217) 544-8473, via e-mail at labeadoh@aol.com, or visit labeadoh.com.

Tammy Powley is a jewelry designer and published author of various jewelry books, blogs, and a Web site. Contact Tammy at tammypowley@yahoo.com. For a list of her links and publications, visit tammypowley.com.

A "56-year-old student of beading," **Karen Price** loves trying new styles and projects. Contact her via e-mail at kap0002@hotmail.com.

Find more of **Chris Prussing**'s work at bead-patterns.com.

Contact **Nancy Sells Puffer** via e-mail at nancysellsglass@juno.com, or visit nancysellsglass.com.

Ludmila Raitzin designed beaded sweaters for more than 15 years, and in the last five years has turned her talents to making jewelry; some has been displayed in the Museum of Art and Design in N.Y. She currently teaches at the Bead Society of N.Y. . Contact her via e-mail at raitzinl@yahoo.com.

Retired engineer **Karen Rakoski** now enjoys the design-and-build process with beads and jewelry components. To share the fun, she teaches and writes about jewelry making in Rochester, N.Y. Reach her via e-mail at knrak@rochester.rr.com.

Stephanie Riger specializes in bead crochet and wirework with semiprecious stones. Contact her through her Web site, stephanieriger.com.

Beading instructor and designer **Noriko Romanko** can be contacted via e-mail at noriko.r@sbcglobal.net.

Irina Serbina is a macramé jewelry artist who creates in Sunnyvale, Calif. View her pieces and patterns on her Web site, macrameboutique. com, or contact her via e-mail at iserbina@gmail.com.

Gwen Simmons sells her beaded jewelry in shops throughout North Carolina and Florida. She also teaches beading classes at The Art Room in Franklin, N. C. Contact Gwen at (828) 644-9681.

Contact **Debbi Simon** via e-mail at debbi@dsimonfineart.com, or visit her Web site, dsimonfineart.com.

Lynne Soto is an Associate Editor of *Bead&Button*. Contact her via e-mail at lsoto@kalmbach.com.

Deborah Staehle has been beading and learning as many new stitches and techniques as she could find for 10 years. She also has taught hundreds of beading classes in the last six years. Contact her at Bead Dreams in Stockton, Calif., (209) 464-2323, or via e-mail at bead_demon@hotmail.com.

Contact **Barb Switzer** via e-mail at beadswitzer@yahoo.com, or visit her Web site, beadswitzer.com.

Contact **Ann Ford Varnes** at (816) 539-0065, via e-mail at info@bobannbeads.com, or visit her Web site, bobannbeads.com.

Carol Ventura fell in love with the colorful tapestry crocheted shoulder bags made in Guatemala in the 1970s. Since that time she has developed a system of diagramming patterns and a variety of projects, featured in her tapestry crochet books and videos. Contact Carol via e-mail at carol@tapestrycrochet.com or her Web site, tapestrycrochet.com.

Contact **Julie Walker** at (937) 395-0590, via e-mail at beadcagequeen@aol.com, or visit her Web site, beadcage.net.

Kat West has been playing with beads for over 35 years, but only started making jewelry eight years ago. It is now her main obsession. Contact Kat via e-mail at katwestbeads@gmail.com, or visit her Web site, kwbeads.com.

Visit **Ny Wetmore**'s Web site, nysjewelry.com.

Jill Wiseman is a full-time bead-weaving designer and instructor in central Texas. Contact her via e-mail at jill@tapestrybeads.com, or visit her Web site, tapestrybeads.com.

June Wiseman is a beadweaver and designer from central Texas who is inspired by her daughter, Jill. Contact her via e-mail at june@tapestrybeads.com, or visit her Web site, tapestrybeads.com.

A jewelry designer for Cosmopolitan Beads in Cave Creek, Ariz., **Barbara Woodall** can be contacted via e-mail at info@cosmopolitanbeads.com, or via the Cosmopolitan Beads Web site, cosmopolitanbeads.com.

Jan Zicarelli beads and teaches around the country. She lives in Tucson, Ariz. Contact Jan via e-mail at jan.zicarelli@comcast.net.

Index

The art to
beauty
lies in
beads

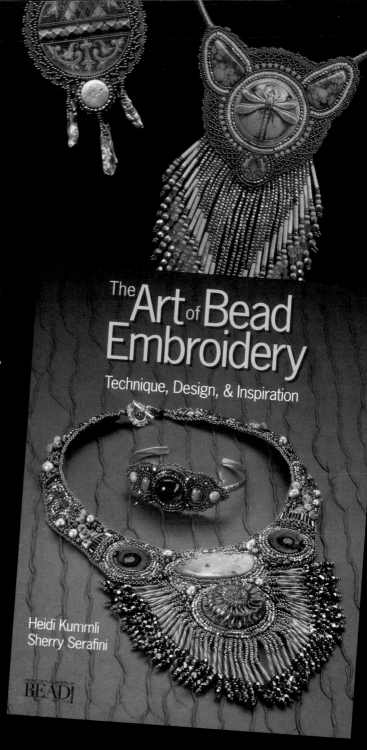

Two talented artists, Heidi Kummli and Sherry Serafini, take you on a tour of bead embroidery through color, texture, and inspiration. They'll teach you which tools to use, what techniques to utilize, and what to pull inspiration from so that you can create beautifully embroidered works of wearable art. 112 pages.

62434 • $21.95

Get creative
with these other
chic guides!

62288 • $29.95

62441 • $29.95

Beading

62253 • $21.95

Order online at www.BeadAndCraftBooks.com or call 1-800-533-6644

Monday-Friday, 8:30 a.m.-5:00 p.m. Central Time. Outside the U.S. and Canada, call 262-796-8776 x661.

BKS-BDB-62625RH